DEFENDING
THE FAITH

DEFENDING THE FAITH

ENGAGING THE CULTURE

Essays Honoring L. Russ Bush

Bruce A. Little
Mark D. Liederbach
Editors

ACADEMIC

Nashville, Tennessee

Defending the Faith, Engaging the Culture:
Essays Honoring L. Russ Bush

Copyright © 2011 by Bruce A. Little and Mark D. Liederbach

ISBN: 978-0-8054-6417-7

Published by B&H Publishing Group
Nashville, Tennessee

Dewey Decimal Classification: 239
Subject Heading: THEOLOGY\APOLOGETICS\DOCTRINAL THEOLOGY

Printed in the United States of America

1 2 3 4 5 6 7 8 9 10 11 12 • '17 '16 '15 '14 '13 '12 '11

VP

Table of Contents

Contributors

Daniel L. Akin President and Professor of Preaching and Theology, Southeastern Baptist Theological Seminary

Mark Coppenger Professor of Christian Apologetics, The Southern Baptist Theological Seminary

James K. Dew Jr. Pastor of Stony Hill Baptist Church in Wake Forest, North Carolina; Adjunct Professor of the History of Ideas, Southeastern Baptist Theological Seminary

Norman L. Geisler Provost, Distinguished Professor of Apologetics and Theology, and Occupant of the Norman L. Geisler Chair of Christian Apologetics, Veritas Evangelical Seminary

Gary R. Habermas Co-chair of Philosophy and Theology Department, Distinguished Research Professor of Apologetics and Philosophy, Liberty University

Kenneth D. Keathley Senior Vice President for Academic Administration, Dean of the Faculty, Professor of Theology, Southeastern Baptist Theological Seminary

Richard Land President, The Ethics and Religious Liberty Commission of the Southern Baptist Convention

Udo W. Middelmann President, Francis A. Schaeffer Foundation; Visiting Professor of Philosophy, The King's College

David P. Nelson Former Senior Vice President for Academic Administration, Dean of the Faculty, Professor of Theology, Southeastern Baptist Theological Seminary

Thomas J. Nettles Professor of Historical Theology, The Southern Baptist Theological Seminary

Paige Patterson President, Professor of Theology, L. R. Scarborough Chair of Evangelism, Southwestern Baptist Theological Seminary

Robert B. Stewart Associate Professor of Philosophy and Theology, Greer-Heard Professor of Faith and Culture, New Orleans Baptist Theological Seminary

Foreword

David S. Dockery

I rejoiced when I heard that Bruce Little, director of the L. Russ Bush Center for Faith and Culture at Southeastern Seminary, was working on a book of essays in honor of Russ Bush. For 30 years, from the fall semester when I entered Southwestern Seminary until Russ was ushered into glory on January 22, 2008, following a two-year battle with cancer, I was privileged to call him a special friend.

Russ Bush was a man who deeply loved Christ and honored His Word. I will always remember the young, dedicated philosophy professor who constantly challenged his students to do their best. He introduced us to the challenging world of Western thought from Socrates to the post-Enlightenment thinkers. During those days, Professor Bush was not necessarily known as a student-friendly instructor. Yet, within God's providence, the door to his office was always a receptive place for me. We often discussed challenging philosophical and theological issues, while also looking for opportunities for lunch or a trip to a Rangers game.

For those who looked on from a distance, Russ Bush often seemed aloof and overly concerned with the minutiae of philosophical arguments. As I mentioned, some thought of him as more interested in his subject matter than in his students. But for many, this was hardly the case. His friends knew him as a soft-spoken, genuinely kind, Southern gentleman; but most of all, Russ was a committed Christ-follower.

Professor Bush was a faithful friend to many, a dedicated husband to Cindy, and a person who deeply loved the gospel of our Lord Jesus Christ. His life and work were deeply rooted in "the faith that was delivered to the saints once for all" (Jude 3 HCSB). Particularly, his work focused on four areas: Christianity and the Bible, Christian Apologetics, Christianity and Science, and Faith and Culture. The essays in this volume were written by friends, students, and colleagues, and they fall into one of these overarching categories. I am grateful for the work of these contributors, and I am sure the readers of this book will be as well. I salute Bruce Little for his fine work in coordinating this project to honor the life, work, and legacy of our mutual friend, Russ Bush.

The lasting contribution of Professor Bush will be the significant work on *Baptists and the Bible* (co-authored with Tom Nettles). His commitment to the truthfulness and the authority of God's Word was a hallmark of all that he was and all that he did. For almost two decades, he served as one of the editors for the *New American Commentary* project. He was also known for his *Handbook for Christian Philosophy* and his compilation of *Classical Readings in Christian Apologetics*. Russ was honored by his colleagues across the evangelical world who elected him as president of both the Evangelical Philosophical Society and the Evangelical Theological Society. The Bush Center on the Southeastern campus, which is led so capably by Bruce Little, is a lasting tribute to his memory and to the quality of his teaching and scholarship.

No one will ever fully know all that Russ Bush did to keep open the doors of Southeastern Seminary during the turbulent years of transition in the late 1980s and early 1990s in his capacity as chief academic officer. Southern Baptists will always owe him a debt of gratitude for his service in this important role.

As I noted earlier, for three decades it was an honor to call him a special friend. We worked together on a number of projects through the years. For the contributors to this volume and many others, Russ was a source of encouragement. Certainly he was such for me. For years I always looked forward to sharing a meal with him each year at the Southern Baptist Convention. While his life seemingly ended before we were ready, we trust God's providential hand and join with his family and friends in rejoicing that Russ's suffering has now ceased. Moreover, we give thanks that he has entered the presence of our Lord, where I am sure he heard the words, "Well done, good and faithful servant." The life of Bruce Little, the lives of these contributors, as well as the lives of other former students and colleagues, along with my own, were blessed and enriched by knowing and learning from our dear friend. I am pleased to join with the contributors and readers of this volume in celebrating the life and influence of L. Russ Rush III (1944–2008).

Preface

L Russ Bush (1944–2008) was a noted apologist, author, professor, pastor, and friend to many people, and he left a wonderfully rich legacy in terms of his personal story, his intellectual integrity, and his personal devotion to his Lord. He spent his life serving the church as a staunch defender of the Christian faith within the organizational framework of the Southern Baptist Convention. His influence, however, extended far beyond Southern Baptists to evangelicals in general. Those who knew Dr. Bush (we always addressed him in that manner) were touched by his conciliatory nature, passion for the truth, and commitment to the inerrancy of the Bible. On January 22, 2008, he was ushered into the presence of the Lord after a valiant two-year effort to overcome the ravages of cancer. This volume serves as an enduring testimony to his life and ministry.

Dr. Bush began his teaching career at Southwestern Baptist Theological Seminary in Fort Worth, Texas (1973–89). In 1989 he moved to Wake Forest, North Carolina, with his wife Cindy and their two children Joshua and Bethany. The purpose of this move was to join the administration at Southeastern Baptist Theological Seminary, where he served as academic vice president, dean of the faculty, and professor of philosophy until 2006. As academic vice president and dean of the faculty, Dr. Bush was an important figure in securing the seminary as a theologically conservative institution committed to training men and women for Christian ministry around the world.

In 2006 Dr. Bush became dean of the faculty emeritus and was appointed by Southeastern Seminary President Danny Akin as the first director of the newly established L. Russ Bush Center for Faith and Culture. For a number of years, Dr. Bush had envisioned a place dedicated to engaging culture and defending the faith, and the Center for Faith and Culture represented the materialization of that vision. It was always his passion to connect Christian theology with the concerns of culture in order to make the gospel of Christ known around the world.

One should not think Dr. Bush's vision was purely a matter of theory or organization. He was deeply committed to the work of missions and loved teaching missionaries. He traveled around the world to encourage them in the work of apologetics in their various ministries. It is of no small significance that the seal he created for the Bush Center has an image of the world, because his heart was to reach the world through personal evangelism, and, according to Dr. Bush, evangelism required apologetics. The Center for Faith and Culture was named for Dr. Bush not simply to honor him, but because he embodied the vision and modeled the ministry of the Bush Center.

Dr. Bush had a wide range of interests that included biblical inerrancy, the importance of apologetics in reaching people for Christ, the role of science in the Western world, and understanding and relating to culture. This explains why the present volume consists of four sections; each section focuses on one of his major interests. A brief article written by Dr. Bush during the last two years of his life introduces each section, followed by three additional essays written by individuals who either had a close personal relationship with Dr. Bush or have a significant current relationship with the Bush Center.

The first section deals broadly with "Christianity and the Bible" and begins with Dr. Bush's short article "Inspiration: The Text or the Men?" The next entry comes from Danny Akin, whose chapter is titled "Jesus, Evangelicals, and the Bible." Akin expounds on the importance of the inerrant Scriptures in the life of the believer who lives under the lordship of Christ. Paige Patterson contributed the third chapter, "Reflections on the Atonement." He argues that the concept of atonement is essential to the Christian message. (Dr. Bush served under both Akin and Patterson during their respective presidential tenures at Southeastern.) The third contributor is Tom Nettles, who was co-author with Dr. Bush of the influential book *Baptists and the Bible*. Nettles' chapter is titled "Apologetics and Scripture: A Lesson from the Early Church," and he discusses decisive treatments of the authority of Scripture by three early apologists: Athenagoras, Justin Martyr, and Origen.

The second section is dedicated to the subject of "Christian Apologetics." Dr. Bush introduces this section with the article "Biblical Apologetics: A 10-Step Methodology." This is followed by Norman Geisler's essay "An Apologetic for Apologetics," which refutes those critics who might suggest that rigorous philosophical and theological arguments are unnecessary in defending the faith.

Geisler writes as one who has devoted his life to the work of apologetics, and the evangelical world bears the fruit of his work in many different ways. Gary Habermas contributes the next essay, which draws on his many years of research into Jesus' resurrection by presenting a critical review of the historical evidence for the post-resurrection appearance of Jesus to the apostle Paul. Habermas' chapter is titled "Jesus' Post-Resurrection Appearance to the Apostle Paul: Can It Withstand Critical Scrutiny?" David P. Nelson, who followed Dr. Bush as Southeastern's academic vice president and dean of the faculty, contributes the next chapter, which is titled "God's Glory among the Nations: Some Reflections on Apologetics and Missions." This essay is of unique importance to this volume because of Dr. Bush's deep interest and personal involvement in missions. Nelson argues that the best apologetic for a missional context is rooted in the grand biblical narrative (GBN) of the Christian Scriptures.

The third section considers "Christianity and Science." Dr. Bush's article "Is Evolution True?" begins this section. Then comes James Dew's chapter on "The Future of Natural Theology: Exploring Alister McGrath's Natural Theology." Dew, a graduate of the Ph.D. program at Southeastern, studied with Dr. Bush. His essay examines the current status of natural theology and its new possibilities in view of the revised understanding suggested by Alister McGrath. Kenneth Keathley, who also studied under Dr. Bush and is the current academic vice president and dean of the faculty at Southeastern Seminary, contributes "Detecting the Invisible Gardener: The Fine-Tuning Argument." This essay examines the evidence from creation as an argument for God's existence. The next contributor is Robert Stewart, whose essay "How Science Works and What It Means for Believers" examines the role of science in Western culture. He explains what science can do, what it cannot do, and how to know the difference.

The final section, titled "Christianity and Culture," begins with Dr. Bush's article "Art: Classical and Popular." Next is Mark Coppenger's essay "The Virtue of Friendliness." Coppenger's chapter is a suggestive piece, sketching out a new area for exploration in relation to how faith in Christ ought to shape the outlook and demeanor of Christians and thus serve as an evangelistic apologetic. Richard Land's essay "Would the Elimination of Nuclear Weapons Make the World More Peaceful and Safe?" considers the crucial cultural issue of nuclear weapons and their place in the civilized world, a subject often discussed between Land and Dr. Bush. Land analyzes and evaluates arguments for nuclear disarmament in an age of terrorism and heightened political instability around the world. The final contribution is by Udo Middelmann of the Francis A. Schaeffer Foundation. His interesting and challenging essay "Nature Is Given, People Create Culture" examines the relationship between nature, which is created by God, and culture, which he argues is created by man from nature. Middelmann's essay deals with a subject of immense interest to Dr. Bush, an interest that was encouraged in no small way by the works of Francis Schaeffer.

The articles in this volume engage subjects that formed the thinking of Dr. Bush and served as the subject matter for many of his conversations, sermons, and books. In the end, they continue the legacy of L. Russ Bush in defending the faith and engaging culture. It is our prayer that this volume will be profitable not only in terms of the content of the essays, but also as a memorial to the stellar work and rich legacy of this evangelical luminary.

Bruce Little and Mark Liederbach, Editors
April 2010

Christianity and the Bible

Chapter 1

Inspiration: The Text or the Men?

L. Russ Bush

Many have debated whether the biblical writers were the objects of inspiration by the Holy Spirit, or whether it is the text (not the men) that was and is inspired. Recently a student e-mail reminded me that in class some years ago I had taught that all Scripture is inspired, or God-breathed, and thus is profitable for all the things listed in 2 Tim 3:16. The men, of course, are only available to us today through their writings. I taught that the Scriptures, not the writers, were inspired.

Being a denominational employee, I am required to affirm Southeastern Seminary's confessional documents, one of which is the Baptist Faith and Message 2000 (BF&M), which clearly states that it was the men (the Scripture-writing prophets and apostles) who were inspired. According to Article I, "The Holy Bible was written by men divinely inspired and is God's revelation of Himself to man." Under that wording, it was the inspired writers who wrote the revealed words, precisely the view I had seemingly questioned in class. The men, I said, were unique in their obedience and sensitivity to the revealed messages from God through the Spirit. They were spiritually guided to write the divine message just as it was given to them, so the resultant text was the infallible Word of God. But the men (the writers) were not personally inspired in such a way that they became holy men who were uniquely infallible in their non-Scripture-writing activities or in their personal lives.

Peter, on the other hand, said that the men (the writers) were being carried along by the Spirit as they gave us the biblical messages (2 Pet 1:20–21). These are similar concepts, but they are not exactly the same. Were these biblical writers great spiritual messengers (like Buddha or Lao Tsu) or mechanically controlled divine messengers or dynamically influenced messengers? Are we reading in the Bible the words of God or those of spiritually minded but fallible men? In a sense, it is both.

A fallible man can write an inerrant word. We do it all the time in nonfiction materials. There is, of course, a difference between inerrant (lacking factual errors in matters affirmed as truthful) and infallible (something that, by definition, not only is not wrong but cannot be wrong). I teach that the authentic text of the Bible is both inerrant and infallible. I do not see any essential conflict between my views as I express them and the more restricted meaning found in the first article of the BF&M. I believe that I express the doctrine of inspiration more clearly than does the BF&M at this point.

In my view, the wording of the original, confirmed, and authenticated text is the original autograph. There are multiple autographs. In other words, Paul may have dictated a letter rather than writing it in his own handwriting (other than perhaps a few words here and there). It is likely that he then read it for editorial revisions. At some point, when his letter read as he intended, he perhaps signed off on that "autographic" copy for additional "autographic" copies to be made and distributed to the churches and the other apostles. Paul's final version is the "original manuscript." Also, every copy or translation that accurately conveys the original meaning is an "original manuscript," no matter who physically put the ink on the paper. Paul authenticated the words, but he was not usually the individual putting the ink on the paper. A professional scribe would do that under Paul's authorization and direction. The letters say what Paul wanted them to say. There is no difference between the "original" and the "copy" if they are verbally identical. If one copy is in Greek and another in French and another in English but the meaning is the same, both translations can be the equivalent of an original Greek autograph. It is not true that only a Greek scholar has access to the true meaning of the New Testament.

It is the text and not the writer that perpetually provides an infallible word from God. When we say the Bible is the Word of God and thus is inerrant in the original manuscripts, we are not pushing infallibility off onto a nonexistent source as liberal Baptists constantly claimed of us in the days of the Southern Baptist Convention's conservative resurgence. Every accurate copy is the equivalent of the original wording. It is the original wording of Scripture that is God-breathed. In the case of the New Testament, that original wording was in Greek. Learn Greek if you can. You will discover many nuances that are hard to translate, but the true message of God's Word can be found in accurate translations, especially those translations produced by evangelical scholars who, like Paul, read and reread their documents to get them right. With an extremely high degree of confidence, we can affirm that the Greek New Testaments we use today are virtually identical to the wording of the initially circulated text.

We have thousands of manuscripts to study wherever textual problems appear. Rarely is the issue of biblical inerrancy one of textual or scribal confusion or copyist errors. In fact, scribal problems are almost always resolved by comparing the many copies we have in order to determine the original text. From there, remaining problems are subject to hermeneutical analysis. Virtually everything is resolvable at that level. An accurate translation of Scripture is always found to be truthful in its teachings and affirmations when it is properly interpreted and understood.

The Bible is a human book, written by humans with their human vocabulary and from their human perspectives. But it is also a divine book, the infallible and inerrant Word of God. Jesus taught this approach to the Scriptures, and we follow His teachings. If He is wrong, we will be wrong. But if He is the Lord, the Son of God Himself, then He will not be wrong about the Bible, the Word of God. I choose to follow His pattern and style of teaching in this regard. Doing so yields a consistent, historically truthful message, the truth of God in written form, preserved without change in message and meaning. When our language changes (and it does), our standard original Greek manuscripts allow us to revise our translations and make them conform to the original meaning of the text left to us by the apostles. This is a wonderful and comforting truth. We have the inerrant and infallible Word of God preserved through thousands of years in multiple ways. We have many original Greek language manuscripts and many good translations based on the old Greek copies. Heaven and earth will pass away, but neither one jot nor the least stroke of a pen will pass from God's original Word. It is the text that has this permanent quality, not the men who wrote the words.

As the rest of the first article of the BF&M says, the Bible

> is a perfect treasure of divine instruction. It has God for its author, salvation for its end, and truth, without any mixture of error, for its matter. Therefore, all Scripture is totally true and trustworthy. It reveals the principles by which God judges us, and therefore is, and will remain to the end of the world, the true center of Christian union, and the supreme standard by which all human conduct, creeds, and religious opinions should be tried. All Scripture is a testimony of Christ, who is Himself the focus of divine revelation.

Chapter 2

Jesus, Evangelicals, and the Bible

Daniel L. Akin

I first met Dr. Russ Bush in the early 1980s as a student at Southwestern Baptist Theological Seminary. I was privileged to take him for the class "Christian Philosophy." It was one of the hardest classes I have ever taken in my life on any level. It was also one of the most rewarding as he challenged me and my classmates to think from the perspective of a Christian worldview.

There is one class period in particular that to this day still stands out in my mind. The topic of the day was the Bible's inerrancy, infallibility, and authority. As he carefully and meticulously laid out his argument, something Dr. Bush always did, he made the statement, "The issue of biblical authority is ultimately a question of Christological identity." He went on to clarify, "What you think about Jesus will ultimately influence what you think about the Bible. Your theology of the 'living Word' [Jesus] and the 'written Word' [The Bible] go hand in hand." Even as a young seminarian I intuitively sensed Dr. Bush was saying something of utmost importance. Now after more than 30 years in ministry, I am absolutely convinced he was correct.

On June 14, 2000, the Southern Baptist Convention met in Orlando, Florida, for its annual meeting. The most important issue on the agenda was the consideration of the Baptist Faith and Message (2000). While the 1925 and 1963 confessions had served us well, many believed certain theological currents and trends made it wise to reconsider, and where necessary, to revise the 1963 statement. Article I of the Baptist Faith and Message (2000) addresses the Scriptures. The following statement, rooted both in Scripture and the language of historic Baptist confessions, is what the Convention overwhelmingly adopted:

> The Holy Bible was written by men divinely inspired and is God's revelation of Himself to man. It is a perfect treasure of divine instruction. It has God for its author, salvation for its end, and truth, without any mixture of error, for its matter. Therefore, all Scripture is totally true and trustworthy. It reveals the principles by which God judges us, and therefore is, and will remain to the end of the world, the true center of Christian union, and the supreme standard by which all human conduct, creeds, and religious opinions should be tried. All Scripture is a testimony to Christ, who is Himself the focus of divine revelation.[1]

From its initial presentation, however, this statement ignited a firestorm of protests among a segment of Southern Baptists. In particular they decried two points: (1) instead of saying that the Bible "is *the record of God's revelation*" as did the 1963 BF&M, the 2000 statement affirmed that the Bible "*is God's revelation*"; and

(2) instead of saying that "the criterion by which the Bible is to be interpreted is Jesus Christ," as did the 1963 BF&M, the 2000 statement affirms, "All Scripture is a testimony to Christ, who is Himself the focus of divine revelation." Both revisions were viewed by the Baptist Faith and Mission Committee (chaired by Adrian Rogers) and the wider Convention as a safeguard against neoorthodox manipulation of the 1963 statement, which manifested itself in two ways: (1) in claiming that only portions of the Bible are God's revelation; and (2) in saying that the teachings of Jesus recorded in Scripture at times should, and even must, be set in opposition to other biblical texts and authors.

During debate at the Convention, a pastor from Texas said to the astonishment of thousands "that while the Bible is true and trustworthy . . . the Bible is still just a book."[2] Later in a telephone interview he told *Baptist Press*, "As I shared, I believe the Bible is a book that God has given us for guidance. It's a book that *points us* to the truth. We're not supposed to have a relationship with a book." These comments, confused and misguided as they are, were mild in comparison to what followed. In an editorial in the *Baptist Standard*, the state paper of Texas, the following was written:

> If the Bible alone is our primary guide, then all parts of the Bible receive equal weight. It is a flat Bible. For example, the words of Moses, Jesus and the Apostle Paul are equally authoritative. If, however, Jesus is the guide to interpreting Scripture, then Jesus' words and clear actions take precedence over their apparent discrepancies with other Scripture passages, such as the Old Testament codes and some of Paul's admonitions.
>
> Some Scriptures, especially portions of the Old Testament, clearly stand in paradox to Jesus' life and teachings, also recorded in Scripture. Other passages, such as

Paul's writings, seem to be at odds with each other, and Jesus' words and actions clarify and separate the timeless and universal from the culturally specific.

Baptists who place Jesus over the Bible still affirm the full authority of the Bible upon their lives, They do not exalt personal experience over Scripture; rather, they base their decisions upon Scripture. But some passages are paradoxical; they say different things about the same subject. In those occasions, Jesus-first people look to Jesus for help in understanding what the biblical norm means for help in applying the Scripture to their lives.

After this rather convoluted argument and exhibition of sloppy theology, the article concludes:

So, the SBC leaders—who trumpeted "biblical inerrancy" as a battle cry to gain and implement control of the convention during the past 20 years—have a high view of Scripture, after all. In fact, it's higher than we thought. Rather than a Trinity, they worship a defacto Quartet: Father, Son, Holy Spirit and Holy Bible, with the Bible acting as the arbiter of the other three.

This is dangerous, for several reasons.

First, it refutes orthodoxy—which asserts the primacy of the Godhead: Father, Son and Holy Spirit—by exalting the Bible to near-divinity and supplanting the influence of Jesus.

Second, by elevating a thing, as precious and authoritative as the Bible is, to such lofty status, it at least implies idolatry, the worship of something other than God.

Third, it denigrates the influence of Jesus and the power of the Holy Spirit to work in lives and guide them toward God's will.

Fourth, it begs a vital question: Who then is to provide the authoritative interpretation of all Scripture?

If Scripture stands over Jesus, then the teachings and actions of Jesus are inadequate.[3]

A local Louisville pastor added, "Not all Scripture rises to the full level of Christ." Later the "BGCT Seminary Study Committee Report" said the BF&M (2000) makes the Bible "equal to God." Even *Christianity Today* chimed in, saying the 2000 statement "is poorer without the rich Christo-centric language of the earlier statement."[4] Strangely, neither this editor nor any other detractor noted that "Jesus as the criterion" does not appear in the 1925 statement, or for that matter any other Baptist confession! R. Albert Mohler Jr. correctly stated:

> The statement [that Jesus is the criterion] was not simply eliminated. It was replaced with a sentence that is far more in keeping with historic confessions of faith. The new sentence affirms that "All Scripture is a testimony to Christ, who is Himself the pinnacle of divine revelation." The language of the 1963 statement is not found in any historic confession of faith, nor did it appear in the 1925 *Baptist Faith and Message* as adopted by the SBC. . . . The 2000 revision is even more Christologically focused than the 1963 statement, and its Christological hermeneutic is stronger, not weaker. In keeping with historic evangelical and Baptist theology, we understand that every single passage of the Bible, in the Old Testament or in the New Testament, is a testimony to Christ. Every word is true, every word is fulfilled in Christ, and Christ affirmed every word of Scripture as fully authoritative.[5]

What should we conclude from the above observations? Have we who affirm the inerrancy and infallibility of Scripture "demoted Jesus" and improperly elevated the Bible to a status "equal to God"? Though there are numerous profitable avenues to pursue this accusation, I want to examine what I believe to be the most important one. I want to answer the question, "What did Jesus believe about the Bible? What was the Savior's view of Scripture?" After all, as the early Clark Pinnock rightly said, "Unreserved commitment to Jesus requires us to look at the Bible through his eyes."[6] We shall call to the witness stand several statements made by our Lord, but in particular I want to give attention to Matt 5:17–18. A careful examination of this text reveals two basic truths about Jesus' view of the Bible.

Jesus Believed that All the Scriptures Point to Him (Matt 5:17)

In the greatest sermon ever preached, the Sermon on the Mount (Matt 5–7), Jesus spoke on the theme of God's kingdom. Matthew 5:17–20, in particular, serves as the introduction to the six great antitheses of 5:21–48. They also explain how we can live out the beatitudes (5:3–12) and be the salt of the earth and the light of the world (5:13–16).

Matthew 5:17 reveals Jesus' high view of Scripture: "Don't assume that I came to destroy the Law or the Prophets. I did not come to destroy but to fulfill" (HCSB). Clearly, what is said here pertains to the Old Testament Scriptures. Nevertheless, what Jesus *affirmed* about the Old Testament He also *promised* about the New Testament. Jesus said:

> "I still have many things to tell you, but you can't bear them now. When the Spirit of truth comes, He will guide you into all the truth. For He will not speak on His own, but He will speak whatever He hears. He will also declare to you what is to come. He will glorify Me, because He will take from what is Mine and declare it to you. Everything the Father has is Mine. This is why I told you that He takes from

what is Mine and will declare it to you" (John 16:12–15 HCSB).

Several points should be made about Jesus' view and use of Scripture. First, Jesus introduced teachings that were new and striking. Indeed, as John 7:46 states, "No man ever spoke like this!" (HCSB). Some may have concluded that His teaching constituted a decisive break with the Old Testament Scriptures. That is certainly the judgment of some scholars today. "Not so," says Jesus. "Do not think [or consider] that I came to destroy [annul, abrogate, disintegrate, demolish] the law." J. A. Alexander noted that the idea is "the destruction of a whole by the complete separation of its parts, as when a house is taken down by being taken to pieces."[7] Jesus said He did not come to tear apart or dismantle the law and prophets (a reference to the OT Scriptures of His day). He did not come to *destroy* (repeated for emphasis) but to fulfill. Note that the antithesis is not between "abolish" and "keep" but between "abolish" and "fulfill." The Scriptures find their fulfillment, their intended purpose, in the life and ministry of Messiah Jesus. He is the one to whom they point. He is the one they predict and anticipate.

Second, Jesus provided not only an emphatic denial but also a positive declaration about the purpose for His coming—He came to fulfill the Scriptures. He came, as the Son, to complete what had previously been delivered in bits and pieces by the Old Testament prophets (see Heb 1:1–2). To set Scripture aside was never His agenda. To bring them to fulfillment and fruition was why He came. Don Carson was correct when he said:

> Jesus fulfills the entire Old Testament in many ways. Because they point toward him, he has certainly not come to abolish them. Rather, he has come to fulfill them in a rich diversity of ways. . . . Jesus does not conceive of his life and

ministry in terms of *opposition* to the Old Testament, but in terms of *bringing to fruition* that toward which it points. Thus the law and the prophets, far from being abolished, find their valid continuity in terms of their outworking in Jesus. The detailed prescriptions of the Old Testament may well be superseded, because whatever is prophetic must be in some sense provisional. *But whatever is prophetic likewise discovers its legitimate continuity in the happy arrival of that toward which it has pointed.*[8]

That our Lord would have affirmed that "all Scripture is a testimony to Christ, who is Himself the focus of divine revelation"—which concludes the BF&M (2000) statement on Scripture—can hardly be questioned:

> You search the Scriptures, for in them you think you have eternal life; and these are they which testify of Me (John 5:39 NKJV).

> Then He said to them, "O foolish ones, and slow of heart to believe in all that the prophets have spoken! Ought not the Christ to have suffered these things and to enter into His glory?" And beginning at Moses and all the Prophets, He expounded to them in all the Scriptures the things concerning Himself (Luke 24:25–27 NKJV).

> Then He said to them, "These are the words which I spoke to you while I was still with you, that all things must be fulfilled which were written in the Law of Moses and the Prophets and the Psalms concerning Me." And He opened their understanding, that they might comprehend the Scriptures (Luke 24:44–45 NKJV).

This truth that Jesus Christ is the theme of the entire Bible is captured well in the anonymous poem, "I Find My Lord in the Book":

I find my Lord in the Bible wherever I chance to look,
He is the theme of the Bible
the center and heart of the Book;
He is the Rose of Sharon,
He is the Lily fair.
Wherever I open my Bible the Lord of the Book is there.

He, at the Book's beginning, gave to
the earth its form.
He is the Ark of shelter bearing the brunt of the storm,
The Burning Bush of the desert, the budding of Aaron's Rod.
Wherever I look in the Bible I see the Son of God.

The Ram upon Mt. Moriah, the Ladder from earth to sky,
The Scarlet Cord in the window, and the Serpent lifted high,
The smitten rock in the desert, the Shepherd with staff and crook,
The face of my Lord I discover wherever I open the Book.

He is the Seed of the Woman, the Savior Virgin-born;
He is the Son of David, whom men rejected with scorn.
His garments of grace and of beauty the stately Aaron deck.
He is a priest forever, after the order of Melchizedek.

Lord of eternal glory whom John, the Apostle saw;
Light of the golden city, Lamb without spot or flaw,
Bridegroom coming at midnight, for whom the Virgins look.
Wherever I open my Bible, I find my Lord in the Book.

Jesus Believed that All the Scriptures Were Perfect in Every Detail (Matt 5:18)

While Matt 5:17 affirms a *promise-fulfillment* understanding of Jesus' view of Scripture, not a *promise-abolish* paradigm, verse 18 provides the Christological and theological rationale. "For I assure you: Until heaven and earth pass away, not the smallest letter or one stroke of a letter will pass from the law until all things are accomplished" (HCSB). Jesus introduces verse 18 with a note of personal authority that transcended the authority of all other rabbis. The word *amen*—variously translated as "assuredly," "truly," "I tell you the truth," or "I assure you"—alerts us that the words that follow are of paramount importance and authority. The phrase "until heaven and earth pass away" means until the end of the age, as long as the present world order persists. "The smallest letter" or "jot" (Gk. *iōta*) is a reference to *yōd*, the smallest letter in the Hebrew alphabet, similar in shape to our apostrophe. One "stroke of a letter" or "tittle" (*keraia*) is the smallest projection or part of a Hebrew letter, similar to that which distinguishes "F" from "E" in English. The phrase "will by no means" is an emphatic negation (using the double negative *ou mē*) to emphasize that God's law will not pass away until all is fulfilled. Luke's parallel says that "it is easier for heaven and earth to pass away than for one stroke of a letter in the law to drop out" (16:17 HCSB).

Jesus affirmed the reliability and truthfulness of the Scriptures in the strongest possible language. He was not saying that the Old Testament contains some truth or that it becomes truth when men and women have a significant encounter with it. He affirmed that "the Scripture cannot be broken" (John 10:35 HCSB), and He proclaimed in His High Priestly prayer, "Your word is truth" (John 17:17 HCSB). H. C. G. Moule well stated that Jesus "absolutely trusted the Bible; and though there are in it things inexplicable and intricate that have puzzled me so much, I am going, not in a blind sense, but reverently, to trust the Book because of Him."[9]

I am no fan of liberal/antisupernatural theology or destructive biblical criticism. I am unimpressed with its worldview, biases, and skewed methodologies. Still, we can learn from those with whom we disagree, and sometimes a breath of scholarly fresh air and honesty blows our way from this camp. When it comes to what Jesus and the early church believed about the Bible, some moderates and liberals would do well to listen to some of their heroes. Rudolf Bultmann said, "Jesus agreed always with the scribes of his time in accepting without question *the authority of (Old Testament) law.* . . . [T]he idea that Jesus had attacked the authority of the law was wholly unknown to the Christian community."[10] Similarly, Emil Brunner stated, "The doctrine of Verbal Inspiration was already known to pre-Christian Judaism and was probably also taken over by Paul and the rest of the Apostles."[11] Kirsopp Lake went even further:

> It is a mistake often made by educated persons who happen to have but little knowledge of historical theology to suppose that fundamentalism is a new and strange form of thought. It is nothing of the kind; it is the partial and uneducated survival of a theology which was once universally held by all Christians: How many were there, for instance, in Christian churches in the eighteenth century who doubted the infallible inspiration of the Scripture? A few perhaps, but very few. No, the fundamentalist may be wrong; I think that he is. But it is we who have departed from the tradition, not he; and I am sorry for anyone who tries to argue with a fundamentalist on the basis of authority. The *Bible* and the corpus theologicum of the Church are on the fundamentalist side.[12]

Four notable examples are cited elsewhere by another author:

> H. J. Cadbury, Harvard professor and one of the more extreme New Testament critics of the last generation, once declared that he was far more sure as a mere historical fact that Jesus held to the common Jewish view of an infallible Bible than that Jesus believed in His own messiahship. Adolf

Harnack, the greatest church historian of modern times, insists that Christ was one with His apostles, the Jews, and the entire early Church in complete commitment to the infallible authority of the Bible. John Knox, author of what is perhaps the most highly regarded recent life of Christ, states that there can be no question that this view of the Bible was taught by our Lord Himself. The liberal critic, F. C. Grant, concludes that in the New Testament, "It is everywhere taken for granted that Scripture is trustworthy, infallible, and inerrant."[13]

A survey of our Lord's teaching in the Gospels indicates that the views of these scholars are on solid ground. Jesus consistently treated the historical narratives of the Old Testament as straightforward records of fact. He referred to Abel (Luke 11:51), Noah (Matt 24:37–39), Abraham (John 8:56), Sodom and Gomorrah (Matt 10:15; 11:23–24), Lot (Luke 17:28–32), Isaac and Jacob (Matt 8:11), the manna (John 6:31), the bronze serpent (John 3:14), David (Matt 22:43), Solomon (Matt 6:29; 12:42), Elijah (Luke 4:25–26), Elisha (Luke 4:27), Jonah (Matt 12:39–41), and Moses (Matt 8:4), among others. Nowhere is there the slightest hint that He questioned the historicity or accuracy of these or any other accounts.

It is interesting to note that Jesus often chose as the basis of His teaching those very stories that many modern skeptics find unacceptable (e.g., Adam and Eve, Noah's flood, Sodom and Gomorrah, and Jonah). For Jesus, Scripture was the final court of appeal in His disputes with the Pharisees and Sadducees. In His battle against Satan in the wilderness, Jesus cited Scripture in such a way that no further argument was possible (Matt 4:1–11). Jesus might set aside or reject the rabbinic or Pharisaical interpretation of the Old Testament (see Matt 5:21–48), but He never questioned its authority or truthfulness.[14]

Again, the early Pinnock saw this clearly:

> Jesus' doctrine of inspiration receives expression in the Sermon on the Mount. Before setting forth his ethical instructions, Jesus explained his intention. "Think not that I have come to abolish the law and the prophets; I have not come to abolish them but to fulfill them" (Mt. 5:17). Evidently he does not want us to think that the thrust of his teaching is to violate or even to devalue Old Testament revelation. The saying which is also contained in Luke (16:17) has an entirely genuine ring to it. Jesus' enemies were eager to pin an "antinomian" label on him if they could. Therefore, Jesus made it clear that the object of his criticisms was not the Bible, but the traditions which the Rabbis had built as a fence around it, traditions which in practice enjoyed an authority actually higher than the written Word. He assures us that his confidence in the divine character of Scripture does not stop short even of its smallest elements. "Not an iota, not a dot, will pass" (Mt. 5:18). He issues a stern warning: "Whoever then relaxes one of the least of these commandments and teaches men so, shall be called least in the kingdom of heaven; but he who does them and teaches them shall be called great in the kingdom of heaven" (v. 19).[15]

The view of liberal scholar James Barr was incorrect when he stated:

> Jesus took Jewish scripture as it was, as his contemporaries did, and he used it as they did in this respect, as a source through which authoritative intimations of divine truth had been given. Thus if Jesus refers to a passage in Exodus or in Deuteronomy with the words "Moses said," it is quite mistaken to read this as if he was placing his own full messianic and divine authority behind the assertion that these books were actually written by the historical Moses. No such question entered his head and there is nothing in the Gospels

that suggests that his teaching was intended to cope with it. Historical questions interested him little.[16]

But Jesus said, "Not a jot or a tittle . . ."

Alan Culpepper, former professor at The Southern Baptist Theological Seminary, was also incorrect when he claimed that "Jesus had remarkably little to say about the nature of Scripture. . . . Jesus demands [in the Sermon on the Mount] a standard of righteousness higher than that set by the Hebrew Scriptures and the traditions of the Pharisees."[17]

The traditions of the Pharisees—yes; the Hebrew Scriptures—no! Our Lord said, "Not a jot or a tittle . . ."

Similarly, Frank Stagg, also a former Southern Seminary professor, was off course when he said that "those who say the Bible is inerrant are lying . . . [and] inerrancy misses the point. If we follow Christ we recognize variant perspectives; we see competing perspectives. You can't go north and south at the same time and Jesus didn't try to. He affirmed much but He rejected much."[18]

However, the Savior said, "Not a jot or a tittle . . ."

Henlee Barnette, another former Southern Seminary professor, was simply wrong when he declared:

1. The Bible is errant with many self-contradictions.
2. The Bible has errors in the field of science.
3. The Bible is not historically accurate.
4. The Bible is errant as to cosmology.[19]

Again, our Lord Jesus Christ said, "Not a jot or a tittle . . ."

Conclusion

My initial theology was heavily influenced and formed by Clark Pinnock. Few lament his theological disintegration more than I. Earlier in his life, he articulated the crux of the matter concerning the relationship between Jesus and the Bible with crystal clarity:

> Shall we follow Jesus in his view of Scripture? In the light of this evidence the question calls for another. How can a Christian even consider *not* doing so? Our Lord's view of inspiration was not an incidental tenet on the border of his theology. His belief in the truthfulness of the Old Testament was the rock on which he based his own sense of vocation and the validity of much of his teachings. The question about the inspiration of Scripture really boils down to the issue of Christology. It is impossible to affirm his authority while at the same time seeking to evade his teachings regarding the divine authority of the Bible. If Christ's claim to be the Son of God is true, his person guarantees the truth of all the rest of his teachings as well. So long as Jesus Christ is confessed, honored, and adored, we may confidently expect a high view of Scripture to persist in the church. And in the light of a considerable defection from that view amongst professed Christians today we boldly appeal for a return to a proper view of the Bible on the basis of the massive fact of our Lord's doctrine of inspiration.[20]

In my early days at Southern Seminary, I had lunch with a former professor. Even though we held significantly different theologies, he was always gracious and supportive of me and I enjoyed the time of fellowship with him. One day as we sat down to eat, he looked at me and said, "I want to ask you a question, and I mean no offense." I replied that he could ask me anything he wished, and his question was this: "How did you turn out theologically the way that you are? I mean, why do you think theologically like you do?" I told him I was not offended by the question at all, but I did not think that my answer would be very satisfying. I shared that when I was a little boy at about the age of eight, I trusted Jesus Christ as my Lord and Savior. As I grew in the faith, I came to understand that to be a Christian meant to live under the lordship of Jesus Christ and that His lordship should permeate every area of our lives. His lordship included what I should think and believe when it comes to matters of theology, including the Bible. I told him that as I had studied Jesus' view of the Bible, I came to the conclusion that I could do nothing other than hold to its complete truthfulness and reliability as He himself had done. To do anything other than that would be to set aside the lordship of Jesus Christ. That professor simply responded by saying, "I have never thought of it like that before, but it does make a lot of sense."

L. R. Scarborough was a great Texas Baptist who succeeded his hero B. H. Carroll as president at Southwestern Baptist Theological Seminary. In his book *Gospel Message*, Scarborough recorded in moving and memorable words the death of this Texas Titan:

> B. H. Carroll, the greatest man I ever knew, as he was about to die, a few days before he died, expecting me, as he wanted me, to succeed him as president of the seminary, I was in his room one day and he pulled himself up by my chair with his hands and looked me in the face. There were times when he looked like he was forty feet high. And he looked into my face and said, "My boy, on this Hill orthodoxy, the old truth is making one of its last stands and I want to deliver to you a charge and I do it in the blood of Jesus Christ." He said, "You will be elected president of this seminary. I want you, if there ever comes heresy in your faculty, to take it to your

faculty. If they won't hear you, take it to the trustees. If they won't hear you, take it to the conventions that appointed them. If they won't hear you, take it to the common Baptists. They will hear you. And," he said, "I charge you in the name of Jesus Christ to keep it lashed to the old Gospel of Jesus Christ." As long as I have influence in that institution, by the grace of God I will stand by the old Book.[21]

This is a great statement. This is a great place to stand. This is a great place to serve. This is a good place to die. I will always be grateful to Russ Bush for helping me see what was at stake in relation to Jesus and the Bible. Eternal destinies hang in the balance. The stakes are too high for us to get this wrong.

Notes

1. Scriptures which attend the article are: Exod 24:4; Deut 4:1–2; 17:19; Josh 8:34; Pss 19:7–20; 119:11,89,105,140; Isa 34:16; 40:8; Jer 15:16; 36; Matt 5:17–18; 22:29; Luke 21:33; 24:44–46; John 5:39; 16:13–15; 17:17; Acts 2:16ff; 17:11; Rom 15:4; 16:25–26; 2 Tim 3:15–17; Heb 1:1–2; 4:12; 1 Pet 1:25; 2 Pet 1:19–21.

2. T. Starnes, "6 Words: 'Defining Moment' between Conservative and Moderate Baptists," *Baptist Press* (June 21, 2000): 2.

3. M. Knox, "Editorial," *Baptist Standard* (June 19, 2000): 5.

4. Editorial, "Do Good Fences Make Good Baptists?" *Christianity Today* (August 7, 2000): 26.

5. Speaking for the *Baptist Faith and Message* study committee at the 2000 Southern Baptist Convention in Orlando, Florida, on June 14, 2000.

6. C. Pinnock, "The Inspiration of Scripture and the Authority of Jesus Christ," in *God's Inerrant Word: An International Symposium on the Trustworthiness of Scripture*, ed. J. W. Montgomery (Minneapolis: Bethany, 1974), 202.

7. J. A. Alexander, *The Gospel according to Matthew* (New York: Charles Scribner and Sons, 1860; reprint, Grand Rapids: Baker, 1980), 126.

8. D. A. Carson, *Sermon on the Mount: An Evangelical Exposition of Matthew 5–7* (Grand Rapids: Baker, 1982), 37; italics added.

9. R. Pache, *The Inspiration and Authority of Scripture* (Chicago: Moody, 1969), 223.

10. R. Bultmann, *Jesus and the Word*, trans. L. P. Smith and E. H. Lantero (London: Scribner, 1958), 61, 63.

11. E. Brunner, *The Christian Doctrine of God* (London: Lutterworth, 1949), 107.

12. K. Lake, *The Religion of Yesterday and Tomorrow* (Boston: Houghton, 1926), 61.

13. K. Kantzer, "Christ and Scripture," *His* 26.4 (1966): 16–20; italics added.

14. For a detailed view of Jesus' view of biblical authority, see J. Wenham, *Christ and the Bible*, 3rd ed. (Eugene, OR: Wipf & Stock, 2009).

15. Pinnock, "The Inspiration of Scripture and the Authority of Jesus Christ," 205.

16. J. Barr, *Beyond Fundamentalism* (Philadelphia: Westminster, 1984), 11.

17. R. A. Culpepper, "Jesus' View of Scripture," in *The Unfettered Word: Confronting the Authority-Inerrancy Question*, ed. R. B. James (Waco: Word, 1987), 26–27.

18. R. Hargus, "Retired Seminary Professor Advises Baptists to Use Bible as Jesus Did," *Baptists Today* (May 23, 1996): 8.

19. H. Barnette, "The Heresy of Inerrancy Continues to Plague Southern Baptists," *Baptists Today* (September 21, 1995): 16.

20. Pinnock, "The Inspiration of Scripture and the Authority of Jesus Christ," 215.

21. L. R. Scarborough, *Gospel Message* (Nashville: Sunday School Board of the Southern Baptist Convention, 1922), 227–28.

Chapter 3

Reflections on the Atonement[1]

Paige Patterson

I n 1979, Southern Baptists began a two-decade struggle between the reigning establishment and those within the denomination who desired to restore the theological commitments of their church forefathers. The public focus was on a discussion about the nature of the Bible and the extent of its inspiration. Russell Bush was a major contributor to the conservative renaissance at many points but especially with Tom Nettles through the publication of *Baptists and the Bible*, a widely read volume that laid historical, biblical, and philosophical foundations for conservatives.[2]

But while the inerrancy of Scripture was the most debated issue, there were others. Ethical concerns like abortion, gender issues, and other theological topics were in view. In 1987 New Orleans Baptist Theological Seminary sponsored a debate on the nature of the atonement. Fisher Humphreys, a faculty member at New Orleans Seminary, argued for a view of the atonement that he called "cruciform forgiveness," while I defended substitutionary atonement. This article is essentially the position I argued in that discussion.

In 1978 Broadman Press released Fisher Humphreys' treatise on the atonement titled *The Death of Christ*. This monograph raised serious questions, which, in the minds of some, remain unresolved. This essay addresses three of these issues raised by Humphreys. The two demanding the most attention focus on the question of the necessity of the atonement, its nature, and especially the important issue of penal substitution. A final consideration is the question of diachronic interpretation. To what degree can contemporary interpreters bridge the gap and grasp what a New Testament author may have intended? Is there a need to create new models in order to interpret the atonement in a world that harbors a radically different perspective from that of the New Testament world?

The Death of Christ is typical of Humphreys' style and approach, characterized by a remarkable ability to entertain abstruse concepts to reduce them to a more popular and readable level yet without sacrificing accuracy. His willingness to indulge in public dialogue on these issues is commendable. Furthermore, his work upholds and explicates themes that are critical for an appropriate theology of the atonement. The concern that Humphreys exhibits to magnify the "costly forgiveness" motif of the New Testament is only one of the many worthy contributions. Notwithstanding these merits, other conclusions drawn by Humphreys appear to be supported inadequately at best and (in at least one case) at worst reflect a misreading of the scriptural emphasis altogether.

The Adequacy of Biblical Models

In assessing the contribution of C. H. Dodd to the understanding of the earliest Christian preaching that is recorded primarily in Acts, Humphreys alleged the following: "The first thing we notice about these sermons is that they are set in a context which is completely foreign to twentieth-century people. Their context is the eschatological hope of Jewish people in the first century that God would bring in a new age and a new world."[3] In point of fact, Humpheys argued that there is only one way that interpreters today can hope to appreciate these sermons: "Only by a deliberate imaginative leap can a modern man appreciate the eschatological way of understanding Jesus' life and death which was so natural for Jews of the first century."[4]

In addition to concerns about the ability of contemporary interpreters to grapple with the eschatological context of early preaching, Humphreys also thought it probable that the sacrifices and rituals of Judaism, which provide the backdrop for New Testament atonement discussions, would prove "foreign and strange" in a modern context.[5] However, he also apparently admitted that the problem may not be limited to a later era since portions of Peter's early preaching "cannot have made his message more palatable to his audience, who were probably no more inclined to believe it than men are today."[6]

This conclusion, in turn, led Humphreys to some rather startling conclusions. The first conclusion is that the New Testament models are inspired; but some models, such as the sacrificial model, are "foreign to us."[7] Therefore, a second conclusion is that one must re-present the teachings of the New Testament as employing modern models instead of biblical ones. Humphreys explained the rationale behind the use of updated models in this way: "Because the presuppositions that accompany them are shared by modern men, they satisfy us, taking the discussion to limits at which we are content to stop."[8]

Humphreys doubtless would stop short of some of the conclusions of Rudolf Bultmann, but he still shared some common assumptions. For example, Bultmann, like Humphreys, considered the preaching of the early church to be unintelligible today. Humphries noted, "To be sure, that preaching was developed in conceptions which are no longer intelligible today, but they do express the knowledge of the finiteness of the world, and of the end which is imminent to us all because we are all beings of this finite world."[9] According to Anthony Thiselton, Bultmann, again like Humphreys, had a problem with the mixture of sacrificial and judicial analogies, which have simply ceased to be tenable for interpreters today.[10] Elsewhere Bultmann wrote:

> In order to describe the significance of the salvation-occurrence, Paul uses a series of terms originating in a number of different thought complexes. One group is composed of statements which understand Jesus' death in terms of Jewish sacrificial practice—and that also means in terms of the juristic thinking that dominated it—regarding his death as a propitiatory sacrifice by which forgiveness of sins is brought about; which is to say: by which the guilt contracted by sins is cancelled.[11]

To Bultmann's credit, he recognized the clear emphasis of the New Testament. However, he was also convinced that this preaching of the apostles needs to be demythologized. Humphreys failed to see the teaching of the Scriptures with the same clarity that Bultmann demonstrated, but he agreed with Bultmann that contemporary men find biblical metaphors and models mystifying and inscrutable. Whereas Bultmann jettisoned the myths, Humphreys just abandoned the models or at least created new ones palatable to contemporary tastes.

Humphreys also joined Bultmann in the latter's conviction that modern men operate from a scientific worldview that differs so radically from the biblical worldview as to make impossible the fusing of the two horizons. As Bultmann put it,

> For modern man the mythological conception of the world, the conceptions of eschatology, of redeemer and of redemption, are over and done with. Is it possible to expect that we shall make a sacrifice of understanding, *sacrificium intellectus*, in order to accept what we cannot sincerely consider true—merely because such conceptions are suggested in the Bible?[12]

Even if Humphreys refrained from alleging that the biblical materials are mythological, the result is still the same. If biblical models are inscrutable to men in our era, then logic would dictate that Bultmann was correct. Portions of the Bible are simply inadequate for a scientifically enlightened era, necessitating the search for new metaphors, models, and modes of expression.

A favorite appeal of Humphreys was the fascinating odyssey of missionary Don Richardson chronicled in *Peace Child*.[13] This readable adventure focuses on the frustrations of Don and Carol Richardson as they attempted to bring the gospel to the Sawi, headhunting cannibals in the Netherlands, New Guinea. Sawi culture was so totally contradictory to every Judeo-Christian concept that often the biblical virtues were Sawi vices, and biblical vices were Sawi virtues. The missionary attempt of the Richardsons would have failed had they not discovered quite by accident the Sawi custom of giving a "peace child" to restore harmony between warring tribes. Seizing this cultural practice, the Richardsons were able to show by way of analogy that God has given a "peace child" to reconcile us to God. According to Humphreys, the new model was essential because the biblical models were culturally inadequate.

Certainly each generation of Christians must explain the gospel to their own age. As a part of that task, new metaphors, analogies, and illustrations are surely permissible in attempts to bridge not only the time gap from biblical times to the modern era but also in overcoming the cultural gaps that exist geographically and ethnically. But does this mean that the biblical symbols and metaphors either are not effective or so encrusted with first-century cultural barnacles as to make them inadequate for the modern era and thus in need of replacement?

While admitting that cultural and linguistic patterns are disparate, this fact in itself does not prohibit correspondence. Humphreys supposed that the concepts of eschatological hope, animal sacrifice, and substitution are hopelessly obscure to moderns. Yet there is constant talk in the Western world of some sort of ominous day of reckoning generally thought to be "the end" and often referred to as "doomsday." Even baseball sports a "sacrifice fly" and a "sacrifice bunt," and almost all competitive events use "substitution" for the disabled or ineffective. Even if ideas belonging to a society removed by 2,000 or more years are not handled with precision by everyone, it is nevertheless inaccurate to suppose that most people cannot get the gist of most of these symbols and ideas.[14]

The case of the "peace child" analogy is indeed instructive. While Don Richardson did discover a cultural custom that became a vehicle of communication, what was ultimately communicated was biblical truth. Richardson used the "peace child" motif to explain John 3:16 and God's giving of a "peace child."[15] Richardson never abrogated biblical analogies and models. He simply employed what he termed the "redemptive analogy" in Sawi culture to gain initial comprehension. From that point, progress to more mature biblical understanding was possible. Furthermore, the Sawi need for a "peace child" for reconciliation is not contrary to, but rather supportive of, the same truth found in the Scriptures. One can and must commend Richardson for his challenge to seek these "redemptive analogies" in every culture. But surely this can be done without suggesting that there is fault or inadequacy in biblical analogies or models.

Another factor apparently missing from Humphreys' assumptions is the role of the Holy Spirit in the interpretive process. Jesus said, "But the Counselor, the Holy Spirit—the Father will send Him in My name—will teach you all things and remind you of everything I have told you" (John 14:26 HCSB). The apostle John, in the Spirit of the Master, added, "The anointing you received from Him remains in you, and you don't need anyone to teach you. Instead, His anointing teaches you about all things, and is true and is not a lie; just as it has taught you, remain in Him" (1 John 2:27 HCSB).

While space prevents further analysis of this question, perhaps more confidence in the ability and understanding of the reader should be a consideration. In addition, the role of the Holy Spirit and His adequacy, in both the initial choice of verbiage in inspiration and in His illuminating task, might inspire greater confidence in the enduring adequacy of the models, symbols, and metaphors of the Bible. Before devising new symbols or models, perhaps the best approach is to elucidate more fully the biblical models chosen by the Spirit of God.

The Necessity of the Atonement

Humphreys expressed concern that Anselm viewed the atonement as "necessary." After erroneously alleging that Anselm's model seems to be "associated with irrational vengeance,"[16] Humphreys proceeded to take issue with the idea of a "necessary" atonement: "Anselm tried to show that the cross was necessary. His title indicates this concern for necessity. I believe it is unwise to seek for a 'necessity' for the cross. It is quite possible to affirm and clarify the importance of the cross without speaking of it as necessary."[17] Humphreys believed that speaking of the atonement as "necessary" is unwise.

For at least two reasons I believe that it is imprudent to allege that to speak of the atonement as "necessary" is "unwise." First, the Scriptures speak of the atonement as necessary. Since the Scriptures prophesied such an event, this word from God of necessity had to be fulfilled. Remonstrating with Peter for his attempted intervention to save Jesus through a violent act, Jesus said, "Do you think that I cannot call on My Father, and He will provide Me at once with more than 12 legions of angels? How, then, would the Scriptures be fulfilled that say it must happen this way?" (Matt 26:53–54 HCSB). Again, Jesus left little doubt about His own perception of the nature and necessity of His mission when at Caesarea Philippi: "Then He began to teach them that the Son of Man must suffer many things, and be rejected by the elders, the chief priests, and the scribes, be killed, and rise after three days" (Mark 8:31 HCSB).

The angels at the empty tomb echoed a similar theme: "He is not here, but He has been resurrected! Remember how He spoke to you when He was still in Galilee, saying, 'The Son of man must be betrayed into the hands of sinful men, be crucified, and rise on the third day'?" (Luke 24:6–7 HCSB).

One of the most interesting avowals of Jesus occurs in John 12:24 when the Lord appears to provide something of a rationale for the essential nature of the atonement, suggesting that unless a grain of wheat die it remains alone. Only by death does it bring forth fruit.

To that striking affirmation can be added the lucid observation of the author of Hebrews who simply declared, "According to the law almost everything is purified with blood; and without the shedding of blood there is no forgiveness" (Heb 9:22 HCSB).

What emerges thus far is that the atonement was in fact necessary in order to fulfill the Scriptures. This alone makes it unwise to say that anyone is unwise to speak of the atonement as necessary! Can it ever be wise to say that something may not be necessary that the Scriptures affirm to be necessary?

Perhaps Humphreys will acknowledge this point but then insist that what he really wanted to avoid was any theory that might put God in a box, a theory that would impose some ontological necessity upon God to the end that God acted in Christ out of necessity rather than out of free, loving compassion. The first point to be made here is that to insist that the atonement is an ontological necessity for God might indeed be injudicious. After all, humility dictates that we exercise a measure of care in stating laws by which God must abide. Law came from God and not the reverse. However, some necessities are attributable to God if He is to be consistent with His own nature. God cannot, for example, do wrong and at the same time remain righteous. The question then becomes one of the preponderance of evidence. Insofar as I can discover, there appears to be no hint in Scripture that the atonement was not essential and somehow bound up in who and what God is.[18] There is certainly no warning in the Scriptures that it might be unwise to speak of the atonement as necessary.

On the other hand, the passages already cited in John 12:24 and Heb 9:22 confer the idea of "necessity" on the atonement more than just a little. Romans 3:23–26 (HCSB), which will be examined later in another context, provides assistance here also:

> For all have sinned and fall short of the glory of God. They are justified freely by His grace through the redemption

that is in Christ Jesus. God presented Him as a propitiation through faith in His blood, to demonstrate His righteousness, because in His restraint God passed over the sins previously committed. He presented Him to demonstrate His righteousness at the present time, so that He would be righteous and declare righteous the one who has faith in Jesus.

What Paul seems to be suggesting here is that the remedy for a fallen race that God pursued enabled Him at once to "declare righteous" those who would believe in Jesus and still be totally "righteous" in doing so. That method is described as "propitiation through faith in His blood." The expression argues strongly for something in the nature of God that apparently necessitated this particular remedy.

Add to these the intriguing scene in Gethsemane when Jesus cried out to His Father for deliverance from the agony of making atonement. What kind of Father is God if He allowed His Son to endure the cross when there remained available to the Father some other options through which He could save men? If it be objected that this removes the atonement from being a free and loving act of God, one must reply that the necessity of a particular action in no way arbitrarily prevents the action from being free or loving.

In any case, the point remains that God will have difficulty avoiding the charge of being a "cosmic sadist" if He failed to exercise other options to save men, while choosing instead to allow His beloved Son to be crucified. This further suggests that Humphreys is on shaky ground when he challenges Anselm on the latter's conviction that the atonement was a necessity. *Unwise* seems to be the most appropriate term to describe the thinking that would raise questions about the necessity of atonement.

John Calvin concurred with this concept of necessity when he said, "In order to interpose between us and God's anger, and satisfy his righteous judgment, it was necessary that he should feel the weight of divine vengeance."[19] Or as J. Stott states the case, "To say that he must 'satisfy himself' means that he must be himself and act according to the perfection of his nature or 'name.' The necessity of 'satisfaction' for God, therefore, is not found in anything outside himself but within himself, in his own immutable character. It is an inherent or intrinsic necessity."[20] So crucial is this issue that J. Denney could even write of the concept as that which separates evangelicals from non-evangelicals: "It is the recognition of this divine necessity, or the failure to recognize it which ultimately divides interpreters of Christianity into evangelical and non-evangelical, those who are true to the New Testament and those who cannot digest it."[21]

A final line of evidence for the necessity of the atonement is discernible in the use of *dei*, the impersonal verb often translated "must" or "it is necessary" in the New Testament. *Dei* signifies necessity or compulsion in regard to an event. Of the 102 occurrences of *dei* in the New Testament, Luke uses it 41 times. In reference to the necessity of the atonement, Jesus says, "The Son of Man must [*dei*] suffer many things and be rejected by the elders, chief priests, and scribes, be killed, and be raised the third day" (Luke 9:22 HCSB). Not only the use of *dei* but also the entire context of Matt 16:21 make abundantly clear the thesis that the atonement was essential. The use of *dei* throughout the New Testament and even its usages in the LXX[22] demonstrate the compelling and unavoidable nature of that to which it refers.[23]

Penal Substitution as Primary Motif

Tackling Anselm is only a portion of Humphreys' agenda. He next turns to J. Calvin and finds his view of penal substitution lacking also. Acknowledging that the idea of substitution "is fundamentally a good idea,"[24] he found the general idea of punishment "much more complicated," as he explained:

> The problem with Calvin's view of punishment is his idea that within God there is a tension between love and righteousness. He felt that though in love God wanted to save men, in righteousness he was required to punish all sins. Only when the demands of righteousness had been met, by punishing Jesus as a substitute for men, was God in a position to forgive. But there is no such tension in God's love.[25]

Humphreys concluded:

> Men today do not ordinarily hold this view of God as simply willing right and wrong, and so they cannot believe that vicarious punishment is either meaningful or moral. No illustration can be given, so far as I can tell, which makes vicarious punishment morally credible to men today. The stories of one soldier punished for another, a child punished for his brother, a man punished for his friend, may be morally praiseworthy from the point of view of the substitute, but they never are acceptable from the point of view of the punisher. It always seems morally outrageous that any judge would require a substitute. However noble the substitute's act might be, the judge's act seems despicable.[26]

Finally, Humphreys objected that "to demand death as a substitutionary punishment is simply morally reprehensible," and he seemed pleased that "almost no one today" holds any longer to Calvin's conclusions on this matter.[27] This avowal will doubtless astonish many contemporary evangelicals. Of course, Humphreys was not the first to find "penal substitution" objectionable. John Stott explained:

> During the last one hundred years a number of ingenious attempts have been made to retain the vocabulary of "sub-

stitution," while rejecting "penal substitution" ("penal" being derived from *poena*, a penalty or punishment). Their origin can be traced back to Abelard's protest against Anselm in the twelfth century, and even more to Socinus' scornful rejection of the Reformers' doctrine in the sixteenth. In his book *De Jesu Christo Servatore* (1578) Faustus Socinus denied not only the deity of Jesus but any idea of "satisfaction" in his death. The notion that guilt can be transferred from one person to another, he declaimed, was incompatible with both reason and justice. It was not only impossible, but unnecessary. For God is perfectly capable of forgiving sinners without it. He leads them to repentance, and so makes them forgivable.[28]

Leaving alone Humphreys' miscalculation about the number of adherents and the categorical affirmation that death as a substitutionary punishment is morally reprehensible (a position for which no evidence is offered), the focus of this investigation rests only on the presence or absence of penal substitution in the Scriptures. In the event that the idea of penal substitution proves to be biblical, a further attempt is made to determine the prominence of this theme in biblical materials.

Surely the concept of penal substitution is present in the Scriptures. A cursory reading of Isa 53 (HCSB), even in English, provides indisputable evidence. Though the Suffering Servant is sinlessly perfect, He is nonetheless "struck down by God and afflicted" (v. 4). He was "pierced because of our transgressions" and the "punishment for our peace" was on Him (v. 5). In fact, "the LORD has punished Him for the iniquity of us all" (v. 6). For the transgressions of Isaiah's people "He was struck" (v. 8); "He will carry their iniquities" (v. 11); and He "bore the sin of many" when He was "counted among the rebels" (v. 12). God is even described as seeing "His anguish" and being "satisfied" (v. 11).

Even granting the poverty of language to describe adequately the ineffable mystery of atoning transaction, nevertheless it is clear that the Suffering Servant of Isa 53 was doing something in His capacity as a substitute, and what He did was accept punishment rightly prescribed for others. Whatever else the atonement may mean, penal substitution is a biblically supported motif. For Humphreys to find Calvin's conviction about penal substitution to be problematic is to find Isaiah's presentation problematic also. To relegate "penal substitution" to a position of little consequence is to differ sharply with the Scriptures.

However, in public discussion Humphreys did affirm that the doctrine of penal substitution was probably taught in Isa 53. Also, Humphreys made clear his conviction that penal substitution is not a major biblical concept or as serviceable as other models, which, like his own model of cruciform forgiveness, might be developed later. But is Humphreys correct? Wolfhart Pannenberg suggested otherwise: "These objections to Luther's doctrine of the penal suffering of Christ do not affect its fundamental insight. Luther was probably the first since Paul and his school to have seen with full clarity that Jesus' death in its genuine sense is to be understood as vicarious penal suffering."[29]

Penal substitution is the major and indispensable model for comprehending what God was doing in Christ. Anselm, Calvin, and the apostle Paul suggest as much. This is not to say that a fully biblical perspective of the atonement would not include such ideas as "example," "reconciliation," "moral influence," and a number of others. However, the thesis is that the foundational understanding of the atonement in the Bible is that of penal substitution. All other aspects of the atoning work of Christ derive their significance from the vicarious suffering of Jesus, who bore our penalty. But can this position be sustained from Scripture?

First, attention must be devoted to the sacrificial system of Israel. According to Exod 29:10; Lev 1:4, and other passages in the law, when a worshipper brought a sacrifice to the tabernacle, he was to place his hand on the head of the animal to be sacrificed. The meaning of this act is suggested clearly in the instructions for the Day of Atonement. Aaron was to "lay both his hands on the head of the live goat and confess over it all the Israelites' wrongdoings and rebellious acts—all their sins. He is to put them on the goat's head and send it away into the wilderness" (Lev 16:21 HCSB).

Clearly the ceremony of placing hands on the head of the animal to be slain or sent away as the scapegoat symbolized transfer and substitution. The worshipper, though guilty, was transferring his penalty to the head of the innocent victim, which would be slain or released alone for certain death in the wilderness. But why was this done? What was intended by these rituals?

Few things are spelled out with greater precision in the Scriptures than this: "the wages of sin is death" (Rom 6:23 HCSB); "on the day you eat from it, you will certainly die" (Gen 2:17 HCSB); "the person who sins is the one who will die" (Ezek 18:20 HCSB). Stott stated the case succinctly:

> Christ died our death, when he died for our sins. That is to say, granted that his death and our sins are linked, the link is not merely that of consequence (he was the victim of our human brutality) but of penalty (he endured in his innocent person the penalty our sins had deserved). For, according to Scripture, death is related to sin as its just reward: "the wages of sin is death" (Rom 6:23). The Bible everywhere views human death not as a natural but as a penal event. It is an alien intrusion into God's good world, and not part of his original intention for humankind.[30]

The ultimate penalty for man's transgression is death. When a worshipper placed his hands on the head of the sacrificial animal, he symbolically transferred his guilt and thus the penalty to the animal. Sentenced to the death penalty, the animal was slain. By any reasonable assessment, this was penal substitution! The sacrificial system pointed inexorably to "the Lamb of God, who takes away the sin of the world!" (John 1:29 HCSB). The death of Jesus was, therefore, one of penal substitution also.

Another line of evidence for this truth is found in the Passover. Exodus 12 stipulates that the death angel would pass through the land of Egypt, exacting the life of the firstborn in each household. The only exception to this rule was in a household where a lamb was slain and its blood sprinkled on the door: "when I see the blood, I will pass over you" (Exod 12:13 HCSB). The transferability of sin's penalty may be less obvious here but certainly not absent. If death is viewed as the universal penalty of sin and if the exodus itself serves as a paradigm of man's sojourn from spiritual slavery to salvific liberation and ultimately promised inheritance, then certainly the clear substitutionary character of the lamb in the place of the firstborn was a "penal substitution," avoiding as it did the judgment of God that fell on the Egyptians and on anyone else who failed to act in faith.

Such thinking was paramount in the mind of Paul when he wrote of the significance of Christ's death in Gal 3:10–13 (HCSB):

> For all who rely on the works of the law are under a curse, because it is written: "Cursed is everyone who does not continue doing everything written in the book of the law." Now it is clear that no one is justified before God by the law, because "the righteous will live by faith." But the law is not based on faith; instead, "the one who does these things will live by them." Christ has redeemed us from the curse

of the law by becoming a curse for us, because it is written: "Cursed is everyone who is hung on a tree."

In this passage the apostle concluded that everyone is "under" (*hupo*) the curse. However, Christ was made a curse "for" (*huper*) us.[31] The result is that He has redeemed us "from" (*ek*) the curse of the law. The salient and poignant teaching of this study shows that there exists a law that, when broken, carries an appropriate penalty or "curse." Since all are lawless, all live under the penalty and its judgment. But Christ was made a curse for us. That this is a reference to His death on the cross is verified by the reference to Deut 21:23 and the curse of one hanged on a tree. Thus, *huper* has been shown to be a preposition that frequently bears the meaning of substitution. Here it clearly involves the transfer of the curse as a result of sin from the guilty to the innocent so that the guilty is purchased "out from" (*ek*) the penalty of the curse. This is penal substitution.

On the point of the curse, Stott observed the following of the apostles:

> Now they were under no necessity to use this language. Peter also spoke of Jesus' "crucifixion," and Paul of his "sufferings" and "execution." So why their references to the "tree" and to his having been "hanged" on it? The only possible explanation is to be found in Deuteronomy 21:22–23, where instructions were given for the body of a man, who had been executed for a capital offence by hanging, to be buried before nightfall, "because anyone who is hung on a tree is under God's curse." The apostles were quite familiar with this legislation, and with its implication that Jesus died under the divine curse. Yet, instead of hushing it up, they deliberately drew people's attention to it. So evidently they were not embarrassed by it. They did not think of Jesus as in any sense deserving to be accursed by God. They must,

therefore, have at least begun to understand that it was our curse which he was bearing.[32]

No less explicit is the crucial passage to which reference was made earlier, Rom 3:23–26. In this passage much of what has been rehearsed in the earlier part of this paper is all brought into focus. All have sinned, but justification and redemption are available through the "propitiation" (Gk. *hilastērion*) of Christ. In the atonement God's righteousness is declared in that He has dealt justly with sin by imposing its full penalty on His Son. At the same time, God justifies sinners who believe in Jesus. No explanation except penal substitution, insofar as I can tell, adequately accounts for this remarkable avowal.

Conclusion

The biblical symbols and models are adequate to convey to men under the prompting and illuminating work of the Holy Spirit the truths of God's act of redemption in Christ. To speak of the atonement of Christ as the way of salvation as necessary is in keeping with the words and the sentiments of Scripture. A plausible argument can even be generated for the necessity of the atonement residing somehow in the very nature of God Himself.

Finally, the cross is a monumental example and has profound moral influence. But neither good example nor moral influence ever gets men to God and to heaven. Sin and its penalty must be addressed. The primary significance of the atonement from which all other meanings draw their dynamic is that of penal substitution. Humphreys' penchant for differing with Anselm or Calvin is certainly permissible even if differing on this particular subject inevitably raises evangelical eyebrows. But differing with the Scriptures is much more serious.

Notes

1. Aside from the brief introductory paragraphs, this article has been revised and edited from its original appearance in the *Criswell Theological Review* 3, no. 2 (Spring 1989): 307–20. Reprinted with permission.

2. L. R. Bush and T. J. Nettles, *Baptists and the Bible*, rev. and exp. ed. (Nashville: B&H Academic, 1999 [1st ed., Moody Press, 1980]).

3. F. Humphreys, *The Death of Christ* (Nashville: Broadman, 1978), 20.

4. Ibid., 21.

5. Ibid., 27.

6. Ibid., 21.

7. Ibid., 43.

8. Ibid.

9. R. Bultmann, *Jesus Christ and Mythology* (New York: Scribner, 1958), 25.

10. A. Thiselton, *The Two Horizons* (Grand Rapids: Eerdmans, 1980), 270.

11. R. Bultmann, *Theology of the New Testament*, vol. 1 (New York: Scribner, 1955), 295.

12. Bultmann, *Mythology*, 17.

13. D. Richardson, *Peace Child* (Glendale: Regal, 1976); cf. Humphreys' use of the story in "The Mystery of the Cross," *Perspectives in Religious Studies* 14 (Winter 1987): 50.

14. One of the dangers inherent in this desire to augment biblical symbols and metaphors with modern ones is demonstrated in Humphreys' uncritical acceptance of a model from liberation theology, in which context is allowed to dictate symbol and analogy to the extent that biblical truth is misrepresented or even contradicted. For example, Humphreys advocated a multifaceted understanding of the atonement that apparently embraces some models that would redefine the Christian faith, citing Jon Sobrino's *Christology at the Crossroads* with approval. This Salvadoran liberation theologian suggests that the cross was a political statement demanding that Christians participate in activities of political liberation (F. Humphreys, "The Mystery of the Cross," 47). Such misrepresentations of the atonement are perhaps inevitable if a controlling emphasis for the significance of the atonement cannot be established.

15. Richardson, *Peace Child*, 212–15.

16. Humphreys, *The Death of Christ*, 54.

17. Ibid., 55.

18. In his 1988 Gheens Lectures at Southern Seminary, L. Morris (*The Cross of Jesus* [Grand Rapids: Eerdmans, 1988], 16) said, "It must be said

quite firmly that God is not subject to any law outside of His own being, but that does not mean that He is lawless or irresponsible. He is not subject to any law, but law is the way He works. To deny this is simply shallow thinking. Law and love go together, else we do not really have love. Apart from law, how are we to distinguish love from caprice?"

19. J. Calvin, *Institutes of the Christian Religion*, vol. 1 (repr. ed.; Grand Rapids: Eerdmans, 1966), 443.

20. J. R. W. Stott, *The Cross of Christ* (Downers Grove: InterVarsity, 1986), 124.

21. J. Denney, *The Atonement and the Modern Mind* (Hodder & Stoughton, 1903), 82.

22. For characteristic uses in the LXX and elsewhere in the NT, see Dan 2:28–29; Luke 17:25; 24:7; Acts 1:16; 3:21; 17:3; Rev 1:1.

23. W. Grundmann. "δεῖ/ δέον, ἐστί," in *Theological Dictionary of the New Testament*, vol. 2, ed. G. Kittel and G. Friedrich (Grand Rapids: Eerdmans, 1964), 21–25.

24. Humphreys, *The Death of Christ*, 59.

25. Ibid.

26. Ibid., 61.

27. Ibid., 61 –62.

28. Stott, *The Cross of Christ*, 141. In addition to Socinus, Stott also noted that the Koran consistently finds the concept of penal substitution unacceptable (*The Cross of Christ*, 41).

29. W. Pannenberg, *Jesus—God and Man*, 2nd ed., trans. L. L. Wilkins and D. A. Priebe (Philadelphia: Westminster, 1968), 279.

30. Stott, *The Cross of Christ*, 64–65.

31. For the use of *huper* as a preposition often clearly implying substitution, see L. Morris, *The Apostolic Preaching of the Cross* (Grand Rapids: Eerdmans, 1965), 59; and A. T. Robertson, *A Grammar of the Greek New Testament in the Light of Historical Research* (Nashville: Broadman, 1934), 631–32.

32. Stott, *The Cross of Christ*, 34.

Chapter 4

Apologetics and Scripture
A Lesson from the Early Church

Thomas J. Nettles

O n April 5, 1972, L. Russ Bush presented a doctoral paper in a class on patristics at the Southwestern Baptist Theological Seminary under Dr. Robert A. Baker. The subject of his presentation was Athenagoras. Russ, a philosophy major, chose the subject of Athenagoras because this second-century Christian writer provided a fascinating window to the world of early Christian apologetics and philosophical method. Bush gave an outline of Athenagoras's works *Embassy* and *Resurrection* and then discussed the "Method of Argument" of this apologetic writer. He emphasized two things. First, Bush pointed out the place of Scripture in providing Athenagoras's fundamental convictions for the standpoint he was set to defend. Second, Athenagoras understandably used Platonic categories as he sought to lay bare the irrationality of the charges brought against Christians by pagans. When some writers suggested that the method of Athenagoras would naturally lead to syncretism, Bush believed that some corrective was in order.

> In defense of Athenagoras at this point it seems only necessary to recall once again the nature of his writing. . . . Obviously he is not trying to develop a theological vocabulary to differentiate Christian faith from Greek philosophy. Rather in this particular work his goal is to make them sound very much alike. The *Embassy* is addressed to the rulers in hopes of making them recognize Christianity as a valid religion and cease the persecution. He is arguing from the authority of Scripture, not for it. The attempt is to make the biblical teachings fit the categories of rationality within philosophical idealism.[1]

This recognition of the Platonic framework of Athenagoras may be seen as normative for most apologetic writers of the second and third centuries. The Jesuit theologian Robert Daly, in his foreword to Hans Urs von Balthasar's work *Origen: Spirit and Fire*, reminded his readers: "The mere fact that Origen's thought can be described as 'Platonizing' is, in itself, only a sign that he was a Christian thinker in the third century. There was at that time no thought system better suited to help Christians in their theological reflection." What must concern one in making this observation is whether the apologist employing the usable skeleton of Platonism "gives sufficient place to the incarnational aspects of Christianity."[2]

This the apologists certainly did in their explanation of Christ and their defense of His resurrection. In addition, they distanced themselves from pure Platonism by their criticism of certain elemental aspects of the system and by their arguments for the distinctive truths of Christianity as coming from the revelatory operations of the Holy Spirit. While space and some philosophical disposition for interaction had been created by the various philosophical schools, the Christian apologists knew well that incarnation and inspiration were at the heart of the message that they set forth.

Henry Chadwick mentioned several themes common to all the apologists through which they could engage their culture in familiar categories. The later apologists stood on the shoulders of those who had preceded them and thus showed continuity and unity in their patterns of argument and content of thought. In addition, they all embraced "the traditional apologetic for Judaism which had been developed in the Hellenistic synagogue" that argued for Moses and the prophets as a source for the Greek philosophers. Moreover, they utilized the debates between the Greek philosophical schools, particularly those between the Stoics and the Platonists. For some of their characterizations of the pagan deities, they used Platonic attacks on the popular *cultus* defended by the Stoics under the influence of Homer. They could just as quickly, however, use some of the thinking patterns of the Stoics in their defense of providence. In addition, Stoicism had created a climate in which the moral arguments pursued by the Christian apologists found a receptive audience, while the Platonic idea of the goal of life to establish "likeness to God as far as possible" allowed great latitude for the presentation of the credibility of Christian truth.[3]

Having a mind congenial to the discovery of philosophical climate and the use of popular culture to make Christian points, Russ Bush found his studies and writings on Athenagoras quite pleasing. Part of the seminary requirement for which Bush's paper was written was an engagement with the ecclesiological contribution, as well as the overall development of Christian theology, of each writer. For the first category of theological contribution, Bush chose the doctrine of Scripture. Though still seven years away from the first outbreak of the Conservative Resurgence, the Broadman Commentary controversy was still fresh and the seminary was abuzz with conversation, in class and out, about the doctrine of inerrancy. Bush took every opportunity to investigate the claim some made that inerrancy was not the historic doctrine of the church. Athenagoras provided an opportunity to look at the patristic era and its view of Scripture. Following Bush's lead, I begin here with Athenagoras as a starting point for engagement with several decisive treatments of the authority of Scripture in three apologists: Athenagoras, Justin Martyr, and Origen.

Athenagoras and Scripture

Arising from what he called "the uncritical gossip of the crowd," Athenagoras identified three charges brought against Christians: atheism, Thyestean banquets (involving cannibalism), and Oedipean unions (incestuous relationships). To the charge of atheism, Athenagoras pointed to the Christian belief in one God. Their dismissal of the multiplicity of deities that inhabited the superstitious minds of the pagans, therefore, caused an uproar of objection. That such resentment brought about the charge of atheism should be understandable. Plato and other philosophers, even Aristotle and the Stoics, said the same thing. "Now if Plato is not atheist when he understands the Creator of all things to be the one uncreated God," Athenagoras reminded the emperor, "neither are we atheists when we acknowledge him by whose Word all things were created and upheld by his spirit and assert that he is God."[4] The views of these philosophers, Athenagoras claimed, as well as a large number of poets, were mere guesses, "each of them moved by his own soul through some affinity with the breath of God to seek, if possible, to find and understand the truth." They gained nothing more than "peripheral understanding," however, since they could not stoop to learn about God from God Himself. Christians, however, "have prophets as witnesses of what we think and believe." These prophets have "spoken out by a divinely inspired spirit about God and the things of God." Would it not be irrational "to abandon belief in the Spirit of God which has moved the mouths of the prophets like musical instruments and to pay attention to human opinions."[5]

Christian convictions reflect, therefore, their belief that they have a revelation from this one God, not only of His existence, but of His attributes and His actions. They describe Him as He has revealed Himself, that is, as a three-personed Godhead, "God the Father, God the Son, and the Holy Spirit." This God has created all things and put them in their proper order and governs them accordingly. The emperor should be persuaded that he was not dealing with atheists, Athenagoras told Marcus Aurelius, precisely because of the "doctrines we hold—doctrines not man-made but ordained and taught by God." What an absurdity it would be to conclude that those are atheists who submit to the authority of a book they believe is inspired by a three-personed Godhead.

Athenagoras frequently supported his philosophical argument with an allusion to the scriptural foundation for the argument by such phrases as "the prophetic Spirit also agrees with this account [our statements]" and "as the prophetic Spirit says."[6] In one particularly assertive passage, Athenagoras appealed to the educational sophistication of the emperor in seeking to convince him that his views were more than just human speculation.

> If we satisfied ourselves with advancing such considerations as these, our doctrines might by some be looked upon as human. But, since the voices of the prophets confirm our

arguments—for I think that you also, with your great zeal for knowledge, and your great attainments in learning, cannot be ignorant of the writings either of Moses or of Isaiah and Jeremiah, and the other prophets, who, lifted in ecstasy above the natural operations of their minds obey the impulses of the Divine Spirit, uttered the things with which they were inspired, the Spirit making use of them as a flute-player breathes into a flute.[7]

Bush, who quoted this particular passage, makes the comment in a footnote, "The term 'inspire' in II Timothy clearly indicates a breathing out by God . . . to which this analogy refers."[8]

Against the charges relative to cannibalism and incest, certainly representations of the grossest kinds of impurity, Athenagoras appealed to the nature of God's holiness, His judgment, and His future blessing for those who suffer here for their confessions of Christ, as well as the future punishment for those who reject the knowledge of God.[9] He pointed out that Christians would rather suffer unjustly than lift their hands against others. The wild variety of worship practices, the distinctions and gradations of deities, the outrageous myths of the activities of the gods with each other all show that the promoters of these gods have "fixed themselves on material things and falling lower and lower divinize the movement of the elements."[10] The worshippers of such deities ("the gods differ in no way from the vilest beasts")[11] become at least as foul as they. "They of all people," Athenagoras marveled, "revile us for vices which they have on their own consciences and which they attribute to their own gods, boasting of them as noble deeds and worthy of the gods."[12]

Christians, however, have "a teaching [that] is not set forth with a view to human laws whose surveillance an evil man may well escape." No, instead, "our doctrine is taught by God."[13] For that reason Christians avoid the provocation of lust, eschew adultery in every form in which it may seek to exert itself, stay clear of a distressing variety of sexual perversions, and avoid even the sight of murderous and vicious spectacles such as gladiatorial contests and animal fights. How can those be murderers or cannibals who will not even view such things? So opposed are Christians to murder and the mistreatment of children that they take a radically counter-cultural stance on the rights of a woman over the child in her body:

> Again, what sense does it make to think of us as murderers when we say that women who practice abortion are murderers and will render account to God for abortion? The same man cannot regard that which is in the womb as a living being and for that reason an object of God's concern and then murder it when it has come into the light. Neither can the same man forbid exposing a child which has been born on the grounds that those who do so are murderers and then slay one that has been nourished.[14]

Athenagoras drew upon his knowledge of philosophy and his substantial familiarity with pagan poets and the myths of the gods, and he subjected these ideas to rational and logical investigation. He also compared Christian behavior and thought to the accusations brought against them by pagans. In the final analysis, however, his discussion of each outrageous error he discerned in pagan thought and behavior along with his explanation of every aspect of Christian thought and behavior flowed from Scripture clearly acknowledged as divine revelation. His knowledge of Scripture and his theological synthesis of a wide understanding of its teachings, with the conviction that God had inspired it all, produced his radical dissent from the prevailing religious commitments of second-century society and his explanation of Christian faith and practice.

In his exalted view of Scripture, and in his formation of an entirely Christian worldview, in opposition to the prevailing philosophical squabbles within pagan culture, Athenagoras built upon the legacy left a quarter of a century earlier by another second-century apologist, Justin Martyr.

Justin Martyr and Scripture

Justin Martyr sought to propagate the Christian faith among both the Jews and the pagans. The charges of atheism, licentiousness, and disloyalty, in addition to a representation of Christianity as being untrue because of its novelty, constituted the major themes that Justin sought to dismiss in his *Apology*. Trained as a philosopher and maintaining the philosopher's garments even after his conversion, Justin employed a variety of arguments, assuming both the vocabulary and framework of middle Platonism, but restructured and redefined by Scripture.[15]

His *logos* doctrine—perhaps inherited from Stoicism and Philo, but in Justin's case clearly dominated by the centrality of the importance of the Word, *Logos*, in its scriptural applications— gave him a Christ-centered concept of general revelation and allowed him to see preparatory ideas in philosophy as well as paganism, and it even suggested to him that such transparent lovers of truth as Socrates were Christians. Thus he could explain how paganism seemed to preempt Christianity in some of its ideas, and at the same time he could emphasize primacy, as well as continuity and originality, for Christianity. By this approach, he destroyed the charge of novelty, while describing also points at which the Christian faith clarified, corrected, and purified the vaguely similar teachings of the pagans by bringing the truth in an absolute form to displace the obscurities of the philosophers and the perversions of the demons.

His knowledge of Christian teaching went far beyond a mere affirmation of tradition received in the context of Christian worship, but developed through an intimate personal study of Scripture. His thoughtful reflection on the pagan culture and Christian suffering and misrepresentation at its hands gave rise to an impressive display of biblical knowledge and confidence in biblical inspiration as fundamental to a legitimate Christian response to culture. In his appeal to Antoninus Pius, Justin called for him not to listen to unjust accusations and mere rumors but to give attention to the truth and investigate the credibility of the charges by seeking to understand the beliefs of Christians.

In opposition to a variety of accusations and misunderstandings connected with the charge of atheism, Justin outlined several aspects of the Christian understanding of God, worship, judgment, punishment, perseverance in the face of persecution, and resurrection. Throughout these descriptions Justin appealed to divine instruction as the means by which these things have been learned. Christians are "persuaded and convinced" of "eternal and pure life" in the presence of God. "This then, to speak briefly," Justin summarized, "is what we look for and have learned from Christ, and teach."[16] The Christian's submission to God in all things, even an unjust death on the basis of irrational and false accusation, is most reasonable since God not only creates but "persuades us and leads us to faith."[17] In addition, Jesus Christ, who is "both Son and Apostle of God the Father," foretold these things: "We are more assured that all the things taught by Him are so, since whatever He predicted before is seen in fact coming to pass; and this is the work of God, to announce something before it happens, and as it was predicted so to show it happening."[18]

To the charge of licentiousness, Justin responded by citing the teachings of Christ as totally antithetical to the ridiculous and ludicrous things of which Christians were accused. Throughout the section setting forth the moral position of Christianity, he presented every moral precept of Christianity as having been derived from Christ Himself through the text of Scripture. "But lest we should seem to deceive," Justin wrote, "we consider it right, before embarking on our promised demonstration, to cite a few of the precepts given by Christ Himself." They, the rulers, should be able to discern quickly whether the Christians abide by these truths of Christ. "Short and concise utterance come from Him," Justin said in commendation of the style of Jesus, "for He was no sophist, but His word was the power of God."[19]

Since Jesus spoke from a reservoir of infinite knowledge and perfect purity, He did not need to engage in long arguments or gilt-edged words, but only short and pithy assertions and commands. He spoke the words of God. He spoke only what was absolutely true. His words emerged from the inexhaustible depth of the powerful wisdom of God. In His words, as well as in His cross, Christ is the wisdom of God and the power of God. For pages, Justin quoted a variety of Jesus' teachings on moral issues interspersed with affirmations of Justin's acceptance of their full authority found in words such as "concerning chastity he said this; And concerning our being long-suffering, . . . this is what he said; And concerning our not swearing at all, but always speaking the truth, He commanded thus; . . . as we have been taught by Him."[20] Life and death are bound up in believing and doing the words of Jesus so that "those who are found not living as He taught should understand that they are not really Christians."[21]

Moreover, Christians believe what seems impossible by nature because whatever Christ has taught, as it derives from the power of God, is reflective of that which God intends to do. Thus the resurrection is true though the philosophers deem it at best implausible and the certainty of eternal punishment in the resurrected body appears most absurd. "We know," however, "that our Master Jesus Christ said, 'the things that are impossible with men are possible with God.'" God is able to cast both body and soul into Gehenna, the "place where those who have lived unrighteously will be punished, and those who do not believe that these things which God has taught us through Christ will come to pass."[22]

The dependence of Justin's apologetic on the truthfulness of divine revelation becomes blatantly clear in the section on prophecy. In order to demonstrate that Jesus was not a charlatan or a magician, Justin believed that if he could demonstrate that Jesus' words, actions, the details of His life and death, and His miracles were prophesied before they happened, this would be sure proof of the genuineness of His mission as sent from God. "We will now offer proof, not trusting in mere assertions," Justin proposed, "but being of necessity persuaded by those who prophesied [these things] before they happened, for with our own eyes we see things that have happened and are happening just as they were predicted; and this will, we think, appear to you the strongest and surest evidence."[23]

In introducing the concept of prophecy to the emperor, Justin recounted the manner in which the Old Testament books containing the prophecies arose. Among the Jews certain persons, prophets of God, "through whom the prophetic Spirit announced beforehand things that were to come to pass before they happened," preserved their utterances as delivered in books. These books, in Hebrew, were also translated into Greek for the sake of the Egyptians. Though these books now are misunderstood by the Jews, a thing that in itself was prophesied, they nevertheless contain such details as should convince anyone that they are inspired and that Jesus is the Christ.

In these books, then, of the prophets we have found it predicted that Jesus our Christ would come, born of a virgin, growing up to manhood, and healing every disease and every sickness and raising the dead, and hated and unrecognized and crucified, and dying and rising again and ascending into heaven, and both being and being called Son of God. [We find it also predicted] that certain people should be sent by Him into every nation to proclaim these things, and that rather among the Gentiles people should believe on Him.[24]

Each one of these points that Justin indicated as having been prophesied is set forth from Old Testament passages. Justin explained how they were fulfilled and interacted with the implications of each element of the prophetic material. After one section of Scripture citation and explanation, Justin remarked: "And that the prophets are inspired by none other than the divine Word, even you, as I think, will agree."[25]

Justin sought to explain that though in the Bible many persons speak, we are not to suppose that the persons themselves speak, but rather "the divine Word who moves them."[26] Scripture has speeches from God the Father, the person of Christ, Moses, David, and others. It is true that each one of these spoke, but it is also true that the Spirit speaks as in the person denominated in the text. "For sometimes He speaks things that are to happen, in the manner of one who foretells the future; sometimes He speaks as in the person of God the Master and Father of all; sometimes as in the person of Christ; sometimes as in the person of the people answering the Lord or His Father."[27]

Justin gave several examples of each of these prophetic modes moving all the way from the virgin birth to the final judgment. He explained how both pagan religion and Greek philosophy mimicked Christian truth at several points through shadowy imitation of the prophetic writings. Christianity alone, therefore, has proof of its doctrines, and those who hear and believe know the truth far beyond the most intelligent of those who do not believe. Justin reminded his readers:

> It is not, then, that we hold the same opinions as others, but that all speak in imitation of ours. Among us therefore these things are heard and learned from those who do not even know the forms of the letters, who are uneducated and barbarous in speech, but wise and believing in mind—some even blind and deprived of sight; so that you can understand that these things are not the product of human wisdom, but are spoken by the power of God.[28]

In his *Dialogue with Trypho*, Justin showed the same zeal for the biblical text. He was able to attract an extended conversation with the Jew because of his evident love of Scripture and divine things. Immediately after Justin related the manner in which he had become a Christian and had had the Scriptures recommended to him, he testified, "Straightway, a flame was kindled in my soul; and a love of the prophets, and of those men who are friends of Christ, possessed me." He wanted others to partake of that same fire and not "to keep themselves away from the words of the Saviour" since they "possess a terrible power in themselves." Trypho was intrigued with this zealous Samaritan and consented to a conversation.[29]

Justin employed many of the same ideas as seen in his *Apology*, seeking to demonstrate that Jesus is the Christ prophesied by the Old Testament Scriptures. The difference, of course, is that in the case of Trypho, as opposed to a Roman emperor, he was dealing with one who already revered the Old Testament as the Word of God. Justin also claimed the Old Testament as his book, and consistently pressed Trypho with the idea that he was blinded to its true meaning because he still looked at it through old-covenant eyes and thus failed to see the reality of the promised new covenant and its inauguration through the coming of the Messiah.

Justin sought to demonstrate through a massive display of biblical knowledge that every type, every Jewish institution, every sacrifice, every prophecy had been fulfilled in Christ. Trypho was impressed with this and stayed with the conversation. That which engaged him so profoundly was Justin's insistence on relating all his interpretations to Scripture. When Justin sought to show through the story of Abraham and Lot that Christ appeared in the Old Testament and was indeed the Lord but numerically distinct from the Father, Trypho replied:

> Prove this; for, as you see, the day advances, and we are not prepared for such perilous replies; since never yet have we heard any man investigating, or searching into, or proving these matters; nor would we have tolerated your conversation, had you not referred everything to the Scriptures: for you are very zealous in adducing proofs from them; and you are of opinion that there is not God above the Maker of all things.[30]

Later in the conversation Trypho asked for Justin to set forth for him his basic proof that "this God who appeared to Abraham, and is minister to God the Maker of all things, being born of the Virgin, became man, of like passions with all, as you said previously." Justin, desiring to do just that, nevertheless requested Trypho to be patient, because he wanted to present a much larger number of proofs on the point before his final demonstration. This accumulation of proofs must necessarily arise from Scripture, Justin maintained:

> I purpose to quote to you Scriptures, not that I am anxious to make merely an artful display of words; for I possess no such faculty, but God's grace alone has been granted to me

to the understanding of His Scriptures, of which grace I exhort all to become partakers freely and bounteously, in order that they may not, through want of it, incur condemnation in the judgment which God the Maker of all things shall hold through my Lord Jesus Christ.[31]

As Justin pressed the conversation toward Scriptures that, according to Justin, spoke of the divine glory of the One in whom the Gentiles would rejoice in the scriptural words "May His glorious name be praised forever" (Ps 72:19 HCSB), Trypho sought to point out a Scripture that seemed to contradict Justin's interpretations: "I am the Lord God; this is my name; my glory will I not give to another." Before Justin gave the interpretation that showed the perfect consistency of this text with all the others he had been treating, he chastised Trypho for a tactic that implied a necessity to admit a contradiction.

> If you spoke these words, Trypho, and then kept silence in simplicity and with no ill intent, neither repeating what goes before nor adding what comes after, you must be forgiven; but if [you have done so] because you imagined that you could throw doubt on the passage, in order that I might say the Scriptures contradicted each other, you have erred. But I shall not venture to suppose or to say such a thing; and if a Scripture which appears to be of such a kind be brought forward, and if there be a pretext [for saying] that it is contrary [to some other], since I am entirely convinced that no Scripture contradicts another, I shall admit rather that I do not understand what is recorded, and shall strive to persuade those who imagine that the Scriptures are contradictory, to be rather of the same opinion as myself.[32]

Justin continued his demonstration that Jesus fulfilled all the messianic Scriptures and types along with explanations, bolstered by prophecy, of the hard-heartedness and blindness of the Jews and their enmity against those who confess that Jesus is the Christ. Near the end he gave an earnest plea to Trypho and his friends concerning their unbelief and, though not worshippers of idols or sacrifices to Baal, yet virtual idolaters because "you have not accepted God's Christ. For he who knows not Him, knows not the will of God; and he who insults and hates Him, insults and hates Him that sent Him. And whoever believes not in Him, believes not the declarations of the prophets, who preached and proclaimed Him to all."[33]

Justin would approach neither pagan nor Jew without a full arsenal of scriptural truth readily at hand. His apologetic to both groups consisted of a continual outlay of biblical material, primarily focused on the facts concerning the birth, life, death, resurrection, and return to judgment of Jesus, along with the consistent theme of the inspired and errorless character of Scripture.

Origen and Scripture

It is quite understandable that Origen's view of Scripture, due to the large liberties that he took in interpretation, might be confusing if not alarming to a present-day inerrantist. It is good to have, therefore, as a cover statement for all of the complexities of his interpretive style his clear affirmation of the full inspiration of Scripture:

> The Scriptures were written by the Spirit of God. . . . Christ, who worked within Moses and whose words are recorded in the Gospels, worked also in Paul and Peter and the other apostles. Thus the just and good God, the Father of our Lord Jesus Christ himself, gave the Law and the Prophets and the gospels, being also the God of the apostles and of the Old and New Testaments.[34]

Origen had such confidence in the inspiration of Scripture that he could state that the one who reads it and understands it "will feel his mind and senses touched by a divine breath, and will acknowledge that the words which he reads were no human utterances, but the language of God."[35] He made a distinction between the bodily and spiritual principles of interpretation and rejected the literalness of some passages as simply incredible and absurd, unworthy of God in their literal meaning. The proper mode of interpretation, therefore, is extremely important for Origen, for "the sacred books are not the compositions of men, but they were composed by inspiration of the Holy Spirit, agreeably to the will of the Father of all things through Jesus Christ."[36]

Though formally oriented toward a three-fold level of interpretation (body, soul, and spirit) and demonstrating this style of interpretation for the sake of illustration, Origen normally considered only the literal, or bodily, and the spiritual, or figurative. If he saw nothing legitimate in the literal, he would deal only with the "soul" and "spirit" of a passage. Passages that mingled all three levels of meaning demanded a careful, reverent, and skillful interpreter. Origen fearlessly asserted that some narrative passages contained things that did not, or perhaps could not, happen. Sometimes only a few words appear that bear a literal interpretation and sometimes many. Sometimes the laws recorded were useful in their own time or are useful in themselves; sometimes what is not useful and sometimes what is impossible is recorded. Do not despair, though, or conclude that the Bible is erroneous, for the Spirit has inspired these parts in order to draw the interpreter into great depths of understanding. These appear purposefully "for the sake of the more skillful and inquisitive, in order that they may give themselves to the toil of investigating what is written, and thus attain to a becoming conviction of the manner in which a meaning worthy of God must be sought out in such subjects."[37]

While one could argue with advantage that Origen sacrificed too much of the historical and too many pertinent facts in his interpretive scheme, that would not be the same as to argue that he believed he had discovered errors in the text. He simply believed that God intended the text to contain sufficient challenge and mystery to draw the interpreter into a spiritual quest for the true understanding of the divine revelation. Sometimes his scheme served the interest of esoteric spiritual ideas unique to Origen, but often they were to help interpret "some of the apparently more 'Christ-distant' realities of the Old Testament." As Robert Daly surmised, "It was the Christian soul following the guidance of the Spirit to look beyond the literal and historical meaning to catch some glimpse of the humanly incomprehensible mystery of the WORD."[38]

An interpretive example that both illustrates and defends that journey of the soul in interpretation is found in Origen's homily on Numbers, treating the passage, "How fair are your houses, O Jacob, your tents, O Israel" (Num 24:5). The house represents activity and work that is complete, steady, stable, and perfected. The tent represents the acquisition of knowledge that is never complete and is indeed inexhaustible, since living in a tent must be the mode of our dealing with Scripture:

> He admires their tents in which they continually wander and make progress; and the more progress they make the more does the road to be traveled stretch out into the measureless. . . . And true it is, when we make some progress in knowledge and gain some experience in such things, we know that when we have come to a certain insight and recognition of the spiritual mysteries, the soul rests there, in a certain sense, as in a "tent." But when it begins to make fresh sense

again of what it finds there and move on to other insights, it pushes on with folded tent, so to speak, to a higher place and sets itself up there, pegged down by strong conclusions; and again the soul finds in the place another spiritual meaning, for which the conclusions from earlier insights have doubtless prepared the way, and so the soul seems always to be pulled on toward the goal that lies ahead (cf. Phil 3:14), moving on, so to speak in "tents." For once the soul has been struck by the fiery arrow of knowledge, it can never again sink into leisure and take its rest, but it will always be called onward from the good to the better and from the better to the higher.[39]

For all the energy Origen dedicated to the intensely metaphysical side of his self-conceived interpretive task, he nevertheless realized that the historical foundations of Scripture held initial and indissolubly important priority. Without the history—the reality of the patriarchs, the history of Israel, the incarnation, the death and resurrection of Christ—no amount of spiritualized interpretation could salvage the Christian faith. This more historically rooted commitment to biblical inspiration characterized Origen's massive refutation of the earlier opponent of Christianity, Celsus, who sought to reduce Christianity to the ridiculous in his book *The True Doctrine.*

Virtually the entirety of *Contra Celsum* presses against Celsus's attempt to depict Christianity as a fabrication or exaggeration unworthy of belief by intelligent persons. In the context of this Origen showed how important an acceptance of the inspiration and truthfulness of the biblical text is for an adequate defense of the faith.

One evidence is that, in moral issues, "God has implanted in the souls of all men the truth which He taught through the prophets and the Saviour; He did this that every man might be without excuse at the divine judgment, having the requirement of the law written in his heart." [40] That the Scriptures give verbal form to those moral goads still resident in the heart gives evidence of its inspiration. Unlike the pagans, Christians, when confronted with evil forces in this life, do not cope through superstitious incantations but through the name of Jesus and all those truths about Him "taken from the divine scripture."[41]

Celsus, as a tactic of intimidation and in an effort to prop up his upcoming misrepresentation of the Christian faith, foolishly asserted concerning his knowledge of Christian beliefs and Scriptures, "I know them all." Origen continually referred to the arrogance implicit in such an attitude throughout the work, but in his immediate response spoke about the absurdity of this confidence and gave an insight into his own love for and reverence for and devoted study of the Scriptures:

> I have to say that if he had read the prophets especially, which are full of admitted obscurities and of sayings of which the meaning is not clear to the multitude, and if he had read the parables of the gospels and the rest of the Bible, the law, the history of the Jews, and the utterances of the apostles, and if he had read with an open mind and a desire to enter into the meaning of the words, he would not have boasted in this way nor have said: *For I know them all.* Not even we, who have spent much time in the study of these books, would say, "I know them all." For we have a love for the truth.[42]

But Celsus had said it, and Origen was determined to demonstrate otherwise.

When Celsus sought an advantage through a criticism of the works of Moses and Christian interpretations of Moses, Origen responded with a demonstration of the superiority of Moses over all the writers to whom Celsus gave credence. Origen presented Moses as a distinguished orator who pays attention to outward form and everywhere keeps carefully the concealed meaning of his words. To the multitudes of the Jews under his legislation he provided no occasions for them to come to any harm in their moral behavior, and yet he did not produce a work which gave no opportunities for deeper study for the few who are able to read with more understanding, and who are capable of searching out his meaning. [In Moses] there dwelt a divine spirit which showed the truth about God far clearer than Plato and the wise men among the Greeks and barbarians.[43]

Origen went on to argue the divine origin of Scripture from its having overcome apparently insuperable opposition. Though Christ was been opposed by the mighty, His doctrine has spread over the whole world, among the vulgar and illiterate as well as among reasonable and intelligent people, since "as the word of God it could not be prevented" but was "stronger than all its adversaries."[44]

Origen also called Celsus's hand on his introduction of a clumsy rhetorical device in an effort to ridicule the Christian understanding of Scripture. Celsus invented an imaginary character, a Jew, who directed "childish remarks" to Jesus and, by extension, to those who have come to God through Christ. Origen spent two books demonstrating that none of Celsus's objections channeled through the Jew are pertinent, for a Jew would never have raised the kinds of objections put into his mouth. For example, Celsus's Jew mentioned the suspicious birth of Jesus, which provided an opportunity for Origen to point to the Jewish, and Christian, belief in prophecy through Isaiah's prophecy of the virgin birth as a sign to Ahaz in Isa 7:14. After discussion of the words, "young woman," the audience to whom the prophecy was directed ("obviously the words to Ahaz were addressed to the house of David") and justifying his argument in light of his speaking supposedly to a "Jew who believes the prophecy," Origen turned his attention to Celsus himself with the challenge to "tell us with what kind of mental apprehension the prophet speaks about the future." If he has told the future, and all evidence points to that fact, "then the prophets possessed divine inspiration."[45]

In response to a challenge issued by Celsus's imaginary Jew of the fantastic nature of some of the stories recorded about Jesus, Origen gave a measured and rational response about the difficulty of "proving" any story to be true. Finally, however, he appealed to the Jew's belief that the stories of Ezekiel's visions and Isaiah's visions were "free from error and that it was by divine inspiration not only that they were seen by the prophet, but also that they were described verbally and in writing." Origen then argued that if such is so with those prophets, how much more do Christians have reason to believe that that level of truthfulness characterizes the accounts of Jesus. "No work of theirs is to be found of comparable importance; whereas the goodness of Jesus towards men was not confined to the period of the incarnation only, but even to this day the power of Jesus brings about conversion and moral reformation in those who believe in God through him." Celsus blundered in placing such a challenge in the mouth of a Jew who believes the entire Old Testament history to be without error "when the event concerned has more historical probability than the stories which he has believed."[46]

Celsus somehow had received the erroneous notion that Christians believed God was corporeal. "If he invents out of his own head ideas which he heard from nobody," Origen wrote, "there is no need for us to concern ourselves with unnecessary argument." Just to settle the issue simply, however, Origen stated simply and forcefully, "The Bible clearly says that God is incorporeal. That is why 'No man has seen god at any time,' and 'the firstborn of all creation is said to be an image of the invisible God.'"[47] Only a proposition from Scripture is needed to correct and refute a criticism of Celsus.

Upon the attempt of Celsus to discredit Christianity by his criticism of "the assertion that the history of Christ Jesus was prophesied by the prophets among the Jews," Origen entered into a lengthy and nuanced discussion of prophecy in light of pagan oracles. Unable to do justice to the entire discussion, we must be content at this point to show the fundamental importance of inspiration for this aspect of Origen's argument. In contrast to what he described as characteristic of the production of pagan oracular sayings, Origen pictures the prophets not only as receiving revelation of truth but being transformed in the process of this interaction with the Holy Spirit. "We prove," he wrote, "that the prophets among the Jews, being illuminated by the divine Spirit in so far as it was beneficial to them as they prophesied, were the first to enjoy the visitation of the superior Spirit to them." Because of this "touch" of the "Holy Spirit upon their soul, they possessed clear mental vision and became more radiant in their soul, and even in body, which no longer offered any opposition to the life lived according to virtue." Origen established a severe contrast between the morals of those that delivered the pagan prophesies and those who had had the "touch" of the Spirit: "Of the Jewish prophets some were wise before they received the gift of prophecy and divine inspiration, while others became wise after they had been illuminated in mind by the actual gift of prophecy itself." This change of life through divine providence made them fit to "be entrusted with the divine Spirit and with the utterances that He inspired." Such a holy and invasive operation of the Spirit gave them a courage that made the work of Antisthenes, Crates, and Diogenes "appear as child's play."[48]

One may notice in reading some of Origen's commentaries that he sometimes takes great liberties in interpretation. Is this consistent with his defense of inspiration and inerrancy? The connection between interpretation and the inspiration that produces an error-free text may be seen in the following response to a misrepresentation by Celsus:

> The prophets, according to the will of God, said without any obscurity whatever could be at once understood as beneficial to their hearers and helpful towards attaining moral reformation. But all the more mysterious and esoteric truths, which contained ideas beyond the understanding of everyone, they expressed by riddles and allegories and what are called dark sayings, and by what are called parables or proverbs. Their purpose was that those who are not afraid of hard work but will accept any toil to attain the virtue and truth might find out their meaning by study, and after finding it might use it as reason demands.[49]

Such interpretations, according to Origen, are in no sense a denial of the text's truthfulness, but are in full accord with the divine intention in the inspiration of the text.

Origen defended the truth of Christianity with a marvelous variety of weapons in his intellectual arsenal. Henry Chadwick made the following observation in the introduction to his translation of *Contra Celsum*:

> In the *Contra Celsum* Origen does not merely vindicate the character of Jesus and the credibility of the Christian tradition; he also shows that Christians can be so far from being irrational and credulous illiterates such as Celsus thinks them to be that they may know more about Greek philosophy than the pagan Celsus himself, and can make intelligent use of it to interpret the doctrines of the Church.[50]

For Origen, moreover, this defense of Scripture went far beyond an entertaining intellectual and polemical exercise. He was driven by a desire for greater spiritual and moral attainments and more profound enlightenment in the truth embodied in the incarnate *Logos*, the Lord Jesus Christ. He is the infinitely bright and shining Light toward which all humanity should be drawn. Central to every aspect of his argument—whether philosophical, moral, theological, rhetorical, or polemical—was a deep and abiding conviction about the divine origin of Scripture. By the Holy Spirit, Christ lived in it and breathed upon humanity through it. The written Scriptures constituted the sphere within which the earnest, pure, and virtuous Christian could explore all truth and enter into his unending quest for knowledge of the true and holy and find himself in an unending expanse of glory. Consequently, Origen believed and taught that this Bible, breathed by the divine Spirit, contains no errors but contains all that we need to know, believe, and obey concerning the knowledge of God and His purposes of transformation and redemption toward man.

Conclusion

Affirming the inspiration and consequently errorless nature of Scripture ruled the apologetic method and colored its outcome for the three figures studied in this chapter. This early method is startlingly distinct from the apologetic method developed by Schleiermacher and subsequent liberalism. The modernist argument for Christianity had no dependence on an objectively inspired Bible and the errorless character of propositional revelation. Under different rubrics of experience and relationship, liberalism minimized the importance of the Bible and viewed it more largely in terms of personal testimonies of the first generation of Christians concerning their experience of the living Christ.

Our writers, however, were all within 200 years of the events that constituted the substance of Christian claims and for which they were being persecuted. These claims included not only the historical events of Christ's life, death, resurrection, and ascension, but the apostolic interpretations of those events and the historical preparation for them by way of prophecy. The truthfulness of Christianity as opposed to paganism, Greek philosophy, or Judaism depended on the credibility of the New Testament accounts and their harmony with the Old Testament prophecies, for on this basis the claim to the divinity of the religion depended. God Himself testified in writing, so the apologists had to claim, to the eternal and exclusive significance of Christ. As His coming and all the events of His coming were prophesied by inspiration, so the interpretation of that coming's meaning was given to the apostles by divine inspiration.

Though the apologists also wrote confidently of the present operations of Christ in converting and sanctifying and strengthening, these experiential aspects of Christianity were inextricably tied to the truthfulness of a text—the Bible. Through Christ, the *Logos*, God has entered into the human condition and redeemed these who will believe; through the Bible, the written *Logos*, God has given a consistent testimony to and exegesis of His redemptive operation in Christ. If we do not have an inspired and errorless Bible, so these early apologists believed, we do not have a testimony worthy of the Redeemer or His work.

Notes

1. L. R. Bush, unpublished doctoral paper, 4; presented April 5, 1972, at the Southwestern Baptist Theological Seminary under Robert A. Baker. I have a personal copy in my possession.

2. R. J. Daly, "Foreword," in H. U. von Balthasar, *Origen: Spirit and Fire*, trans. R. J. Daly, S. J. (Washington: The Catholic University of America Press, 1984), xiv.

3. H. Chadwick, "Introduction," in Origen, *Contra Celsum*, trans. H. Chadwick (Cambridge: University Press, 1965), ix–xi.

4. R. Macmullen and E. N. Lane, *Paganism and Christianity 100–425 C.E.* (Minneapolis: Fortress, 1992), 176. They have included large sections of Athenagoras's work *Legatio*, also known as *Embassy*.

5. Ibid., 178.

6. Ibid., 179, 183.

7. Athenagoras, *Embassy* 9. Lane and McMullen did not include this section in their edited version of Athenagoras.

8. Bush, unpublished doctoral paper, 13.

9. Lane and McMullen, *Paganism and Christianity*, 195; cf. Athenagoras, *Embassy*, 31.

10. Ibid., 189.

11. Ibid., 185.

12. Ibid., 197.

13. Ibid., 196.

14. Ibid., 197–98.

15. L. W. Bernard, *St. Justin Martyr: The First and Second Apologies* (New York/Mahwah, NJ: Paulist Press, 1997), 12–21. References to Justin's *Apology* are made from this text using the received paragraph numbering of the text.

16. *Apology*, 8.

17. Ibid., 10.

18. Ibid., 12.

19. Ibid., 14.

20. Ibid., 15–17.

21. Ibid., 16.

22. Ibid., 19.

23. Ibid., 30.

24. Ibid., 31.

25. Ibid., 33.

26. Ibid., 36.

27. Ibid.

28. Ibid., 60.

29. "Dialogue of Justin, Philosopher and Martyr, with Trypho, a Jew," in *The Ante-Nicene Fathers*, vol. 1, ed. [and trans.] A. Roberts and J. Donaldson (Grand Rapids: Eerdmans, 1985), 8. This number indicates the chapter number in "Dialogue" and is the manner of citation used in this chapter.

30. Ibid., 56.

31. Ibid., 57–58.

32. Ibid., 65.

33. Ibid., 136.

34. Origen, "De Principiis," in *the Ante-Nicene Fathers*, vol. 4, trans. F. Crombie (Grand Rapids: Eerdmans, 1956), 241.

35. Ibid., 354.

36. Ibid., 357.

37. Ibid., 1–15.

38. Daly, "Foreword," xvi.

39. Origen, "Homily on Numbers," cited from von Balthasar, *Origen: Spirit and Fire*, 26.

40. Origen, *Contra Celsum*, 9. The location according to the numbering of books and chapters is I.4. This location system is followed in subsequent notes unless Chadwick is quoted in his introductory remarks.

41. Ibid., I.6.

42. Ibid., I.12.

43. Ibid., I.18–19.

44. Ibid., I.27.

45. Ibid., I.28, 35.

46. Ibid., I.43–44.

47. Ibid., VII.27.

48. Ibid., VII.4, 7.

49. Ibid., VII.10.

50. Ibid., xii.

Section Two

Christian Apologetics

Chapter 5

Biblical Apologetics
A 10-Step Methodology

L. Russ Bush

Apologetics is not just one thing. If we are witnessing to Larry King, the talk show host and a famous agnostic, we may need to explain why we believe in God. The resurrection of Christ, by the way, is a good argument for the existence of God. To a Muslim, we would not need to argue for God's existence. He or she would already believe in God. But we would clearly need to set forth the case for Christ and His resurrection. To a secularist, we may want to point out evidence for creation. To a skeptic, we would defend the reality of the supernatural. So we do not have a set starting point in practice, but in theory we do have an order of priority for how the elements of gospel faith should be defended. We need first to defend the possibility of truth, followed by the reliability of the Bible, the uniqueness of Christ, the historicity of the resurrection of Jesus, the reality of God, and the fact of creation. These are the essentials in the right order.

To implement a biblical apologetic with integrity, we should follow a 10-step pattern. This is an overall strategy and is not intended to set forth a simple chronology for witness. First, the goal of Christian apologetics is reaching people with the gospel of Christ. By "reaching" we mean enabling them to hear and reflect upon the claims of Christ. The Holy Spirit works on the heart and mind from the inside, and our task is to provide from the outside the full body of truth as we are able. There is an evangelistic purpose and potential for apologetics, but there is also an overwhelming need for apologetics in discipleship ministries and in spiritual growth.

Second, biblical apologetics must be person-centered. The gospel is the same for all, but each person has a different context, heritage, and culture within which they hear and evaluate spiritual claims. We must take this into account when we give our witness to the truthfulness of the gospel. We never change the message, but we may need to approach the issues in a different way, depending on the situation.

Third, there is essential content for gospel witness. God is real. The world was created by the God who is there, and thus it is a real world, not an illusion or a divine dream. Jesus is the unique incarnation of God in human flesh. He died for us in Jerusalem and was raised the third day. Then He ascended back into heaven from which He will one day return. Each element of this comprehensive gospel witness must be included in a comprehensive apologetic. Not every encounter will lead to a full discussion of each issue, but the Christian apologist should be prepared in every essential area of gospel truth. The essential context for meaningful discussion is the theistic worldview. Here alone truth is an intellectual option. If everything is mere opinion or viewpoint only, the alternative claims cannot be differentiated.

Fourth, the historical testimony about the incarnation of God is found in a set of historical documents (the biblical Gospels). The Bible is the authentic record of God's revelation to mankind. The biblical text is also the means of revelation to us, because it has been preserved accurately and the narratives describe real history. If these texts do not report the facts accurately, we are left without a reliable account or testimony regarding Christ and we have no non-subjective, non-relative way of knowing the truth of Christian claims. The Gospels themselves are set in a historical context, and Christ is described as the One who fulfilled the meaning of the message of the Old Testament. The factual content of the Hebrew Bible is the essential context that must be defended in order to honestly establish the reliability and value of the New Testament Gospels, the book of Acts, and the epistles. God could supernaturally persuade someone to believe without reference to the body of biblical evidences, but to the extent that we can learn and verify the facts that compose the favorable body of biblical evidence, we are making the rational case stronger and stronger for the truthfulness of the entire biblical testimony. We obviously cannot externally verify every fact or detail of the entire Bible, but we have a large body of evidence supporting the claim that the Bible is trustworthy and reliable. It is a theological move to go on to the claim of biblical infallibility and inerrancy. This is a defensible claim on theological grounds, but the reality of the gospel is the basis for, not the result of, such theological claims.

Fifth, the testimony we give may well include a personal experience, but the truthfulness of biblical faith is not a result of our experience. The validity of our experience depends on the prior authenticity of the biblical claims. We do not deny the power and validity of a testimony of conversion, but we do not consider that to be a significant element in the biblical case for faith. Virtually all religions have special confirming experiences, including healings and purported miracles or supernatural events. World Christianity also includes many seemingly miraculous sightings of Mary or other mysterious events, and many artifacts are considered to be authenticated relics. None of these claims have any significant role to play in a biblical apologetic method.

Sixth, a very important way to understand the world and the context in which the gospel witness comes is through the study of human culture. This includes studies of art, music, literature, architecture, drama, film, sculpture, and modern media (both print and electronic), as well as the history of science. We study the views of life and meaning and value that artists reveal in the body of their work. We see cultural trends reflected and at times forecast in the arts. We find great insight into the modern mind by reviewing popular culture (modern art, music, novels, television, movies, and the Internet). The history of scientific research and discovery at times seems to be a threat to faith, but we believe the doctrine of creation is the best framework for understanding the world that God has made, and a theological understanding of nature is essential. Today, more than ever, Christians must respond to the strides in medicine and the resulting ethical dilemmas that we face in biotechnology. Astronomy and physics, as well as biology, should also be understood within a creationist framework.

Seventh, the apologist must not shy away from the classical philosophical problems. Why is there so much suffering in the world? What is the origin of evil? Where is history going? What about the problem passages in the Bible? What is the proper basis and role of religious authority? How does the Christian understand the history of Western thought? Is there an objective basis for ethics and political philosophy? Can systematic theology be sustained as a valid rational enterprise? Why should anyone need or want a theological education (see 2 Tim 3:14; 4:5)? What are the fundamental presuppositions of false philosophy (Col 2:8)?

Eighth, the best approach to gospel witness is one that practices sound thinking. While principles of logic are not the only valid principles for thinking, they are important for us to show that we are claiming that Christian faith is true, not simply a useful viewpoint. Critical thinking is not essential for faith, but it is essential for the development of the strongest case for faith. This is important because human beings did not lose the image of God when they sinned, and the ability to consider the evidence and to be persuaded by the evidence is a human trait given to us by God from the very beginning. The Holy Spirit is active throughout the process of gospel witness, but the Holy Spirit does not go beyond the knowledge level of the individual. How can they believe in one of whom they have never heard (Rom 10:14)? The answer is, they cannot.

Ninth, the apologist is wise to study worldviews and to use this conceptual framework to organize the proper analysis of alternative views and to test and verify the true views. The apologist will always address worldview issues whether this vocabulary is used by the apologist or not. Theism, naturalism, and idealism are the commonly held worldviews.

Tenth, the apologist knows and evaluates the classical evidences, including the traditional rational arguments for the existence of God. The cosmological arguments are considered the strongest, but the teleological arguments seem to be equally if not more persuasive. Evolution, however, is the most serious naturalistic alternative to teleology and design. Other classical evidences are biblical prophecy and biblical miracles. The apologist defends biblical truth in the whole and in the part with all appropriate rational and empirical evidences. The ultimate miracle (which is also a fulfillment of biblical prophecy) is the historical and factual resurrection of Christ. The evidence for this event is exceptionally strong, and every student of apologetics should be familiar with this body of evidence regarding the resurrection of Christ.

Comprehensive and effective explanations are best based on truth, and false views may be revealed by their weak explanatory power. A final test for comprehensiveness is related to pragmatic values, but these are never foundational to the argument.

Chapter 6

An Apologetic for Apologetics[1]

Norman L. Geisler

C hristianity is under attack, and it must be defended. There are attacks from within by cults, sects, and heresies. And there are attacks from without by atheists, skeptics, and other religions. The discipline that deals with a rational defense of the Christian Faith is called apologetics. It comes from the Greek word *apologia* (1 Pet 3:15), which means to give a reason or defense.

Objections to Defending the Faith: Biblical and Extra-Biblical

Many objections have been offered against doing apologetics. Some offer an attempted biblical justification. Others are based on extrabiblical reasoning. First, let's take a look at those based on biblical texts.

I. Objections to Apologetics from Within the Bible

A. The Bible does not need to be defended. One objection often made about apologetics is the claim that the Bible does not need to be defended; it simply needs to be expounded. Hebrews 4:12 is often cited as evidence: "The word of God is living and active" (NIV).[2] It is often said that the Bible is like a lion; it does not need to be defended but simply let loose. A lion can defend itself. Several things should be noted in response.

First, this begs the question as to whether or not the Bible is the Word of God. Of course, God's Word is ultimate, and it speaks for itself. But how do we know the Bible is the Word of God, as opposed to the Qur'an, the Book of Mormon, or some other book? One must appeal to evidence to determine which of the many conflicting books really is the Word of God.

Second, no Christian would accept the claim of a Muslim without question that "the Qur'an is alive and powerful and sharper than a two-edged sword." We would demand evidence. Likewise, no non-Christian should accept our claim without evidence.

Third, the analogy of the lion is misleading. A roar of a lion speaks with authority only because we know from previous knowledge what a lion can do. Without the tales of woe about a lion's ferocity, its roar would not have the same authoritative effect on us. Likewise, without evidence to establish one's claim to authority, there is no good reason to accept that authority.

B. Jesus refused to do signs for evil men. Some have argued that Jesus rebuked people who sought signs. Hence, we should be content simply to believe without evidence. Indeed, Jesus did on occasion rebuke sign seekers. He said, "A wicked and adulterous generation asks for a miraculous sign!" (Matt 12:39; cf. Luke 16:31). However, this does not mean that Jesus did not want people to look at the evidence before they believed. There are many reasons this is so.

First, even in this very passage Jesus went on to offer the miracle of His resurrection as a sign of who He was: "But none will be given it except the sign of the prophet Jonah" (Matt 12:39). Likewise, Paul gave many evidences for the resurrection (1 Cor 15), and Luke referred to "many convincing proofs" (Acts 1:3) of the resurrection.

Second, when John the Baptist inquired whether He was the Christ, Jesus offered miracles as proof: "Go back and report to John what you hear and see: The blind receive sight, the lame walk, those who have leprosy are cured, the deaf hear, the dead are raised, and the good news is preached to the poor" (Matt 11:4–5). When replying to the scribes, He said: "'But that you may know that the Son of Man has authority on earth to forgive sins.' . . . He said to the paralytic, 'I tell you, get up, take your mat and go home'" (Mark 2:10–11). Nicodemus said to Jesus, "Rabbi, we know you are a teacher who has come from God. For no one could perform the miraculous signs you are doing if God were not with him" (John 3:2).

Third, Jesus was opposed to sign-seeking or entertaining people by miracles. Indeed, He refused to perform a miracle to satisfy King Herod's curiosity (Luke 23:8). On other occasions He did not do miracles because of the unbelief of the people (Matt 13:58), not wishing to "cast pearls before swine." The purpose of Jesus' miracles was apologetic, namely, to confirm His message (Exod 4:1ff; John 3:2; Heb 2:3–4). This He did in great abundance, for "Jesus of Nazareth was a man accredited by God to you by miracles, wonders and signs, which God did among you through him" (Acts 2:22).

C. Paul was unsuccessful in his use of reason on Mars Hill and later discarded the approach. Some opponents of apologetics have argued that Paul was unsuccessful in his attempt to reach the thinkers on the Areopagus or Mars Hill (Acts 17), discarding the method and later telling the Corinthians that he wanted to "know Jesus and Him only" (see 1 Cor 2:2). However, this interpretation is based on a misunderstanding of the text.

For one thing, Paul did have results in Athens since some of them were converted, including a philosopher. The text says clearly, "A few men became followers of Paul and believed. Among them was Dionysius, a member of the Areopagus, also a woman named Damaris, and a number of others" (Acts 17:34).

Second, nowhere in either Acts or 1 Corinthians does Paul indicate any repentance or even regret over what he did in Athens. This is reading into the text what simply is not there.

Third, Paul's statement about preaching Jesus and Jesus only is not a change in the content of Paul's preaching. This is what he did everywhere. Even to the philosophers "Paul was preaching the good news about Jesus and the resurrection" (Acts 17:18; see v. 31). So there was nothing unique about what he preached; it was simply how he did it.

Paul tailored his starting point to where the audience was. With the heathen at Lystra he began by an appeal to nature (Acts 14) and ended by preaching Jesus to them. With the Jews he began with the OT and moved on to Christ (Acts 17:2–3). But with the Greek thinkers Paul began with creation and reason to a Creator and on to His Son Jesus who died and rose again (Acts 17:24ff).

D. Only faith, not reason, can please God. Hebrews 11:6 insists that "without faith it is impossible to please God." This would seem to argue against the need for reason. In fact, it would appear that asking for reasons, rather than simply believing, would displease God. In response to this argument against apologetics two important points must be made.

First of all, the text does not say that with reason it is impossible to please God. It says without faith one cannot please God. It does not eliminate reason accompanying faith or a reasonable faith.

Second, God in fact calls on us to use our reason (see 1 Pet 3:15).

Indeed, He has given "clear" (Rom 1:20) and "convincing proofs" (Acts 1:3 NASB) so that we do not have to exercise blind faith.

Third, Heb 11:6 does not exclude "evidence" but actually implies it. For faith is said to be "the evidence" of things we do not see (Heb 11:1 NKJV). For example, the evidence that someone is a reliable witness justifies my believing his testimony of what he saw and I did not. Even so, our faith in "things not seen" (Heb 11:1 NKJV) is justified by the evidence we have that God does exist, which is "clearly seen, being understood from what has been made" (Rom 1:20).

E. Paul said God cannot be known by human reason when he wrote, "The world by wisdom knew not God" (1 Cor 1:21 KJV). However, this cannot mean that there is no evidence for God's existence, since Paul declared in Romans that the evidence for God's existence is so "plain" as to render even the heathen "without excuse" (Rom 1:19–20). Further, the context in 1 Corinthians is not God's existence but His plan of salvation through the cross. This cannot be known by mere human reason but only by divine revelation. It is "foolish" to the depraved human mind.

What is more, the "wisdom" of which he speaks is "the wisdom of this world" (1 Cor 1:20 NKJV), not the wisdom of God. Paul called a sophist the "disputer of this age" (v. 20). A sophist could argue for argument's sake. This leads no one to God.

Further, Paul's reference to the world by wisdom not knowing God is not a reference to the inability of human beings to know God through the evidence He has revealed in creation (Rom 1:19–20) and conscience (Rom 2:12–15). Rather, it is a reference to man's depraved and foolish rejection of the message of the cross.

Finally, in this very book of 1 Corinthians Paul gave his greatest apologetic evidence for the Christian faith—the eyewitnesses of the resurrection of Christ that his companion Luke called "many convincing proofs" (Acts 1:3 NASB).

Indeed, even though man knows clearly through human reason that God exists, he nevertheless "suppresses" or "holds down" this truth in unrighteousness (see Rom 1:18). Thus, it is the presence of such strong evidence that leaves him "without excuse" (Rom 1:20).

F. *The natural man cannot understand spiritual truths*. Paul insisted that "the man without the Spirit does not accept the things that come from the Spirit of God" (1 Cor 2:14). They cannot even "know" them. What use, then, is apologetics? In response to this argument against apologetics two things should be observed.

First, Paul did not say that natural persons cannot *perceive* truth about God, but only that they do not *receive* it (Gk. *dechomai*, "welcome"). Indeed, Paul emphatically declared that the basic truths about God are "clearly seen" (Rom 1:20). The problem is not that unbelievers are not aware of God's existence but that they do not want to accept Him because of the moral consequences this would have on their sinful lives.

Second, 1 Cor 2:14 says they do not "know" (Gk. *ginōskō*), which can mean to know by experience. In other words, they know God in their mind (Rom 1:19–20), but they have not accepted Him in their heart (Rom 1:18). The Bible says, "The fool says in his heart, 'God does not exist'" (Ps 14:1 HCSB).

G. *Only the Holy Spirit can bring someone to Christ*. The Bible says that salvation is a work of the Holy Spirit. He alone can convict, convince, and convert (John 16:8; Eph 2:1; Titus 3:5–7). This is certainly true, and no orthodox Christian denies this.[3] However, two things must be kept in mind.

First, the Bible does not teach that the Holy Spirit will always do this apart from reason and evidence. It is not either the Holy Spirit or reason. Rather, it is the reasonable Holy Spirit using good reason to reach rational people. God is always the efficient cause of salvation, but apologetic arguments can be an instrumental cause used by the Holy Spirit to bring one to Christ.

Second, apologists do not believe that apologetics saves anyone. It only provides evidence in the light of which people can make rational decisions. It only provides evidence that Christianity is true. One must still place his faith in Christ in order to be saved. Apologetics only leads the "horse" to the water. Only the Holy Spirit can persuade him drink.

H. Apologetics is not used in the Bible. It has been objected by some that if apologetics is biblical, then why do we not see it done in the Bible? There are two basic reasons for this misunderstanding.

First, by and large the Bible was not written for unbelievers but for believers. Since they already believe in God, in His Son Jesus Christ, and so on, they are already convinced these are true. Hence, apologetics is directed primarily to those who do not believe so that they may have a reason to believe.

Second, contrary to the claim of critics, apologetics *is* used in the Bible. (1) The first chapter of Genesis confronts the mythical accounts of creation known in that day. (2) Moses' miracles in Egypt were an apologetic that God was speaking through him (Exod 4:1–9). (3) Elijah did apologetics on Mount Carmel when he proved miraculously that Yahweh is the true God, not Baal (1 Kings 18). (4) As we have shown in detail elsewhere,[4] Jesus was constantly engaged in apologetics, proving by signs and wonders that He was the Son of God (John 3:2; Acts 2:22). (5) The apostle Paul did apologetics at Lystra when he gave evidence from nature to the heathen that the supreme God of the universe existed and that idolatry was wrong (Acts 14). (6) The classic case of apologetics in the NT is Acts 17, where Paul reasoned with the philosophers. He not only presented evidence from nature that God existed but also from history that Christ was the Son of God. Indeed, he cited pagan thinkers in support of his arguments.

II. Objections to Apologetics from Outside the Bible

In addition to these internal objections there are some from external sources. These objections against apologetics are geared to show its irrationality, inadequacy, or fruitlessness. Many come from a rationalistic or skeptical point of view. Others are fideistic, which denies that reason should be used to support one's faith.

A. Human reason cannot tell us anything about God. Some critics assert that human reason cannot give us any information about God. First, it says that reason does not apply to questions about God. But this statement itself is offered as a reasonable statement about the issue of God. In order to say that reason does not apply to God, one has to apply reason to God in that very statement. So reasoning about God is inescapable. Reason cannot be denied without being employed.

Second, purely hypothetical reason itself does not tell us anything exists, including God. But since something undeniably exists (e.g., I do), then reason can tell us much about existence, including God. For instance, if something finite and contingent exists, then something infinite and necessary must exist (i.e., God).[5] And if God exists, then it is false that He does not exist. And if God is a necessary Being, then He cannot not exist. Further, if God is Creator and we are creatures, then we are not God. Likewise, reason informs us that if God is omnipotent, then He cannot make a stone so heavy that He cannot lift it. For whatever He can make, He can lift. These and many more questions are answered in my book with Ravi Zacharias, *Who Made God? And Answers to 100 Other Tough Questions of Faith.*[6]

B. Reason is useless in religious matters. Fideism argues that reason is of no use in matters that deal with God. One must simply believe. Faith, not reason, is what God requires (Heb 11:6). Several points can be made in response.

First, even from a biblical point of view God calls on us to use our reason (Isa 1:18; 1 Pet 3:15; cf. Matt 22:36–37). God is a rational being, and He created us as rational beings. God would not insult the reason He gave us by asking us to ignore it in such important matters as our beliefs about Him.

Second, this fideistic position is self-defeating, for either it has a reason that we should not reason about God or it does not. If it does, then it defeats itself by using reason to say we should not use reason. If fideism has no reason for not using reason, then it is without reason for its position, in which case there is no reason why one should accept fideism. Furthermore, to claim reason is just optional for a fideist will not suffice. For either the fideist offers some criteria for when we should be reasonable and when we should not, or else his view is simply arbitrary. If he offers some rational criteria for when we should be rational, then he does have a rational basis for his view, in which case he is not really a fideist after all. Reason is not the kind of thing in which a rational creature can choose to participate. By virtue of being rational by nature one must be part of rational discourse. And rational discourse demands that one follow the laws of reason.

A major contribution made by Francis Schaeffer was his emphasis on the need for a reasoned approach to apologetics. In his *Escape from Reason* he showed the futility of those who attempt to reject reason. He constantly chided those who make a "dichotomy between reason and non-reason."[7] He also criticizes those who forsake reason for a "lower story" materialism or an "upper story" mysticism.[8]

C. You cannot prove God or Christianity by reason. According to this objection, the existence of God cannot be proven by human reason. The answer depends on what is meant by "prove." First, if "prove" means to demonstrate with mathematical certainty, then most theists would agree that God's existence cannot be proven in this way. The reason for this is that mathematical certainty deals only with the abstract, and the existence of God (or anything else) is a matter of concrete, real existence. Mathematical certainty is based on certain axioms or postulates that must be assumed in order to get a necessary conclusion. But if God's existence must be assumed in order to be proven, then the conclusion that God exists is only based on the assumption that He exists, in which case it is not really a proof at all. Mathematical certainty is deductive in nature. It argues from given premises. But one cannot validly conclude what is not already implied in the premise(s). In this case one would have to assume God exists in the premise in order to validly infer this in the conclusion. But this begs the question.

Second, if by "prove," however, we mean "give adequate evidence for" or "provide good reasons for," then it would seem to follow that one can prove the existence of God and the truth of Christianity. Indeed, many apologists have offered such proofs, and people have become Christians after reading their writings.[9]

D. No one is persuaded of religious truths by reason. According to this argument, no one is ever persuaded to accept a religious truth by reason. Psychological, personal, and subjective factors prompt religious decisions, not rational arguments. But this objection is patently false for many reasons.

First of all, whoever became a believer because he thought it was irrational and absurd to do so? Certainly, the vast majority of people who believe in God or accept Christ as their personal Lord and Savior do so because they think it is reasonable.

Second, this objection confuses two kinds of belief: *belief in* and *belief that*. Certainly, religious belief in God and in Christ is not based on evidence and reason. But neither is it done without them. Every rational person looks to see if there is evidence that the elevator has a floor before he steps in it. Likewise, all rational people want evidence that an airplane can fly before they get in it. So *belief that* is prior to *belief in*. Apologetics deals with the former. It provides evidence that God exists, that Christ is the Son of God, and that the Bible is the Word of God. A religious decision is a step of faith in the light of the evidence, not a leap of faith in the dark—in the absence of evidence.

III. The Reasons for the Need to Defend the Faith

There are many good reasons for doing apologetics. First of all, God commands us to do so. Second, reason demands it. Third, the world needs it. Fourth, results confirm it.

A. God commands the use of reason. The most important reason for doing apologetics is that God told us to do it. Over and over the New Testament exhorts us to defend the faith. First Peter 3:15 says, "But in your hearts set apart Christ as Lord. Always be prepared to give an answer to everyone who asks you to give the reason for the hope that you have." This verse says several important things.

First, Peter said that we should be ready. We may never run across someone who asks the tough questions about our faith, but we should still be ready just in case. But being ready is not just a matter of having the right information available; it is also an attitude of readiness and eagerness to share with others the truth of what we believe.

Second, we are to give a reason to those who ask the questions (Col 4:5–6). It is not expected that everyone needs pre-evangelism or reasons before he accepts the gospel, but when they do need it, we must be able and willing to give them an answer.

Finally, it links doing pre-evangelism with making Christ Lord in our hearts. If He is really Lord, then we should be obedient to Him by "destroying speculations and every lofty thing raised up against the knowledge of God, and . . . taking every thought captive to the obedience of Christ" (2 Cor 10:5 NASB). In other words we should be confronting issues in our own minds and in the expressed thoughts of others that are preventing them from knowing God. That is what apologetics is all about.

In Phil 1:7 Paul spoke of his mission as one of "defending and confirming the gospel." He added in verse 16, "I am put here for the defense of the gospel." And we are put where we are to defend it as well.

Jude 3 declares: "Beloved, while I was making every effort to write to you about our common salvation, I felt the necessity to write to you appealing that you contend earnestly for the faith which was once for all handed down to the saints" (NASB). Jude's original audience had been assaulted by false teachers, and he needed to encourage them to protect (Lit. "agonize for") the faith as it had been revealed through Christ. Jude made a significant statement about our attitude as we do this: "have mercy on some, who are doubting" (v. 22 NASB). Apologetics, then, is a form of compassion.

Titus 1:9 makes knowledge of Christian evidences a requirement for church leadership. An elder in the church should be "holding fast the faithful word which is in accordance with the teaching, so that he will be able both to exhort in sound doctrine and to refute those who contradict" (NASB). In 2 Tim 2:24–25 Paul declared that "the Lord's bondservant must not be quarrelsome, but be kind to all, able to teach, patient when wronged, with gentleness correcting those who are in opposition, if perhaps God may grant them repentance leading to the knowledge of the truth" (NASB). Anyone attempting to answer the questions of unbelievers will surely be wronged and be tempted to lose patience, but our ultimate goal is that they might come to a knowledge of the truth that Jesus has died for their sins.

Indeed, the command to use reason is part of the greatest command. Jesus said, "'Love the Lord your God with all your heart and with all your soul and with all your mind.' This is the first and greatest commandment" (Matt 22:37–38).

B. Reason demands it. God created us with human reason. It is part of His image in us (Gen 1:27; Col 3:10). Indeed, it is that by which we are distinguished from "brute beasts" (Jude 10 NKJV). God calls upon us to use our reason (Isa 1:18) to discern truth from error (1 John 4:6), to determine right from wrong (Heb 5:14), and to discern a true from a false prophet (Deut 18:19–22).

A fundamental principle of reason is that we should have sufficient grounds for what we believe. An unjustified belief is just that—unjustified. Being created rational creatures and not "unreasoning animals" (Jude 10, NASB), we are expected to use the reason God gave us. Socrates said, "The unexamined life is not worth living" (Plato, *Apology*, 38a). Likewise, the unexamined faith is not worth having. Therefore, it is incumbent upon Christians "to give a reason for their hope" (see 1 Pet 3:15). This is part of the great command to love God with all our mind, as well as our heart and soul (Matt 22:36–37).

C. The world needs it. Many people refuse to believe without some evidence, as indeed they should. Since God created us as rational beings, He does not expect us to live irrationally. He wants us to look before we leap. This does not mean there is no room for faith. But God wants us to take a step of faith in the light—in the light of evidence. He does not want us to leap in the dark.

We should have evidence that something is true before we place our faith in it. For example, no rational person steps in an elevator unless he has some reason to believe it will hold him up. Likewise, no reasonable person gets on an airplane that has a broken wing and smoke coming out the tail end. Remember that *belief that* is prior to *belief in*. Evidence and reason are important in establishing *belief that*. Once this is established, one can place his *belief in* it. Thus, the rational person wants some evidence that

God exists before he places his faith in God. Likewise, rational unbelievers want evidence for the claim that Jesus is the Son of God before they place their trust in Him.

We are all aware that the world needs to hear the gospel (Matt 29:18–20) since it alone is the power of God unto salvation (Rom 1:16). But the fact is that much of the world does not believe the prerequisites of the gospel, namely, that a theistic God exists, that miracles are possible, and that the New Testament documents are historically reliable. Without these preconditions, the gospel does not seem credible to many people. The apostle Paul exhibited this need for pre-evangelism in Athens (Acts 17) when he found it necessary to reason with the Epicurean and the Stoic philosophers.

D. Results confirm it. There is a common misnomer among many Christians that apologetics never helps to bring anyone to Christ. This is a serious misrepresentation of the facts, and here are some examples where apologetics has been instrumental in someone's conversion.

The Conversion of St. Augustine. There were several significant rational turning points in Augustine's life before he came to Christ. First, he reasoned his way out of Manichaean dualism. One significant turning point here was the success of a young Christian debater of Manicheans called Helpidius.[10] Second, Augustine reasoned his way out of total skepticism by seeing the self-defeating nature of it.[11] Third, were it not for studying Plotinus, Augustine stated, he would not have even been able to conceive of a spiritual being, let alone believe in one.[12]

The Conversion of Frank Morrison. This skeptical attorney set out to disprove Christianity by showing the resurrection never occurred. The quest ended with his conversion and a book titled *Who Moved the Stone?* in which the first chapter was titled "The Book That Refused to Be Written"![13] More recently another unbelieving attorney, Lee Strobel, had a similar journey, which he narrates in his widely read book *The Case for Christ*.[14]

The Conversion of Simon Greenleaf. At the turn of the century, Simon Greenleaf, a professor of law at Harvard Law School who wrote the book on legal evidence, was challenged by students to apply the rules of legal evidence to the New Testament to see if its testimony would stand up in court. The result was a book titled *The Testimony of the Evangelists* in which he expressed his confidence in the basic documents and truths of the Christian faith.[15] Many other unbelievers have experienced similar conversions, including C. S. Lewis,[16] Josh McDowell,[17] and Jay Budziszewski.[18]

The Results of Debates. Many people have been led toward or to Christianity as a result of debates I have had with atheists and skeptics. After debating Berkley University philosopher Michael Scriven on "Is Christianity Credible?" the University of Calgary audience voted three to one in favor of Christianity. The campus newspaper report read: "Atheist Fails to Convert Campus Christians!" Following a debate on the rationality of belief in Christianity with the head of the philosophy department at the University of Miami, the Christian student leadership held a follow-up meeting. The atheist professor attended and expressed doubts about his view expressed at the debate. It was reported that some 14 people who had attended the debate made decisions for Christ.

After a debate on the Moonie religion at Northwestern University in Evanston, Illinois, a Moonie girl asked some questions about Christianity. I could see that she had been convinced that the Unification Church was not teaching the truth. After talking with her briefly, I introduced her to a female seminary student who led her to Christ.

When we shared the gospel with Don Bly, an unbeliever in our community, he told us that he was an atheist. After we reasoned with him from atheism to open-minded agnosticism, he agreed to read Frank Morrison's book. The evidence for Christ's resurrection convinced him, and we had the privilege of leading him to Christ. He has since then raised his family for Christ and become a leader in a church south of St. Louis.

The Results of Reading Apologetic Writings. I have received a number of letters and reports of people who have been converted to belief that God exists or to belief in Christ after reading apologetics works. God used its arguments as an instrument to bring people toward and to Christ.

Antony Flew, one of the world's most widely known atheists, wrote this about his conversion to theism: "Nor do I claim to have had any personal experience of God or any experience that may be called super-natural or miraculous. In short, my discovery of the divine has been a pilgrimage of reason and not of faith."[19] Noted former atheist Francis Collins said, "After twenty-eight years as a believer, the Moral Law still stands out for me as the strongest signpost to God. More than that, it points to a God who cares about human beings, and a God who is infinitely good and holy."[20]

Since many of my books are widely circulated, I often get letters from readers. Recently, a college student wrote: "God sent me your book 'I Don't Have Enough Faith to Be an Atheist.' . . . I opened the book thinking I would rip it apart with my superior viewpoint and about one quarter of the way through I ended up apologizing to God and accepting him into my heart. I have since grown exponentially in Christ, and I thought I would thank you for your inspiring book."[21] Another reader wrote this to me about his conversion: "I just got done reading *Why I Am a Christian*, and I was blown away. It is perhaps the most powerful and influential Christian book I've ever read. It was exactly what I was looking for. It provided the answers to the roadblocks that were guarding against my faith. . . . Your book pressed the red button setting off the nuclear bomb of my faith."[22]

Conclusion

Christianity is under attack today and must be defended against these attacks from within by cults and heresies and from without by skeptics and other religions. As we have seen, the objections to doing apologetics are without foundation in Scripture. Further, there are many reasons for doing apologetics, including: (1) God commanded it; (2) reason demands it; (3) the world needs it; and (4) results confirm it.

We have a reasonable faith, and the Bible has commanded that we give reasons for it. As perhaps the greatest apologist of the twentieth century, C. S. Lewis, said:

> To be ignorant and simple now—not to be able to meet the enemies on their ground—would be to throw down our weapons, and to betray our uneducated brethren who have, under God, no defense but us against the intellectual attacks of the heathen. Good philosophy must exist, if for no other reason, because bad philosophy needs to be answered.[23]

The reason we need to defend the true religion is because there are false religions. The reason we need to stand for authentic Christianity is that there are counterfeit forms of Christianity.

Notes

1. This article is a revision of a previously unpublished article called "The Need for Apologetics."

2. Unless otherwise noted, all quotations from the Bible are taken from the New International Version of the Bible (NIV).

3. See N. L. Geisler, "Holy Spirit, Role in Apologetics," in *Baker Encyclopedia of Apologetics*, ed. N. L. Geisler (Grand Rapids: Baker, 2000), 330–36.

4. See N. L. Geisler and P. Zukeran, *The Apologetics of Jesus* (Grand Rapids: Baker, 2009).

5. N. L. Geisler, *Christian Apologetics* (Grand Rapids: Baker, 1976), 47–64.

6. R. Zacharias and N. L. Geisler, *Who Made God? And 100 Other Tough Questions of Faith* (Grand Rapids: Zondervan, 2003).

7. F. Schaeffer, *He Is There and He Is Not* Silent (Wheaton: Tyndale, 1972), 46.

8. Ibid., 56.

9. See L. R. Bush, ed., *Classical Readings in Christian Apologetics: A.D. 100–1800* (Grand Rapids: Zondervan, 1983); W. Corduan, *No Doubt About It: The Case for Christianity* (Nashville: B&H Academic, 1997); Geisler, *Christian Apologetics*; N. L. Geisler and F. Turek, *I Do Not Have Enough Faith to Be an Atheist* (Wheaton: Crossway, 2004); P. Kreeft and R. K. Tacelli, *Handbook of Christian Apologetics (*Downers Grove: InterVarsity, 2004).

10. See St. Augustine, *Confessions*, Oxford World Classics, trans. H. O. Chadwick (New York: Oxford University Press, 2009).

11. See St. Augustine, *Against the Academics*, Ancient Christian Writers, trans. J. J. O'Meara (Mahwah, NJ: Paulist, 1978).

12. See Augustine, *Confessions*.

13. See F. Morrison, *Who Moved the Stone?* (London: Faber and Faber, 1996).

14. See L. Strobel, *The Case for Christ: A Journalist's Personal Investigation of the Evidence for Jesus* (Grand Rapids: Zondervan, 1998).

15. See S. Greenleaf, *The Testimony of the Evangelists: Examined by the Rules of Evidence Administered in Courts of Justice* (Grand Rapids: Baker, 1984).

16. See C. S. Lewis, *Mere Christianity* (New York: Macmillan, 1943).

17. See J. McDowell, *More Than a Carpenter* (Carol Stream, IL: Tyndale, 1987).

18. J. Budziszewski, *The Revenge of Conscience: Politics and the Fall of Man* (Dallas: Spence, 1999).

19. A. Flew, *There Is a God: How the World's Most Notorious Atheist Changed His Mind* (New York: Harper One, 2007), 93.

20. F. Collins, *The Language of God: A Scientist Presents Evidence for Belief* (New York: Free Press, 2006), 218.

21. Ryan, letter to N. L. Geisler, November 10, 2006.

22. J. Warmels, letter to N. L. Geisler, June 27, 2005.

23. C. S. Lewis, *The Weight of Glory* (New York: HarperOne, 2001), 50.

Chapter 7

Jesus' Post-Resurrection Appearance to the Apostle Paul

Can It Withstand Critical Scrutiny?

Gary R. Habermas

When it comes to the conversion of the apostle Paul, we are faced with an apparent anomaly. No New Testament witness to Jesus' resurrection appearances is taken more seriously by critical scholars, but comparatively few seem to challenge or even look closely at this apostle's own experience. Why?

In this essay, I discuss the New Testament reports of Jesus' post-resurrection appearance to Paul, considering a range of critical responses over the last century and a half.[1] My chief purpose is to ascertain if Paul's testimony can survive examination.

The Priority of Paul

Critical scholars almost unanimously hold that at least seven of the epistles in the New Testament that bear Paul's name were written by him: Romans, 1 and 2 Corinthians, Galatians, Philippians, 1 Thessalonians, and Philemon. Even skeptical scholars refer to these texts as the "undisputed letters"[2] or as those writings that are "generally accepted as genuine without doubt."[3] Their compositions by Paul occurred in the decade of the AD 50s.[4]

Paul mentioned on several occasions that the risen Jesus, after His death by crucifixion, appeared to him. This experience is cited as the specific call whereby Paul was commanded to take the gospel message to the Gentiles (Gal 1:16).[5] On another occasion, Paul cited Jesus' appearance to him as providing the necessary credentials for his identification as an apostle (1 Cor 9:1). Further, he placed His appearance at the end of a very early official list of other appearances (1 Cor 15:3–8), fully recognizing that the lateness of his experience was a temporal anomaly. This last report is the most evidential statement of resurrection appearance data in the New Testament.

Secondary summaries of Jesus' appearance to Paul are recounted three times in Acts (9:1–9; 22:1–11; 26:9–19). Luke, the best prospect for the authorship of Acts, as well as Paul's traveling companion, presumably heard the apostle tell his own story more than once.

That this event inaugurated Paul's becoming a follower of Jesus Christ is seldom denied. Yet such a drastic turnaround from his previous path as an exceptional young scholar and chief persecutor of the church (1 Cor 15:9; Gal 1:13–14; Phil 3:4–7) to an apostle certainly demands an adequate explanation. Paul explained forthrightly that he had met the risen Jesus.

The unanimity among critical scholars is really quite amazing. It is generally acknowledged that Paul certainly was the recipient of a real experience that he believed deeply to be an appearance of the risen Jesus. Such an experience would surely account for his incredible transformation and motivation to spread the gospel message. For reasons like these, Paul's statements are regarded as eyewitness reports of his experience. For example, atheistic philosopher Michael Martin said, "However, we have only one contemporary eyewitness account of a postresurrection [sic] appearance of Jesus, namely Paul's."[6]

Why is the appearance of the risen Jesus to Paul given this place of priority? Jesus Seminar member Roy Hoover explained that Paul's writings are the proper place to launch such a study: "The reason for starting here is simple and compelling: Paul's testimony is the earliest and the most historically reliable evidence about the resurrection of Jesus that we have."[7] Hoover then added, "The most important evidence about the resurrection with which Paul provides us is . . . a direct claim that he has seen the risen Jesus."[8]

Martin and Hoover are not alone here; other skeptical scholars also agree on the crucial nature of Paul's witness.[9] Actually, historian Donald Akenson charged that critical scholars need to take Paul even more seriously than they do! For Akenson, this pride of position holds for similar reasons to those mentioned by Hoover.

Paul's authentic letters are the earliest sources for the historical Jesus, and they are the only New Testament writings whose authorship is clearly known. Yet Akenson found fault with both liberal and conservative scholars for not being even more thoroughly committed to this Pauline conclusion. He thought that liberals fail to give Paul his full due for two reasons: (1) the centrality of the crucifixion and resurrection in his writings; (2) they give equal and perhaps even prior commitment to the so-called Q pre-gospel source. Akenson faulted conservatives even more for preferring Paul without realizing that this apostle contributed plenty to an understanding of the historical Jesus. He suggested placing Paul firmly in the primary position ahead of the Gospels and Acts until the latter can be confirmed by Paul.[10]

Importantly, critical scholars are generally in agreement today: Paul is the best authority with regard to what we can learn about Jesus and the earliest church. To be sure, various scholars argue especially for particular details taken from Mark, Q, or the other Gospel sources. However, the preference for Paul usually holds, even in spite of the various theological differences that are present.

Older Naturalistic Approaches to Paul's Resurrection Experience

Throughout the nineteenth and the first decades of the twentieth century, much of theology was dominated by the so-called old German Liberalism. This broad movement generally eschewed two sorts of New Testament reports: dogmatic theology and supernatural events. These scholars often recognized or accepted the general text of a Gospel pericope as long as it did not offend one of these two sensibilities, especially when there was a contemporary moral to the story or some other point of congruence that might be made with their own generation.

When it came to a miraculous report itself, liberalism tended to accept the general outline, while elaborating some natural account that may actually have happened instead of the reported supernatural component. After all, so it was reasoned, ancient peoples were often mistaken and rather gullible in their openness to miracles. For example, the account of Jesus walking on the water could have been a case where Jesus walked the shoreline, though this was undetected by His disciples during the storm.[11]

In keeping with this spirit, Jesus' miracles must be explained in natural terms. Likewise, when it came to what happened to Paul on the road to Damascus, the overall outline could be kept intact, while the miraculous element would be expunged. So Paul could well have been on his way to Damascus in order to persecute the early Christian sect, traveling with several companions who would presumably help in rooting out this blasphemous cult. However, rather than meeting the risen Jesus, any number of other natural suggestions were substituted in order to explain his conversion to Christianity. As J. Gresham Machen observed, critical attempts in his day included suggestions that Paul perhaps suffered some sort of heat stroke and that a violent thunderstorm may have played a role. Likewise, epilepsy, nervous exhaustion, and hallucinations were all posited as potential natural occurrences.[12]

One very popular example is the work of prominent German New Testament scholar F. C. Baur of Tübingen University. In one of the most influential analyses of the nineteenth century, Baur rejected popular external options in his time, such as Paul's encounter with a flash of lightning while he was on his way to Damascus. Rather, Baur postulated that Paul's conversion was the result of a private, subjective experience that was expressed objectively. This occurrence resulted from Paul's "downcast, introspective" personality and was due to his conviction of his sins from the recent events in his life. Through a real experience that he believed was an appearance of the risen Jesus, just like what had happened to Jesus' disciples, Paul's life changed dramatically. However, he did not actually see anyone, since nothing had happened in the "real" world.[13]

Another example is that of prominent Jewish scholar Joseph Klausner, who researched and wrote his classic work on Paul between the years 1929 and 1939. He concluded that while traveling on the road to Damascus, Paul, a devout and zealous Pharisee, was thinking about his role in Stephen's martyrdom.

Suddenly, Jesus was standing before him, although not in reality. This experience was sufficient to cause his conversion. For Klausner, this occurrence was "clearly" due to Paul having suffered from a case of epilepsy. Most likely, Paul was contemplating the new and revolutionary idea of Jesus as the suffering Messiah just prior to his epileptic attack. This disease would therefore explain the subjective experience of a "heavenly light" and would align Paul with the "long list of epileptics" throughout history.[14]

This is an example of what was mentioned above, namely, the propensity of the older liberal studies to accept the majority of the New Testament account, while explaining naturally the supernatural component. While the differences between these approaches and more recent studies are generally more pronounced regarding the resurrection appearances to the other followers of Jesus, accounts of Paul's conversion do not differ so much.

Recent Trends Regarding Paul's Resurrection Appearance

During the last few decades, the approach to Paul's conversion has been more positive than what we have just seen. Critical scholars tend to discuss Paul's experience in a more straightforward manner, usually without attempting to get behind the text and extrapolate concerning what "must really have occurred." Still, some scholars have ventured explanations that sound very much like those of Baur and Klausner.

For example, while discussing the nature of Paul's conversion, historian Michael Grant noted that the descriptions in Acts 9, 22, and 26 cannot be totally trusted, even though the variations between the accounts are rather minor. Without being dogmatic about the actual cause, Grant apparently believed that the possibilities include storms with thunder and lightning, heat, exhaustion, or thirst. Likewise, a medical condition such as epilepsy or mental disturbances that approach some sort of breakdown could also explain the situation. At any rate, Paul apparently experienced a luminous, mystical incident of some sort, perhaps due to his nervous and highly suggestive state of mind.[15]

One recent trend, however, has been rather steady during the last two centuries. The tendency among arguably the majority of commentators is to conclude that, whatever one decides regarding the other resurrection appearances of Jesus, Paul's experience is usually taken to be less than the sighting of the actual body of Jesus. Generally, it is argued that, at most, Paul witnessed a disembodied, glorified vision of the exalted Jesus. However, during the last decade or two, a dramatic trend has emerged, which argues that Paul at least thought he had encountered the raised body of Jesus, as had his fellow apostles.[16]

Most intriguingly, this last position is even preferred by several major researchers who doubt or deny actual resurrection appearances but still think that the appearance of the risen Jesus to Paul was bodily in nature. For example, Gerd Lüdemann held that Paul's appearance was a subjective vision, but he thought that Paul's language requires at least that he *believed* that the risen Jesus appeared as an actual body.[17]

Likewise, after juxtaposing the Acts descriptions with Paul's own brief comments, John Dominic Crossan and Jonathan Reed opted for the latter since they are the primary texts, while the Acts accounts are secondary. Taken along with Paul's view of the resurrection body, they argue that Paul held to bodily resurrection appearances.[18] This follows another analysis of the issue by Crossan.[19]

Although I cannot pursue this detailed argument here, the recent trend in scholarship is to recognize that, taking the entirety of Paul's language regarding the resurrection body of both Jesus and believers strongly favors that Paul taught the notion that Jesus appeared after His death in an actual, physical body. Nevertheless, Paul's treatment in 1 Cor 15 and elsewhere indicates that Jesus had also changed, exhibiting a spiritual component (cf. Phil 1:21). Therefore, we must do justice to both terms in Paul's concept of "spiritual body" (1 Cor 15:42–44). Some researchers have even gone as far as to argue that Paul thought of his own appearance as even "more 'objective' and 'physical'" than the other resurrection appearances![20] This is certainly a remarkable about-face from the research during the last two centuries.

Still, many contemporary theologians seem rather slow to criticize or even question the reality of the resurrection appearance to Paul. Generally, the experience is often simply stated in a straightforward manner and left there. Nonetheless, enough questions have been raised in the past two centuries to require a historical response.

Countering the Negative Criticism

It is impossible in a single essay to respond adequately to all the questions regarding Jesus Christ's resurrection appearance to Paul. In this section I have noted three general problems with the critical attempts to explain or marginalize Paul's experience in natural terms. Then I turn to some suggestions on constructing the parameters of the appearances to Paul. First, the vast majority of naturalistic approaches to the appearance of the risen Jesus to Paul during the last 200 years postulate the presence of normal conditions or situations such as coincidental storms with lightning, heat stroke, epilepsy, a remorseful and guilty conscience, a highly suggestive or nervous personality type, or psychological conditions such as hallucinations. These phenomena certainly occur, sometimes even at strange times. But the chief problem is the lack of data to confirm that any such conditions were actually true of the apostle Paul at these precise moments and in such a way that they were capable of explaining the major components of his experience. In other words, while such conditions *could* have been the case, how do we separate these alternative scenarios from simple, ad hoc suggestions in order to avoid the miraculous? It is virtually impossible to prove that any of these conditions ever applied to Paul or that they could best explain his experience.

To choose perhaps the most frequent example from the list above, it is often postulated that Saul of Tarsus suffered overwhelming guilt and remorse due to his persecution of Christians, propelling him in the direction of Christianity. However, Paul's own testimony after the fact is that his actions towards believers were performed with enthusiasm, based on his faultless standing regarding the Old Testament law. His persecution of Christians was exceptionally zealous (Acts 22:3; Gal 1:13–14; Phil 3:4–6). There is no indication whatsoever of any regret prior to his conversion.

Moreover, the proposal that Paul suffered excessive remorse and guilt would constitute a very weak foundation for the apostle's unyielding Christian transformation and conviction, even as he faced death on numerous occasions. It is difficult to see how this projected remorse would extend throughout his life and overcome every obstacle that Paul faced, from multiple beatings to shipwrecks to a stoning where he was left for dead (2 Cor 11:23–28; see 4:8–12). Yet throughout the entire group of undoubted "authentic" Pauline epistles, there is never even an inkling that Paul questioned his conversion, considered reverting to Judaism, or ever experienced any remorse and guilt.

Actually, Paul's former passionate obsession for the law and his potent training in Judaism could more easily have resulted in some sort of backlash at some later time against his more recent Christian convictions. Yet, all we witness, and repeatedly so, is his exceptional enthusiasm and the personal conviction of his Christian faith.

But could the persecution of Christians have produced such guilt in Paul prior to his conversion? Again, while such a scenario is *possible*, where is the *evidence* in favor of these and other such claims? All indications that would make these conditions obtain for Paul are lacking, and severely so. Actually, the information that we do possess argues otherwise and is clearly contrary to the thesis of exceptional guilt and remorse causing the apostle's change of heart. A lack of evidence does not trump the presence of data.

It might be countered that Paul was spinning his situation in the best light in each of these contexts. But again, this is mere conjecture; the issue is that we have no *evidence* to support the natural theses, and some data, especially of the firsthand variety like Paul's, is far better than no data at all. In other words, Paul's description is better than no description at all.

Remarkably, critical scholars not only frequently acknowledge the lack of evidence for their counterproposals, but also recognize the weakness of postulating responses in such a vacuum. For example, Baur noted the "unsatisfactory" nature of alternative suppositions when there are no supporting indications! Later, he complained that these critical responses are "really mere hypothesis, and as it not only has no foundation in the text, but is rather opposed to the acknowledged tone of the author, we shall make here no further mention of it."[21] Yet, incredibly, his own admonition did not keep him from venturing precisely such a proposal just a few pages later![22] Likewise, Grant stated,

"Our evidence is too fragmentary, and enigmatic, to allow us to do more than guess at an answer." Nonetheless, this admission did not keep him from venturing just such a naturalistic speculation.[23] As Machen asserted, since these counterproposals have "totally insufficient data . . . no real basis . . . not the slightest evidence," the critical scholar who employs such maneuvers "is in grave danger of becoming untrue to his own critical principles."[24]

Second, closely related but beyond the critic's lack of evidence is the need to psychologize Paul. Not only do we lack the evidence to establish the critical hypothesis on its own grounds, but *we could never get into Paul's head and properly extrapolate his internal moods, conflicts, and motivations, regardless of his state of mind.* Worse yet, even if our revised suppositions about him were true, we could never know it. Crucially, the problem is that new knowledge is necessary to reconstruct a probable situation that opposes Paul's own testimony. As Machen stated, "The fundamental objection to all these theories of psychological development is that they describe only what *might* have been or what ought to have been, and not what actually *was*."[25] Constructing a counter-hypothesis depends on our knowing Paul's mind-set, beyond his clear testimony, and that can never be established in a vacuum.

Third, while many scholars are generally quite critical of the book of Acts, they frequently either affirm or at least find little fault with the three descriptions of Christ's resurrection appearance to Paul in Acts 9, 22, 26. For instance, while Lüdemann concluded that large portions of Acts, including the apostolic speeches, are often the construction of the author and hence unhistorical or legendary,[26] he still thought that the accounts of Paul's conversion are fairly accurate, at least in their broad details.[27] In this respect, Lüdemann is unlike Crossan and Reed, who "bracket" the details of the Acts accounts of a visionary light experience in favor of Paul's own eyewitness comments that he actually saw Jesus, without any reference to the light phenomena.[28] Machen even agreed that we need to be critical of scholars who reverse their own procedure and elevate the Acts narratives over Paul's own testimony.[29]

However, approaches such as those of Crossan, Reed, and Machen are in the minority. Hence the inconsistency here: rather than interpreting the secondary source according to the primary texts, which is almost always the accepted procedure in research, critics who seem to have a personal hypothesis at stake often prefer to elevate the secondary, much later writing, apparently because of the presumed benefits of presenting Jesus Christ's appearance to Paul as a visionary experience from heaven. Besides the inconsistency itself, this move raises the possibility that the Acts accounts are more reliable than critical scholars often allow. What this might say, in turn, about the reliability of the resurrection narratives in the third Gospel is also affected by the conclusion here.

I bring my general considerations to an end by pointing out some of the overall problems that are frequently evident in critical scholars who would downplay or explain away the appearance of the risen Jesus to Paul. For such critics to carry out their skeptical agenda, they must postulate conditions that are unsupported by the evidence, ignore the early and authoritative data that we already possess, and psychoanalyze Paul without ever being able to ascertain whether he possessed an alternative mind-set other than what the data dictate. The inconsistency of generally ignoring Acts except when accounts are needed is a further issue. It is sufficient to note the faulty conceptual and methodological underpinnings of the typical moves to explain away Paul's appearance.[30]

Taking Steps Toward a Positive Case

Several principles are more helpful in establishing the nature of Jesus' appearance to Paul. Here are a few of the signposts.

First, in light of the data in the previous section regarding the skeptical preference for the Acts accounts of Jesus' resurrection appearance to Paul while minimizing or even rejecting the reliability of the book as a whole, critical scholars appear to be riding the horns of a dilemma, and in more than one area.

If the stories in Acts regarding Paul's conversion are thought to be reliable, then this moves the interpreter in a direction that many critics may not want to embrace. However one accounts for these descriptions, the data indicate that it is definitely not the case that Paul experienced a hallucination or some other subjective perception.

Although Acts says that Paul's companions neither saw Jesus (9:7) nor understood the words of His voice (22:9), to emphasize these more subjective elements ignores the objective comments found in the very same accounts. Acts also says that the other travelers heard at least the sound of the voice—although possibly without comprehension (9:7). But they clearly saw the supernatural light (22:9; 26:13), and, like Paul, they also responded by falling down to the ground (26:14). Additionally, Paul was blinded for three days (9:8–9; 22:11). Moreover, against those who suggest that Paul only witnessed a heavenly light, the texts also affirm that he saw Jesus (9:17; 9:27; 22:14–15; 26:16).

But why relish the more subjective elements here while disregarding the larger number of objective aspects in the same contexts that head in a different direction? To dismiss the objective components is to sacrifice the subjective elements too. Conversely, neither can the subjective aspects be ignored. These accounts are challenging to all sides, precisely because both aspects are present. But the more objective perceptions in the real world argue strongly against hallucinations and other subjective phenomena, since the latter have no corresponding objective or veridical referents. The bottom line here is this: if these Acts accounts are accepted, then the objective elements also follow, ruling out purely subjective hypotheses. But if these texts are rejected, then there is virtually no reason to categorize Paul's experiences as subjective.

So it would seem that to accept the general reliability of the Acts accounts of Paul's conversion experience would be to embrace both subjective and objective qualities. But the common critical move to use these texts to argue more subjectively is to play fast and loose with the data. For such a response often downplays the book as a whole, as well as ignoring or minimizing the unwanted objective elements in the very accounts that are accepted.

Second, as many have noted, Paul's own personal comments take precedence over secondary summaries, and he specifically stated that he had seen the risen Jesus (1 Cor 9:1; 15:8). As N. T. Wright argued, the language in 1 Cor 9:1 particularly refers to normal sight and needs to be taken in a straightforward manner.[31]

Third, beyond the Acts accounts, there are other serious problems with categorizing Jesus' resurrection experience to Paul as a hallucination or some other subjective experience by Paul. There are three reasons for this: (1) It is very difficult to identify what impetus would have caused Paul to hallucinate or otherwise imagine a vivid experience of the glorified Jesus in whom he did not even believe! (2) To the contrary, we *do* know that Paul's conversion produced his powerful commitment to Jesus Christ that ended in martyrdom, with no evidence whatsoever that he reexamined his faith or recanted later, while exhibiting the complete assurance that Jesus had appeared to him. Such total life-changing transformations are rarely connected with hallucinations. (3) Paul reported the early creedal message that Jesus appeared to more than 500 believers at one time (1 Cor 15:6), as well as to other groups (vv. 5,7), so he plainly did not think Jesus' appearances were internal and subjective events. Moreover, a subjective experience also fails to explain viably (v. 4) the empty tomb[32] or (v. 5) James' conversion (1 Cor 15:7) from skepticism, which demands its own viable explanation.

Fourth, while I said earlier that this cannot be defended here in any detail, given the many solid reasons for believing that Paul conceived of Jesus' resurrection appearance to him as bodily in nature,[33] this would virtually rule out any notion that he considered Jesus' appearance to have been that of a disembodied, heavenly figure. This argument alone is sufficient to cause several skeptical scholars, such as Lüdemann and Crossan, to conclude that Paul conceived of this event in bodily terms. This is clearly warranted by the straightforward language that is employed in the relevant texts.

Therefore, the view that Paul actually saw a bodily appearance of the risen Jesus has the strongest case. Opposing hypotheses build their cases on the decided absence of evidence, are unable to know the inner workings of Paul's mind beyond his own clear statements, and frequently elevate the Acts accounts of Paul's conversion. The natural case is characterized by stringing together a series of "what if" comments—all without any factual foundation. Not only are the data lacking, but there is no means of confirming the required suppositions.

On the other hand, while the Acts accounts are challenging, especially with regard to what Paul's companions saw, it seems abundantly clear in the relevant texts that Paul actually saw the risen Jesus. Such a thesis is supported by the overall tenor of the

Acts accounts and Paul's own straightforward statements, as well as the many compelling reasons to doubt that Paul's experience was subjective. Further, the vast majority of our evidence indicates that Paul also believed that Jesus' resurrection appearances were bodily and that he had witnessed one, and both are exceptionally strong deterrents to his having taught anything else. In short, the evidence that we actually have favors strongly this conclusion, so it must remain by far the best option.

Notes

1. This study does not pretend to be exhaustive. Rather, I have limited the discussion to a select number of the better-known critical attempts to undermine Paul's claims.

2. B. D. Ehrman, *The New Testament: A Historical Introduction to the Early Christian Writings* (New York: Oxford University Press, 2000), 290.

3. H. Koester, *History and Literature of Early Christianity*, vol. 2 of *Introduction to the New Testament*, trans. H. Koester (Philadelphia: Fortress, 1982), 52.

4. Koester preferred AD 50–56 (*History and Literature*, 103–4), while Ehrman preferred the more general AD 50–60 (*The New Testament*, 44).

5. Although it is sometimes disputed both whether Paul spoke in this particular passage about his actual appearance and, if so, what sort of experience he described.

6. M. Martin, *The Case Against Christianity* (Philadelphia: Temple University Press, 1991), 81, 89.

7. R. W. Hoover, "A Contest between Orthodoxy and Veracity," in *Jesus' Resurrection: Fact or Figment?* ed. P. Copan and R. Tacelli (Downers Grove: InterVarsity, 2000), 129.

8. Ibid., 130–31.

9. G. Lüdemann, *What Really Happened to Jesus* (Louisville: WJK, 1995), 4; R. Funk, *Honest to Jesus* (San Francisco: Harper Collins, 1996), 36, 40; M. Borg, "Thinking about Easter," *Bible Review* 10 (1994): 15; N. Perrin, *The Resurrection According to Matthew, Mark, and Luke* (Philadelphia: Fortress, 1977), 80, 83; J. S. Spong, *Resurrection: Myth or Reality?* (San Francisco: Harper Collins, 1994), 47.

10. D. H. Akenson, *Saint Saul: A Skeleton Key to the Historical Jesus* (Oxford: Oxford University Press, 2000), 122–25, 137–43, 166–70.

11. A. Schweitzer, *The Quest of the Historical Jesus: A Critical Study of Its Progress from Reimarus to Wrede*, trans. W. Montgomery (New York: Macmillan, 1968), 51–53.

12. J. G. Machen, *The Origin of Paul's Religion* (Grand Rapids: Eerdmans, 1925), 58–60.

13. F. C. Baur, *Paul the Apostle of Jesus Christ: His Life and Works, His Epistles and Teachings*, vol. 2 (Peabody, MA: Hendrickson, 2003), 67–81, 264.

14. See chap. 11 of J. Klausner, *From Jesus to Paul*, trans. W. F. Stinespring (New York: Macmillan, 1944), 322–30.

15. M. Grant, *St. Paul: The Man* (Glasgow: William Collins Sons, 1976), 104–13.

16. For a survey of recent scholarship on this contrast, see G. R. Habermas, "Mapping the Recent Trend Toward the Bodily Resurrection Appearances of Jesus in Light of Other Prominent Critical Positions," in *The Resurrection of Jesus: John Dominic Crossan and N. T. Wright in Dialogue*, ed. R. B. Stewart (Minneapolis: Fortress, 2006).

17. G. Lüdemann, *What Happened to Jesus? A Historical Approach to the Resurrection*, trans. J. Bowden (Louisville: WJK, 1995), 103.

18. J. D. Crossan and J. L. Reed, *In Search of Paul: How Jesus's Apostle Opposed Rome's Empire with God's Kingdom* (San Francisco: Harper Collins, 2004), 8–9; cf. 173, 296–97, 341–45.

19. J. D. Crossan, "The Resurrection of Jesus in Its Jewish Context," *Neotestamentica* 37 (2003): 42–43, 48–51.

20. D. Wenham, *Paul: Follower of Jesus or Founder of Christianity?* (Grand Rapids: Eerdmans, 1995), 369.

21. Baur, *Paul the Apostle of Jesus Christ*, 63–64, 71.

22. Ibid., 75.

23. Grant, *St. Paul*, 109.

24. Machen, *The Origin of Paul's Religion*, 59, 61, 65.

25. Ibid., 65; italics added.

26. G. Lüdemann, *Early Christianity According to the Traditions in Acts: A Commentary*, trans. J. Bowden (Minneapolis: Fortress, 1987), 47–49.

27. Ibid., 106–16.

28. Crossan and Reed, "The Resurrection of Jesus in Its Jewish Context," 5–10.

29. Machen, *The Origin of Paul's Religion*, 61.

30. I have responded elsewhere to other recent questions regarding Paul's experience, such as Evan Fales's contention that Paul may have converted in order to move up the social ladder (!) or that Paul manifested a case of conversion disorder (which has nothing to do with religious

conversion). For my response to Fales, see G. Habermas, "On the Resurrection Appearances of Jesus," *Philosophia Christi*, New Series 3, no. 1 (2001): 76–87. My critique of the conversion disorder hypothesis may be found in G. Habermas, "Explaining Away Jesus' Resurrection: The Recent Revival of Hallucination Theories," *Christian Research Journal* 23, no. 4 (2001): 26–31, 47–49.

31. N. T. Wright, *The Resurrection of the Son of God* (Minneapolis: Fortress, 2003), 381–82.

32. Assuming that Paul was aware of it, as per the implication of 1 Cor 15:3–4 and what is often thought to be another early traditional passage in Acts 13:34–37, which is more explicit.

33. For one of the best treatments of this, see Wright, *The Resurrection of the Son of God*, especially Part 2.

Chapter 8

God's Glory among the Nations

Some Reflections on Apologetics and Missions

David P. Nelson

D
r. Russ Bush was my teacher, dean, and friend. Among many things I learned from him was the relationship of apologetics and missions, since we shared a passion for the Great Commission. I fondly recall discussions with him about the most effective strategies for communicating the gospel to people from varied religious backgrounds, including Hindu, Buddhist, Muslim, and animist cultures. My purpose in this chapter is to offer some insights into the relationship of apologetics and missions and to honor Russ Bush. I admit that I am neither a philosopher nor a missiologist. I am a theologian who cares deeply for the nations and who appreciates the work of philosophers, like Russ, who employ their skills to penetrate the important questions related to a careful explanation of the gospel to inquirers and skeptics alike, along with believers

whose strength is so often strengthened by the witness of apologists.

My argument is simple: The best apologetic for a missional context is rooted in the grand biblical narrative (GBN) of the Christian Scriptures. Discussions about Christian apologetics tend to revolve around certain philosophical issues, and in our day they typically focus on epistemological matters, such as whether one is an adherent to evidentialism, foundationalism (of some sort), or reformed epistemology. Those discussions are not insignificant or unimportant, but they are not my concern in this essay. Rather, I am concerned to lay out some thoughts about how the overarching narrative of the Bible leads to a manner of being and way of life that provide the basis for an effective apologetic in varied sociocultural contexts.

The Grand Biblical Narrative and the Reason for the Hope within Us

Evangelicals often begin discussions of apologetics with reference to 1 Pet 3:15: "Always be ready to give a defense to anyone who asks you for a reason for the hope that is in you" (HCSB). The emphasis is usually placed upon the notion of making a "defense" (Gk., *apologia*).[1] Such apologies focus on certain questions raised about Christianity and formulate answers to those questions in a reasoned and sometimes highly intellectual manner. Peter did urge us always to be ready to give an answer to those who raise such questions, and it is true that our answers should be reasonable. While this is the case, I am not sure that we often enough offer reasons that are rooted in the "hope" that is in us. That is, we often answer the questions raised without reference to or in the context of the redemptive narrative of Scripture that most fully explains Christian hope, which is counter to the very reason that we offer an *apologia*—to explain to the unbeliever the hope of the gospel of Jesus.

The biblical narrative involves the story of God's creation, man's fall, God's redemption in Christ, and His ultimate restoration of all things. This story tells the truth about God, about His world, about us, and about God's purposes for His creation. The redemptive work of Jesus Christ is the center of the biblical narrative, showing how the incarnation of the Son—His life, death, and resurrection—alters the story of every man. It is because of Christ that we have hope, so our account of the hope within us involves the narration of this story and the introduction of skeptics and inquirers alike to Jesus Christ.

My proposal about the significance of the GBN has great significance in the missiological context. People explain the world in light of certain controlling narratives, and these are often religious in nature. The answers to ultimate questions—such as, How did the world come to be? What are the nature and purpose of man? What is wrong with the world? and Is there any hope?—are answered in varied ways by these narratives. The Christian narrative, of course, is true. It provides the only truly hopeful answers to such questions, and it leads us to the One who is to be trusted with such questions—the One who is to be trusted with our very lives. The Christian apologetic must lead people to find hope in Christ, and I maintain that retelling the GBN is the most compelling way to offer reasonable answers in the missional context. With this in mind, I have traced below some of the ways in which the GBN helps to form an effective apologetic with respect to missions.

The Virtue of Cultural Awareness

The Bible gives considerable attention to the subject of human culture.[2] The opening chapters of Genesis assume the significance of cultural development in the world God made and in which He placed the creature made in His image and likeness. Man, male and female, was given dominion over God's creation (Gen 1:28), and God instructed man to cultivate the garden that He created for man's dwelling and sustenance (Gen 2:15). Beginning with the Torah, the Bible narrates the development of human culture in its various aspects, both good and evil.

The GBN shows how God exercises sovereignty over His world and how He ultimately restores the world in the age to come. That world, God's restored world, is itself inclusive of human culture, including a city, a center of human culture. Not only does the Bible describe culture in various ways; it also commends an understanding of culture that permits an appropriate gospel response. In Romans 14 this means that believers possess an awareness of both Christian doctrine and human cultural practices to make wise judgments about "opinions"—about matters that may be disputed. Such matters include, in this context, what food is eaten and what special days are observed. These are cultural practices that are not themselves matters of biblical command nor in themselves matters of good and evil. Paul's instructions imply a sense of cultural awareness, not to mention scriptural acumen, which enables the church to make wise decisions. This allows those within the church to live in relation to one another in a way consistent with the gospel.

In 1 Cor 9 we see another significance of cultural awareness for the sake of the gospel. There Paul referred to the exercise of his liberty, not for his own personal benefit but in order to discharge faithfully the gospel stewardship entrusted to him. Paul was willing to contextualize,[3] to communicate in appropriate ways cross-culturally for the sake of the gospel. This allows the church to live in relation to unbelievers in a manner consistent with the gospel. Such contextual sensitivity prompts believers to listen carefully to the controlling narratives of those in a given culture, to understand the cultural and philosophical orientations of people in that context, and to communicate to those in the culture in ways that answer the questions raised within these controlling narratives and orientations. The gospel functions in a subversive manner in such contexts. It does answer certain questions that naturally arise in a given context, but it introduces new questions as well, overturning philosophical presuppositions and telling a superior narrative of the divine and the world, the true story of the Creator who redeems.

To relate to one another within the church and to relate to unbelievers in such culturally appropriate ways demands a certain cultural awareness. The cultivation of such cultural awareness is virtuous, and it is integral to an effective apologetic. Such cultural awareness, however, is of little value apart from a vital relation to the GBN, which provides not only the content of an effective apologetic but also enables the church to frame valid answers to the questions raised by those who ask. The GBN also enables the church to determine which questions are of most importance and to formulate those questions appropriately in a given cultural context.

For example, questions about the problem of evil, prominent in apologetics, are not rightly framed apart from reference to the doctrines of creation and redemption, two major features of the GBN. Yet many do not think to ask questions about evil in the context of a biblical framework, nor should we expect them to. The unbeliever may well reject biblical teachings about God, creation, man, and sin that help us to understand properly the existence of evil in the world. The Buddhist, for example, does not understand the world in terms of God and creation in any way like the Christian. So each person's answers to questions about evil differ significantly.

To answer such questions adequately, we have to form both questions and answers from the standpoint of the GBN. This is precisely the way Russ Bush offered his apologetic for the problem of evil. Bush stated: "It is from Scripture that we learn the true nature of God's goodness and God's power, and it is to Scripture that we must turn to find a viable solution to the problem of evil."[4] Bush proceeded to trace a series of biblical themes culminating in the cross of Christ and God's triumph over evil in the resurrection and the promise of life in Christ in the age to come. It is this sort of appeal to the GBN that provides the most meaningful apologetic, because it situates answers to ultimate questions in the context of God's revelation about Himself, His world, His people, and His purposes.

The Necessity of Theological Fidelity

Cultural awareness, as important as it is, is of little value apart from proper relation to the Bible. The Bible is a theological book. It is theological in the sense that the Scriptures are God's revelation of Himself and of His relation to the world, and to man in particular. An effective apologetic is dependent on faithfulness to the theology of the Scriptures, which is formed by the GBN.[5] I find this to be a point of great significance: the form[6] of the Scriptures is materially theological. By this I mean that the Bible is not simply the means of God's revelation, but that the form of the Bible is itself revelation. The Scriptures include narrative, historical writings, prophetic texts, poetry, wisdom literature, and epistles. This suggests that theological fidelity includes faithfulness to the doctrines of Scripture[7] along with the recognition that the doctrines are themselves formed by the forms of Scripture that narrate God's revelation. Here I suggest a few ways that this point bears significance for apologetics.

First, the prominence of narrative in the Scriptures indicates something of the nature of the forms of communication that are effective in communicating the truth about God. The Bible is written, in part, in the form of logical argument, but it is mainly written in narrative form. Yet our apologetics are often largely focused on logical argument to the neglect of narrative. One must ask, given the nature of Scripture itself, if a narrative approach to our apologetic answers should receive our consideration. For example, the opening of the Torah narrates the creation of the world, and it does so in a way that not only establishes that God Himself is the Creator, but that He is ruler of all creation, including those parts of creation that are so often worshipped in various religions. Yet according to the opening chapters of Genesis, the living creatures, birds and cattle alike, are mere creatures. The moon, the stars, and the sun itself are not divine; they merely serve the function assigned them by the Creator. Perhaps the retelling of this story, in a manner faithful to both the form and content of Scripture, is a compelling way to offer a reason for the hope within us to those in missional contexts, whether in a tribal setting in Africa, in a Buddhist setting in the Far East, or in a pagan setting in North America.

Second, we should pay careful attention to the other literary forms in the Bible and consider how they might frame the nature and form of our apologetics. The poetry of the book of Psalms provides guidance for us in this respect. Psalms contains theological texts, and it has been rightly argued that all the major teachings of Scripture are to be found in these poems.[8] These texts answer some of the most significant apologetic questions raised by humans, including the existence of God, the creation of the world, the reality of human lament related to evil and suffering, and the absurdity of human existence. Psalms answers these questions in clearly theological terms but does so with an aesthetic sensibility that should not be lost in our apologetics. It is the case that some who need to hear reason for the hope within us are primarily asking intellectual questions related to their doubts. It is also the case that some are primarily answering emotional questions related to their doubts. Psalms provides answers to both, and its teachings are set in the form of artful poetry that speaks deeply to the human soul. We would do well to mine the varied forms of Scripture, like the Psalms, to see what ways they might shape the forms of apologetic responses we offer to those with questions about the faith.

Third, attention to the theology formed by the GBN should foster an awareness of the central biblical-theological themes present in the Scriptures. Due attention to the entire scope of the Bible ensures that our apologetic includes key themes that will substantially aid our efforts. Such awareness of these themes will fund our apologetics with the resources of the doctrines of God and creation so that the answers we form will be rightly theological. As well, this awareness will ensure that our apologetic is rightly Christocentric, including the doctrines of Jesus' death and resurrection that provide ultimate answers to certain questions raised about Christianity.

Fourth, attention to theology reminds us to frame our apologetic with reference to the Scriptural emphasis on the age to come, central to our explanation of the hope that is within us. This eschatological dimension of Christian apologetics is determinative in a certain sense. By that I mean that whether or not we account for the eschatological dimension determines whether our apologetic is truly Christian. By "eschatological" I do not mean what some evangelicals typically think of when that term or the terminology "last things" is mentioned. That is to say, I am not thinking of arguments about the millennium, the tribulation, or the rapture of the church. I am focusing on the more central biblical-theological matters related to death and the life to come, with respect both to the personal and cosmic dimensions of those subjects. The reality of death is ubiquitous. As David Bentley Hart elegantly put it:

> The natural world overwhelms us with its splendor, its beauty, its immensities and fragilities, its incalculable diversity, its endless combinations of the colossal and the delicate, sweetness and glory, minute intricacies and immeasurable grandeurs. . . . But, at the same time, all the splendid loveliness of the natural world is everywhere attended—and, indeed preserved—by death.[9]

Finally, our apologetics will be incomplete—and it will certainly lack theological fidelity—if we answer the intellectual questions of inquirers but fail to point them to the life in Christ that is the biblical gospel. Christ came to give life, and the life He offers is wholly unique; it is unlike any other way of life. Christian apologetics must show the difference, the beauty, and the superiority of life in Christ. We are not, after all, hopeful people because we simply know certain truths. We are hopeful people because Christ has redeemed us from death and sin and has given life in the Spirit by which we will possess an inheritance with God "to the praise of His glory" (Eph 1:14 HCSB).

The Noetic Effects of Love

When we offer answers to those who ask, we are conscious of the need to help questioners acquire knowledge of some sort. Accepting the gospel surely involves knowledge of the truth, and God Himself desires people to come to such knowledge (1 Tim 2:4). The church is "the pillar and foundation" of this truth (1 Tim 3:15). We tend to think of this knowledge of the gospel primarily in intellectual terms. And there is, to be sure, a noetic[10] quality to the gospel in the intellectual sense. But knowledge is not limited to the intellectual sense. As humans we operate with a number of faculties and capacities, including the mental, the physical, the emotional, and the linguistic. We should account for the whole human person when we develop our apologetics. One significant aspect of human nature is the capacity to love and be loved. This is, I think, a central way in which we reflect the image of God. I want to point out how the Scriptures speak to the noetic effects of love with respect to the gospel.

While 1 Pet 3:15 tells us that we should give a reasoned answer to those who ask, 1 Pet 3:16 explains how we should offer that answer. It is to be done with gentleness and respect to the end that the Christians who explain the hope of the gospel do so consistent with the good associated with Christ. It is significant that in this passage some of those inquiring of the Christians appear to be hostile to the church in a visible way. Even they are worthy of gentleness and respect. This is consistent with Jesus' instructions to the apostles in John 13:35: "By this all people will know that you are My disciples, if you have love for one another" (HCSB). It is by observing love between followers of Jesus that others gain knowledge. In this case, they learn that the disciples' identity is real due to the nature of their love. This noetic effect of love is demonstrated throughout the GBN. In fact, the love of God in Christ is a central message of the GBN, and any biblical apologetic must account for it. A missional apologetic should have such an appreciation for the noetic effects of love at its center.

The Primacy of Trust in Christ

Apologetics as practiced by many evangelicals today are focused significantly on concepts, ideas, and sometimes abstractions.

When someone asks about the existence of God, we appeal to certain arguments, such as teleological or design arguments, to help remove barriers to belief and to demonstrate plausibility of belief. These arguments are by nature typically conceptual. Such arguments are useful to the extent that people are struggling with conceptual difficulties related to Christianity. There is, however, a potential danger with these sorts of arguments, in that we encourage people to trust in concepts rather than the person of Christ. Consider, for example, the typical manner in which we employ the "five ways" of Thomas Aquinas as apologetic tools. We lay out the five "arguments," as we like to call them, the argument from motion, the argument from efficient causes, the argument from necessity, the argument from gradation of being, and the argument from design. We note how each one, given the reality that there can be no infinite regress of causes, leads to the conclusion that God must exist. What is notable about such arguments is that, while they may demonstrate the legitimacy of belief in God, they do not lead us to know which god exists. Without further instruction, the one hearing this apologetic is left a good ways short of hearing the gospel to which the Scriptures bear witness. I find it somewhat ironic, by the way, that Aquinas himself began this section of his *Summa Theologiae* by quoting from the Bible, adducing Exod 3:14 before he even laid out his "five ways."[11] We might learn a lesson from Thomas, who set his explanation for the existence of God in the context of the witness of Scripture that calls the hearer to trust the God who is I AM, just as Moses did. Attention to the GBN, then, offers a corrective to the problem of overly conceptualizing our apologetics as proper attention to the GBN leads to an understanding of the gospel as trust in a person, not in an idea or concept.

I think this corrective benefits our apologetic approach in at least a few ways. First, it rightly associates the conceptual and the personal. We cannot say that the gospel is personal and not conceptual. Nor can we say that the gospel is conceptual and not personal. It is, of course, both, and the Scriptures keep us on the path that rightly relates the two. Second, it prompts the apologist to consider more sensitively the possible array of questions being asked by inquirers. Not every skeptic is asking intellectual questions. They are sometimes asking emotional questions. Regardless, to only point them to arguments, concepts, and ideas is to fail to explain the hope that is within us. Our hope is not in an argument, a concept, or an idea; our hope is in Jesus Christ. Third, it reminds us that apologetics is for believers as well as unbelievers. This means that the church needs to be reminded of the truths of the gospel continually (Eph 2:11). The Bible was written for God's people, and the GBN rehearses the gospel continually for them, strengthening their faith amidst the doubts that commonly arise.

Conclusion

Russ Bush believed the Scriptures, and he believed they are the very revelation of God.[12] He believed that Jesus is the only Savior and that He graciously saves sinners who call on His name. And he believed that sinners, from every tribe and language and people and nation, deserve to hear of the One who died for them, and that they deserve honest answers to their questions, no matter how skeptical they may be, so they might come to faith and give glory to God. Russ Bush had good reason to hope, and he was eager to offer an *apologia* for the hope that was in him. Of course for him that faith is now sight, and it remains for his students and the literally thousands upon thousands who are students of his students, to take up the Book he loved and to offer reason for the hope within us to the nations for whom Christ died.

Notes

1. The *apologia* is a verbal defense or speech. Paul made such a speech when he was arrested in Jerusalem (Acts 22:1), and he also referred to the "defense of the gospel" in his letter to the Philippians (1:7,16).

2. By "culture" I refer to the various ways in which man works with the material of creation. In Gen 2:15 man is told to work and keep the good earth made by God. We "cultivate" land and materials given to us by God, and different groupings of people form shared patterns of thought, values, and practices in the process of such cultivation, which we call "culture."

3. Definitions of "contextualization" vary. I appreciate David Clark's attempt to unfold a "dialogical" model of contextualization that improves upon some of the shortcoming of the "decode/encode" model of contextualization, which mainly focuses on decoding and encoding what is considered the "transcultural meaning of the Bible." In this way, contextualization appears mainly to be concerned with transmitting principles or concepts, and it seems to assume that the messenger can himself decode and encode the message. Drawing on the work of William Dyrness, Clark presented a more nuanced and, I think, holistic model of contextualization that includes "thought" and "life." Significantly, Clark argued that contextualization must concern itself with understanding and answering the concerns of a given culture, and it must also transform those concerns. This is done in dialogical fashion, with the messenger communicating in dialogue with the hearer. See D. K. Clark, *To Know and Love God: Method in Theology* (Wheaton: Crossway, 2003), 110–22. In this vein, I describe contextualization as the task of communicating the biblical narrative (the whole and its parts) of God's work in His world in terms faithful to Scripture itself such that the gospel may be heard, and so that manners of being and modes of thought are transformed, to the end that hearers may trust Christ and enact a particularly Christian way of life.

4. L. R. Bush, *A Handbook for Christian Philosophy* (Grand Rapids: Zondervan, 1991), 171.

5. I should clarify the manner in which I use the terms "theology" and "theological." Of course, in the most basic sense I use those terms to refer to our reflections about God. But in the more specific sense I mean, with reference to the Bible and theology, our reflection that has the Bible as its primary source (I dare not say *only* source, because rarely does anyone form theology *only* from the Scriptures, whether one realizes this fact or not) and that forms a distinctively Christian way of life. Scripture, then, is God's discourse about Himself, and theology is man's discourse about God. And theology is further discourse that leads to a particular way of

life, formed by the Scriptures. By "theological fidelity," then, I refer to those formulations, patterns of thought, and forms of life that are formed by and consistent with the GBN.

6. By "form" I mean the nature and structure of the writings of Scripture. This includes but is not limited to the varied genres of the Bible. For example, the nature of the Bible as a collection of writings that display magnificent intertextual referents informs our way of thinking about the unity and coherence of Christian theology.

7. We might understand this to be, in a classical theological sense, something like the *regula fidei*, the "rule of faith." It is common for us to appeal to certain theological loci, like those common to systematic theology, to understand these doctrines. These are useful ways to organize the teachings of Scripture. My one worry about such systems is the way in which they might strip away the significance of the biblical forms of communication. My point here is one drawn from the doctrine of inspiration. Why is it that God has revealed Himself in *these* texts? Why did God not reveal Himself in other forms, including well-formulated arguments like those we seem to prefer in our apologetics. Or, for that matter, why was it not the "fullness of time" during the video age so we could have "cinematic" revelation of Christ? Instead, God revealed the Word by words, by His Spirit to be sure, but by words—and the words of humans guided by the Spirit at that. If we take the doctrine of inspiration seriously, we will consider the forms of revelation seriously and think carefully about how those forms might contribute to our apologetic.

8. See Athanasius, "The Letter to Marcellinus on the Interpretation of the Psalms."

9. D. B. Hart, *The Doors of the Sea: Where Was God in the Tsunami?* (Grand Rapids: Eerdmans, 2005), 49–50.

10. By "noetic" I refer to the mental or intellectual capacities of the human person.

11. The "five ways" are found in *Summa Theologiae* part 1, question 2, article 3. For a brief, yet very helpful explanation of the five ways that provides good correctives to the unfortunate and common errors about Aquinas, see B. Davies, *The Thought of Thomas Aquinas* (New York: Oxford, 1992), 25–31.

12. See L. R. Bush and T. J. Nettles, *Baptists and the Bible*, rev. and exp. ed. (Nashville: B&H Academic, 1999).

Section Three

Christianity and Science

Chapter 9

Is Evolution True?

L. Russ Bush

D arwinian evolution is the most widely held theory of biological change. Small changes in living organisms supposedly happen naturally and randomly and frequently. These small changes (if favorable to the organism) supposedly accumulate, and over time it is thought that these small changes result in larger changes, even to the point of transforming one species into another. This process of accumulating "small beneficial" changes and eliminating "nonbeneficial" changes is called natural selection (as opposed to divine selection).

No doubt biological organisms do change over time in response to environmental stimuli, and these changes sometimes seemingly accumulate so that new groupings of animals appear. The stickleback fish seem to have gone through such a change (there are now two varieties of these fish where there used to be only one), and the so-called walking stick insects apparently have recently developed a new variety. A strain of bacteria may develop a resistance to certain antibiotic medicines. For some, these are convincing examples of "evolution."

For most scientists the term "evolution" means that these kinds of changes are inevitable and persistent, and they believe that these changes illustrate how all biological change occurs. Darwinism is the theory that all of these small, natural changes have been added up over time so that original single-cell life-forms eventually transformed into all the multicellular life-forms known on Earth today. According to Darwin's theory, by the accumulation of small changes invertebrates became vertebrates, reptiles became birds, and the amoeba changed into a man.

There are, however, several problems with this theory. First, the Darwinian theory of evolution does not explain how life began. In the laboratory we can "spontaneously" generate large quantities of amino acids, the building blocks of life, but even our carefully designed efforts result in useless mixtures, not the uniform series of amino acids that are necessary for life. The stereo-chemistry is always wrong when we make these molecules by chance processes. Even if we could get all the chemicals right, we still would not have life. At the moment of death, the chemicals are all still there, but life is not. Life requires a certain level of chemical complexity, but that chemical complexity is not the same as nor does it explain life; it only permits life. Life does not spontaneously arise from nonlife, even if all the necessary chemicals are there.

Second, the fossil record does not show the gradual changes predicted by the Darwinian theory of evolution. Fossilized transitional forms simply do not appear frequently in the fossil record, if at all, though if Darwin were right there should be millions of such forms.

Third, the organized complexity of even the simplest living cell is such that it cannot be built up by small accumulated changes. Life is not found in the parts but only in the whole, and even the simplest whole is made up of many complex parts that would not arise and/or combine in the necessary specified manner through random nonliving natural processes.

Fourth, a genetic code exists in the DNA molecule of the cell. This DNA molecule is not merely chemistry. It is an encoded message that provides the blueprints for building all of the proteins necessary to make the living organism. Encoded information is evidence of intelligent design.

Fifth, there are numerous systems that are essential for life and yet are hard if not impossible to account for on Darwinian premises. The ozone layer is one of those systems. The ozone layer, high in the atmosphere, acts as a filter for deadly radiation and thus makes life possible on the Earth. Yet ozone is a by-product of living things. Without ozone already being there, living things could not exist. Yet life must exist in order to form and replenish the ozone layer. Naturalistic theories have a difficult time explaining the origin of this relationship.

Sixth, the Earth is an open system, but even the sun's energy alone is not sufficient to account for the necessary rise in complexity required by evolutionary theory. In reality things tend to simplify and wear out. The rise in complexity proposed by evolutionary theories simply does not happen in nature unless there are a plan and a mechanism to capture and organize the available energy. Neither of these is inherent within nature.

Seventh, the Bible says that God created the heavens and the Earth, and that He made all of the animals and established that in this world they would reproduce after their kind. All of the evidence is consistent with this claim. Stickleback fish and walking sticks now have two varieties, and certain bacteria have become resistant to some drugs; but the fish are still stickleback fish, the insects are still insects, and the bacteria are still bacteria. There is simply no evidence that one kind of creature has ever naturally transformed itself into some other kind of creature. Darwin was wrong.

The Bible says the world is not the source of life. The living God created the life we know and have, and the same eternal and all-powerful God sustains that life for His own purposes and for His own glory. The best and most consistent claim is the one God Himself made. He told us that He created all things and that He saw that everything He finished was good. God is the Creator and Sustainer of all things. Evolution in its purely natural form has no starting point. Natural selection is a real process, but it doesn't account for the origin of anything.

Chapter 10

The Future of Natural Theology

Exploring Alister McGrath's Natural Theology

James K. Dew Jr.

Prior to the mid-twentieth century, natural theology was a regularly accepted aspect of Christian theology and apologetics. Thinkers like Thomas Aquinas[1] with his "Five Ways" and William Paley[2] with his design argument argued for God's existence via nature and reason. However, the philosophical arguments of David Hume[3] and Immanuel Kant,[4] accompanied by Charles Darwin's theory of evolution,[5] caused the practice of natural theology to fall on hard times.[6] Furthermore, in the early twentieth century theologians like Karl Barth suggested that natural theology was inappropriate since it allowed theology to develop autonomously from Scripture.[7] By the beginning of the twentieth century, the practice of natural theology was generally viewed as an impossible and inappropriate discipline.

In the last 40 or 50 years, however, there has been a revival of natural theology.[8] With new discoveries about the cosmos and its origins, the emergence of the anthropic principle, skepticism as to whether or not Barth's criticisms of natural theology are valid, and the lingering metaphysical questions that arise from the study of nature, theologians and philosophers are once again giving significant attention to natural theology. This does not mean that natural theology has been revived in its old form without modifications and adaptations; it is also being refurbished and revised in light of the lessons learned from the past. Even Alvin Plantinga admitted that this project may be useful in some capacity, though he is often portrayed as being opposed to natural theology.[9]

Among evangelicals, Alister McGrath stands out as the most significant theologian advocating a new version of natural theology.[10] With the publication of his three-volume *A Scientific Theology*,[11] two additional works devoted specifically to natural theology titled *The Open Secret* and *A Fine Tuned Universe*,[12] and several other works that give considerable attention to the subject,[13] McGrath's may be the most significant contribution to natural theology in recent times. But is his approach of any value to evangelicals today? This chapter examines McGrath's natural theology and considers why his particular approach may be advantageous in the contemporary setting.

McGrath's Approach to Natural Theology

McGrath's work on the relationship between theology and science in general, and natural theology in particular, may be his most important work since it represents the culmination of his 30-year career. During this time, he has developed a theological method called "scientific theology" that integrates both scientific and theological perspectives. At the heart of his scientific theology is a renewed vision for natural theology. McGrath is fully aware that natural theology has been abandoned by modern theologians and philosophers. He noted, "If my personal conversations with theologians, philosophers, and natural scientists over the last decade are in any way representative, natural theology is generally seen as being like a dead whale, left stranded on a beach by a receding tide, gracelessly rotting under the heat of a philosophical and scientific sun."[14] Nevertheless, he contended that natural theology, when properly conceptualized, still has an important role to play in Christian theology. As such, he devoted much attention to a renewed natural theology throughout most of his recent works.

The Theological Basis of McGrath's Natural Theology

One cannot understand McGrath's approach to natural theology without understanding his theology of nature. Some critics have suggested his natural theology is nothing more than a theology of nature,[15] but this is not accurate. To be clear, McGrath does look at nature through theological lenses—and this is essential to his natural theology—but this is not all that his approach does. His view of nature, however, is the appropriate place to begin when considering his natural theology.

Whereas nature is generally thought of as being a fixed term with an objective meaning shared by all people and all groups, McGrath contended that nature is actually a fluid concept variously understood by different groups. "Nature," he said, "far from being a constant, robust, autonomous entity, is an intellectually plastic notion."[16] This important consideration is given fullest attention throughout his works on scientific theology. He argued that the concept itself is ambiguous since each group uses its own socially constructed ideas to understand the concept. Thus, from one group to the next, the term *nature* may be employed with different meanings, leading to great confusion and equivocation. He illustrated this by pointing to the various ways the term *nature* has been used in the last 2,000 years. One brief example comes from the twentieth century. He pointed out these various twentieth-century ways of viewing nature:

- nature as a mindless force, causing inconvenience to humanity and demanding to be tamed;
- nature as an open-air gymnasium, offering leisure and sports facilities to affluent individuals who want to demonstrate their sporting prowess;
- nature as a wild kingdom, encouraging scuba-diving, hiking, and hunting;
- nature as a supply depot—an aging and increasingly reluctant provider that produces (although with growing difficulty) minerals, water, food, and other services for humanity.[17]

McGrath said that prior to the twentieth century, nature was viewed as a mindless force by the pre-Socratics, as feminine by medieval thinkers,[18] as a stage by Shakespeare and the poets, as a book by Pierre Viret and Francis Bacon,[19] and as a machine during the Enlightenment.[20]

Since nature is such an ambiguous term, McGrath argued that the "Christian theologian is not under any obligation to accept a normative definition of nature originating from outside the Christian tradition. Instead, Christian theology may deploy and explore its own distinctive understanding of what others call nature, but which the Christian tradition prefers to name 'creation.'"[21] To be clear, McGrath is doing more than just replacing one term with another. He is suggesting the use of the term *creation* because of the meaning that lies behind it and because the word *nature* is very ambiguous. Moreover, he contended that the Christian doctrine of creation is a preferred way of thinking about nature since it offers advantages to both science and theology.

Scientifically, McGrath believed that certain scientific ideas find rational support from the Christian doctrine of creation. For example, natural scientists accept that the universe is rational and that this rationality can be discovered and explained by human beings, but it can offer no satisfying reason why this is the case.[22] He said:

> One of the most significant parallels between the natural sciences and Christian theology is a fundamental conviction that the world is characterized by regularity and intelligibility. . . . So important is this notion that it could be argued that the natural sciences are founded on the perception of explicable regularity to the world, which is capable of being represented mathematically. In other words, there is something about the world—and the nature of the human mind—which allows patterns within nature to be discerned and represented.[23]

He later added:

> What the natural sciences are forced to assume—in that it cannot be formally demonstrated without falling into some form of circularity of argument or demonstration, the Christian understanding of "wisdom" allows to be affirmed on the basis of divine revelation, and correlated with the existence of a transcendent creator God, responsible both for the ordering of the world and the human ability to grasp and discern it.[24]

McGrath also thought that the notion of creation is helpful for theological purposes since it allows insights gained from creation to play a part in the development of theology. He noted, "If God made the world, which therefore has the status of being 'creation' as well as 'nature', it is to be expected that something of the character of God might be disclosed through that creation."[25] He further noted:

> The Christian understanding of creation leads directly to the conclusion that there is a correspondence—the degree of which requires clarification—between the works of God and the being of God. . . . For the Christian, the creation is not divine, but bears the hallmarks of divine crafting. The fundamental assumption of a responsible natural theology . . . is that we are authorized by Scripture to seek a partial disclosure of the glory of God through the works of God in creation. God is rendered in and through the creation.[26]

This is also reaffirmed by McGrath in his more recent works on natural theology wherein he deals with the *analogia entis*— "analogy of being." "On this reading," he suggested, "the *analogia entis* is based upon a rigorously Christian doctrine of creation which on the one hand affirms the absolute distinction between creator and creation, yet on the other posits a created capacity on the part of the analogy to model God."[27] As a created entity, nature is contingent and thus qualitatively distinct from the creator. Yet, because it originates from the creator, nature reflects the creator in a limited way. If this is correct, then McGrath believed that the doctrine of creation gives natural theology a firm theological basis.

Thus, since nature is such an ambiguous concept, and because there are scientific and theological advantages with the Christian concept of creation, McGrath preferred to speak about creation instead of nature. Simply put, his theology of nature—creation— plays an enormous role in both his scientific theology and his natural theology.

The Starting Point of McGrath's Natural Theology

McGrath defined natural theology as the "enterprise of seeing nature as creation, which both presupposes and reinforces fundamental Christian theological affirmations."[28] As such, one can immediately recognize that this approach is distinct from other contemporary approaches to natural theology. William Lane Craig, for example, defined natural theology as "that branch of theology which seeks to provide rational warrant for the proposition that God exists on the basis of argument and evidence independent of authoritative divine revelation."[29] There are two important aspects of Craig's approach: (1) natural theology is defined as an attempt to support religious beliefs; and (2) natural theology must proceed by reasons or evidences that are isolated from, or independent of, the Bible or any other revealed article of faith.[30]

McGrath, however, deviated from the latter by placing natural theology within the context of the Christian faith and starting with certain theological assumptions. He argued:

> Natural theology gains its plausibility and derives its intellectual foundations from within the Christian tradition. Its roots lie *intra muros ecclesiae*, even if its relevance extends *extra muros ecclesiae*. It is not a tradition-independent or autonomous intellectual discipline, in that its legitimation rests upon a Christian doctrine of creation—including the related concepts of the contingent ordering of the created world, and the epistemic and spiritual capacities of human nature.[31]

There are important reasons McGrath believed this revision to natural theology is necessary. Most significantly, he thought that his approach repairs some of the damage inflicted on natural theology during the Enlightenment when it was forced to proceed on neutral ground and serve as a foundation for Christian belief. Due to the rise of biblical criticism, growing criticism of church authority, distaste for organized religion, and the immense success of the natural sciences, the practice of natural theology was changed as Christians felt pressure to find ways of dialoguing with their culture without recourse to the Bible. McGrath noted, "The church, realizing that it was increasingly difficult to base a dialogue with English academic thought upon the Bible, sought an alternative common ground for its apologetic discourse—and found it in the realm of nature. Natural theology thus rapidly became an apologetic tool of no small importance."[32] Thus, in the Enlightenment, theologians "saw a rational appeal to the natural order, without reference to revelation, as a means of defending the Christian faith at a time of intellectual ferment."[33] In short, during the Enlightenment, theologians attempted to use natural theology as an objective basis for justifying theological beliefs.

The problem with this approach is that it assumes that nature is an objective concept with fixed meaning and fails to recognize the various ways that it is understood. If different concepts of nature are in play, then various theological conclusions will be drawn. For example, deists like Voltaire, who strongly emphasized the design argument and the watch analogy, came to mechanistic theological conclusions that understood God as the creator of the universe but who is now far removed from and disinterested in the world.[34] By contrast, theologians like Paley, who also emphasized the design argument and the watch analogy, came to much different theological conclusions. In Paley's approach, nature was used to support the existence of the God of Christian theism.[35] To state it briefly, when employed in this fashion, McGrath thought that natural theology can lead to a wide variety of different conclusions. In his famous *Dialogues Concerning Natural Religion*, Hume noted how nature might just as easily point to polytheistic conclusions as opposed to trinitarian ones. He contended, "A great number of men join in building a house or ship, in rearing a city, in framing a commonwealth: Why may not several deities combine in contriving and framing a world?"[36]

Thus, since the word *nature* seemed to point in various theological directions, the Enlightenment approach to natural theology, which assumed one fixed meaning for the concept of nature, is rejected by McGrath as more problematic than beneficial. In his mind, natural theology should be thought of as "natural *Christian* theology, which interprets natural theology as something that is both historically located in the life of and death of Jesus of Nazareth and theologically interpreted by the church."[37]

The Form of McGrath's Natural Theology

Unlike other natural theologians, McGrath did not use arguments for God's existence such as the cosmological, teleological, or ontological. He did briefly mention these arguments in his general work on *Christian Theology*: "The general consensus within Christian theology seems to be that, although reason does not bring individuals to faith in God, believers are nonetheless able to give rational reasons for their belief in God."[38] This, coupled with McGrath's defense of Aquinas's "five ways" as valid since they are merely "offering support for faith from within the context of an existing faith,"[39] suggests that McGrath is not opposed to natural theology being used to support theological beliefs. His most recent work on natural theology, *A Fine-Tuned Universe*, adds further confirmation to this since the second half of the book makes a number of observations about the universe that seem to confirm Christian belief.[40]

McGrath did not develop these arguments. He simply pointed to various features of the cosmos and humanity that make more sense within a theistic framework as opposed to naturalism. For him, "Abduction, not deduction, is as characteristic of natural theology as it is of the natural sciences."[41] This means that natural theology operates with a particular way of reasoning that searches, not for logical certainty in its conclusions, but for the best empirical fit or best explanation from inference. In his works on scientific theology, McGrath pointed to the laws of nature, or what he calls the "big picture,"[42] as well as other important phenomena such as man's religious inclinations, sense of wonder, sense of goodness, and quest for meaning, as things that make the most sense when considered from within a Christian perspective.[43] This emphasis was continued in one of his more recent works on natural theology where he noted that the ordering of the universe and humanity's awareness of the transcendent are best explained by the Christian view of reality.[44]

In addition, McGrath also pointed to the "anthropic principle" and argued that these phenomena have particular resonance with a Christian understanding of the world. He stated, "The smallest variation in the constant of universal gravitation, or the mass of a neutron, or change of the electron, would have changed everything, making the emergence of human observers impossible."[45] McGrath was also careful to note that the "anthropic principle" is not just a phenomenon of the cosmic world, but that "in recent years, similar phenomena have been identified in chemistry, biochemistry, and evolutionary biology."[46] In the final analysis, McGrath takes a more broad approach to natural theology by focusing on the whole spectrum of phenomena within creation, while others like Craig focus on specific details of creation to develop arguments for God's existence. McGrath simply claims that reality itself is best explained by Christianity.

Finally, since his approach to natural theology makes use of abduction as opposed to deduction, it does not yield logical certainty that God exists. Instead, McGrath intended to offer insights from nature that serve as confirmation of Christian theism. Though he did not offer logical proof for God's existence, he insisted that "the existence of a God such as that proposed by the Christian tradition makes sense of what may be observed of the world."[47] Simply put, McGrath's approach offers assurance or confirmation of a Christian view of the universe.

An Assessment of McGrath's Natural Theology

McGrath's approach to natural theology is distinct from other contemporary approaches because (1) it assumes a particular view of nature, which is creation; (2) it starts from within the Christian faith instead of trying to begin on neutral grounds; and (3) it does not take the form of an argument such as the cosmological, teleological, or ontological arguments do. His approach is firmly grounded within a Christian perspective and attempts to give natural theology a new lease on life in the twenty-first century.

Concerns

One of the most significant objections to McGrath's approach is that it seems to be of little apologetic value since it assumes what it sets out to prove, namely, that the Christian view of reality is correct. By affirming the Christian doctrine of creation at the outset, McGrath began with a significant theological assumption and offered nothing more than a circular argument. William Abraham raised this objection after the publication of McGrath's first volume of *A Scientific Theology*. In particular, Abraham suggested that McGrath's use and development of natural theology is inadequate since it does not give the unbeliever any reason to believe that nature is God's creation in the first place. For Abraham, McGrath's approach to natural theology works fine for the believer, but there is nothing about it that would cause the unbeliever to accept it.[48]

Is Abraham's assessment of McGrath's position valid? McGrath did not think so. In an essay responding to Abraham and others, McGrath defended his approach.[49] In short, McGrath believed his approach does have apologetic value, even if he started from within the Christian tradition. For one thing, Abraham's objection assumes that one can start from premises that are universally accepted about nature. But this is the very thing that McGrath questions throughout his works on scientific theology and natural theology. If, as McGrath argued, each group has its own understanding of nature, then one cannot begin from a universally accepted vantage point. Since each person comes to nature with his own understanding of what this is, McGrath thought that the Christian is justified to begin with his understanding of nature as creation.

Furthermore, Abraham's objection would only be legitimate if there were no correspondence between what Christianity claims about reality and reality itself. But, as McGrath argued, there is a very high level of correspondence between the world and what Christianity says about it. In fact, throughout his works on scientific theology and natural theology, McGrath highlighted areas of correspondence and showed how the phenomena of reality are best explained by a Christian view of reality, as opposed to other belief systems. Based on the strength of these areas of correspondence, McGrath's approach to natural theology has apologetic value. His approach may not offer absolute proof that Christianity is true, but it does offer confirmation and assurance that this particular view of reality is correct.

A second concern with McGrath's approach comes from the fact that he often seems to blur the lines between natural theology and natural revelation. As noted, he officially defined natural theology as "the enterprise of seeing nature as creation, which both presupposes and reinforces fundamental Christian theological affirmations."[50] But when he elaborated on what this means, it often sounds as if he were really describing what is traditionally thought of as natural revelation. This is especially true in his works on scientific theology. For example, when discussing John Calvin's "natural theology," McGrath said that Calvin was "arguing that the created order is a 'theatre' or a 'mirror' for the displaying of the divine presence, nature, and attributes."[51]

The problem here is not that Calvin did not teach this, for clearly he did.[52] Rather, the concern is that what McGrath described here sounds much more like natural revelation than natural theology. Just as one would make a distinction between the Bible as a source of revelation and the theology that is derived from that revelation, it seems that one must also make a distinction between natural revelation and natural theology.[53] For evangelicals, this is an important consideration since divine revelation is held to be reliable and accurate in all that it teaches, whereas a particular theological affirmation can be true or false.[54] Yet, lack of distinction between the two is a minor concern and not detrimental to his project as a whole. Those who wish to follow McGrath's approach can note this distinction and move forward without any problem.

A final concern that might be raised with McGrath's approach is that he is a theistic evolutionist. This is abundantly clear in *A Fine-Tuned Universe*, where he argued that the process of evolution makes most sense within a theistic framework.[55] But this should not cause one to reject McGrath's approach to natural theology. The fact is that the universe is rational and there are great examples of order, structure, and beauty that can be identified by anyone. One does not have to be a theistic evolutionist to argue that these phenomena resonate particularly well with the teachings of Christianity. Here again, the concerns with McGrath's natural theology should not be overly problematic.

Positives

In spite of these concerns, there are advantages to McGrath's approach to natural theology. First, by locating natural theology within the Christian tradition the way he did, McGrath moved beyond the Enlightenment approach to natural theology where it was used as the starting point for religious belief. In Craig's defense of classical apologetics, for example, he suggested that one could use natural theology as a first step to religious belief and then, as a second step, use other evidences to show that it is Christianity, as opposed to another religious system, that is ultimately true.[56] In this case, natural theology is used as the basis for belief in God. Because of this, people such as Alvin Plantinga have associated natural theology with classical foundationalism and questioned the appropriateness of this kind of natural theology.[57]

Today it is widely recognized that one cannot really have this kind of objective vantage point. In fact, there is now widespread recognition that each of us is affected cognitively by our surrounding, education, background, and much more. As Christians, we do see the world in a particular way. As such, instead of trying to begin from an objective vantage point, perhaps one should simply try to determine if the Christian view of reality fits with reality itself. If it does, then this is significant confirmation of the Christian worldview. This is precisely where the strength of McGrath's approach is found.

Second, McGrath's approach brings some much needed relief to natural theology from the heavy and unreasonable demands that it must achieve absolute certainty to be of any value. As John Hedley Brooke explained, "Since the Enlightenment, natural theology has often been characterized as the attempt to construct rational 'proofs' for God's existence and attributes."[58] But it is widely noted today that demanding certainty of a proposition before it can be counted as intellectually justified is dangerous and unproductive since much of what we claim to know does not fall within the bounds of epistemological certainty. Furthermore, when arguments fail to produce the certainty that they promise, the impression is left that the argument is of no value. Yet when natural theology is recast as an enterprise that looks for probability or confirmation, it has some apologetic value. Again, one of the strengths of McGrath's approach is found in his insistence that natural theology offers confirmation of God's existence, but not logical proof.

Finally, McGrath's approach is significant in that it expands natural theology by focusing on "big picture" issues of reality, instead of just the beginning of the universe and instances of design, typical of cosmological and teleological arguments. McGrath considered the "anthropic principle" on cosmic and microbiological levels, man's sense of the divine, the shared religious quest of mankind, beauty, rationality, meaning, and a host of other phenomena of the world to make his case. As such, McGrath reminded us that "the *logos* through which the world was created is embedded in the structures of the created order."[59] Because of this, those doing natural theology can point to much more than just a few arguments to support their faith. It is the whole of creation's phenomena that corresponds to the teachings of Christianity.

Conclusion

McGrath's approach to natural theology is clearly unique in comparison with other evangelical approaches to natural theology. How it will affect the future of natural theology remains to be seen. There are a few aspects of his natural theology where further clarification or development would be helpful. While some will surely be uncomfortable with his "new vision for natural theology," others, like myself, think that McGrath is on to something and that there is apologetic value to be gleaned from his work.

Notes

1. T. Aquinas, *The Summa Theologica*, trans. Father of the English Dominican Province (Notre Dame: Christian Classics, 1948), 1.2.3.

2. W. Paley, *Natural Theology* (Oxford: Oxford University Press, 2006).

3. D. Hume, *Dialogues Concerning Natural Religion* (New York: Penguin Books, 1990).

4. I. Kant, *Critique of Pure Reason*, trans. J. M. D. Meiklejohn (Amherst: Prometheus Books, 1990).

5. C. Darwin, *On the Origin of Species* (Cambridge: Harvard University Press, 2003).

6. Of course, there are a number of other thinkers who were instrumental in the demise of natural theology, though the ones mentioned here were of greatest significance on this matter.

7. K. Barth, "No!" in E. Brunner and K. Barth, *Natural Theology*, trans. P. Frankel (Eugene, OR: Wipf and Stock, 2002), 75.

8. See J. Polkinghorne, *Science and Theology: An Introduction* (Minneapolis: Fortress, 1998), 71; and E. T. Long, ed., *Prospects for Natural Theology*, vol. 25 (Washington, DC: Catholic University of America Press, 1992), vii.

9. A. Plantinga, "The Reformed Objection Revisited," *Christian Scholar's Review* 12, no. 1 (1983).

10. McGrath began his academic pursuits as a convinced atheist who later converted to Christianity and ultimately earned doctoral degrees in both the natural sciences and Christian theology. He earned his first doctorate (D.Phil.) from Oxford in December of 1977 in molecular biology and his second doctorate (D.Div.) from Oxford in 2001. McGrath shared the details of his early academic pursuits and Christian conversion in a number of places, but most briefly in A. E. McGrath, "Contributors: An Appreciation and Response," in *Alister E. McGrath and Evangelical Theology*, ed. S. W. Chung (Devon, Exeter, UK: Paternoster, 2003), 333–67.

11. A. E. McGrath, *A Scientific Theology*, 3 vols. (Grand Rapids: Eerdmans, 2001–2003).

12. A. E. McGrath, *The Open Secret: A New Vision for Natural Theology* (Oxford: Blackwell, 2008); and A. E. McGrath, *A Fine-Tuned Universe:*

The Quest for God in Science and Theology (Louisville: Westminster-John Knox, 2009).

13. See A. E. McGrath, *The Science of God* (Grand Rapids: Eerdmans, 2004); A. E. McGrath, *The Foundations of Dialogue in Science and Religion* (Oxford: Blackwell, 1998); A. E. McGrath, *Science and Religion: An Introduction* (Oxford: Blackwell, 1999); A. E. McGrath, *The Order of Things: Explorations in Scientific Theology* (Oxford: Blackwell, 2006).

14. McGrath, *A Fine-Tuned Universe*, 5.

15. Ibid., 36.

16. McGrath, *The Open Secret*, 9.

17. McGrath, *Science of God*, 38.

18. Ibid., 37–38.

19. McGrath, *A Scientific Theology*, 1:103.

20. McGrath, *Science of God*, 37–38.

21. Ibid., 45.

22. McGrath, *The Science of God*, 59–71.

23. McGrath, *A Scientific Theology*, 1:218.

24. Ibid., 222.

25. McGrath, *A Scientific Theology*, 1:21.

26. Ibid., 193.

27. McGrath, *The Open Secret*, 188.

28. McGrath, *The Science of God*, 113.

29. W. L. Craig, "Natural Theology," in *Philosophy of Religion*, ed. W. L. Craig (New Brunswick: Rutgers University Press, 2002), 69.

30. Craig's approach to natural theology seems quite common among contemporary evangelical natural theologians. E.g., C. S. Evans, *Philosophy of Religion* (Downers Grove: IVP, 1982), 38; and W. P. Alston, *Perceiving God* (New York and London: Cornell University Press, 1991), 289.

31. McGrath, *A Scientific Theology*, 2:74. That is, natural theology arises inside the walls of the church, but its significance extends beyond the walls of the church.

32. McGrath, *The Open Secret*, 145–46.

33. McGrath, *The Science of God*, 76.

34. See A. Kenny, *A Brief History of Western Philosophy* (Oxford: Blackwell, 1998), 244–55; and McGrath, *The Science of God*, 56–57.

35. Paley, *Natural Theology*.

36. Hume, *Dialogues Concerning Natural Religion*, 77.

37. McGrath, *The Open Secret*, 15.

38. A. E. McGrath, *Christian Theology: An Introduction*, 4th ed. (Oxford: Blackwell, 2007), 183–84. He also added, "It will be clear that the traditional 'kalam' argument has been given a new lease on life by the Big Bang

theory of the origins of the universe. . . . However, the philosophical issues which are raised are likely to remain disputed. A similar debate focuses on the question of whether the universe can be said to be designed" (190).

39. McGrath, *A Scientific Theology*, 1:266.

40. McGrath, *A Fine-Tuned Universe*, 99–216. Many evangelicals would be uncomfortable with what McGrath did in this section of the book since he is a theistic evolutionist. Here McGrath argued that the natural processes of creation can be used not to disprove God, but to show uniformity and rationality in nature that actually confirm theistic belief.

41. Ibid., 218.

42. McGrath, *A Scientific Theology*, 3:195.

43. Ibid.

44. McGrath, *The Open Secret*, 237.

45. Ibid., 241–42.

46. Ibid., 242. McGrath unpacked this observation most fully in chaps. 10–12 of *A Fine-Tuned Universe*.

47. McGrath, *The Open Secret*, 233. McGrath affirmed this multiple times in all of his works on scientific theology and natural theology.

48. W. J. Abraham, "Revelation and Natural Theology," in Chung, *Alister E. McGrath and Evangelical Theology*, 266–72.

49. McGrath, "Contributors," in Chung, *Alister E. McGrath and Evangelical Theology*, 333–67.

50. McGrath, *The Science of God*, 113.

51. Ibid., 72.

52. J. Calvin, *Institutes of the Christian Religion*, ed. J. T. McNeill, trans. F. L. Battles (Louisville: WJK, n.d.), 1.3.1, 1.5.1–2.

53. There is a distinction between revelation as an epistemological source given from God and theology that men infer from divine revelation.

54. For example, in almost all areas of theology, scholars debate positions and affirmations. The history of the church involves the practice of debate while believers wrestled with what to believe. In the end, some doctrines have been abandoned as heresy; some have held firm through the centuries.

55. McGrath, *A Fine-Tuned Universe*, 155–201.

56. Craig, "Classical Apologetics," in *Five Views on Apologetics*, ed. Steve B. Cowan (Grand Rapids: Zondervan, 2000), 26–55.

57. A. Plantinga, "Is Belief in God Properly Basic?" in *Contemporary Perspectives on Religious Epistemology*, ed. R. D. Geivett and B. Sweetman (Oxford: Oxford University Press, 1992), 134.

58. J. H. Brooke, "Natural Theology," in *Science and Religion*, ed. G. Ferngren (Baltimore: Johns Hopkins, 2002), 163–64.

59. McGrath, *The Open Secret*, 233.

Chapter 11

Detecting the Invisible Gardener

The Fine-Tuning Argument

Kenneth D. Keathley

Recently, a flurry of books has come out promoting atheism. Authors such as Richard Dawkins, Daniel Dennett, and Christopher Hitchens rail against religion in general and Christianity in particular with a fevered, evangelistic zeal. The "new atheists," as they are sometimes called, exhibit vitriol unseen before, or at least not for some time. One might think that such aggressiveness signals a rise in atheism as an intellectual movement. However, there could be another, opposite reason: the advent of the Intelligent Design (ID) movement and its concomitant arguments has atheists feeling threatened. Many have shielded their atheism with the veneer of scientific respectability, and ID arguments—such as the case for fine-tuning—peel away the façade.

A case in point is Anthony Flew, who, at the time of this writing, is in his late eighties. For the past 50 years, Flew has been arguably the most significant writing atheist. In 1950, while a student at Oxford University, he presented a paper titled "Theology and Falsification" at a meeting of the Socratic Club, a meeting presided over by C. S. Lewis. In the paper Flew presented his (in)famous Parable of the Invisible Gardener.[1] It tells of two men who are attempting to discern whether or not a clearing in the woods is a deliberate garden or a clearing that happened by chance. One man believes there is a gardener, but the other is skeptical. They go step-by-step through increasingly elaborate processes trying to determine whether or not the gardener exists. They put up a barbed-wire fence, they electrify it, they use bloodhounds, but no gardener is found. After each failure the skeptic asserts that there is no gardener while the believer conjures up an even more convoluted explanation. The believer contends the gardener is invisible, impervious to fences, and undetectable by dogs. Eventually, the hypothesis of the invisible gardener is thus "killed by inches, the death by a thousand qualifications."[2] The point of the parable is that a god who cannot be perceived, discerned, or detected in any way is no different from no god at all. The reader may be surprised to learn that Flew is now a theist, and as we will see, the "fine-tuning" argument played no small part in his conversion.

In 1998 L. Russ Bush took part in my comprehensive orals that all Ph.D. students at Southeastern Baptist Theological Seminary are required to pass at the conclusion of the residency portion of the program. At the end of the exam, Dr. Bush asked me a question about a subject that he knew had my attention: "What is the impetus behind the ID movement?" The answer I gave then serves now as the thesis statement for this essay: if one looks at the empirical evidence, while temporarily sidelining a prior commitment to philosophical naturalism or an allegiance to any revelatory record, that person will conclude that the world is very old and very well designed. The world appears ancient and created. In other words, examining the physical world alone leads one to embrace some type of old-earth creationism. Darwinists and young-earth creationists both concede that this indeed is the way the cosmos appears, but they also contend that this appearance is an illusion. The two parties disagree about which part of the evidence is misleading—the appearance of age or the appearance of design. Darwinists contend that the world is indeed old, but rather than being created it is the product of unguided forces. Adherents of young-earth creationism affirm creation, but they argue that all appearances of age are misleading. ID takes a different tack—one that is more doggedly committed to the empirical findings. ID's focus remains on the physical evidence, and as such has built a remarkable case for the design inference—much to the consternation of Darwinists and the chagrin of young-earth creationists.

During the last half century, two lines of discovery have given the design argument (and in turn, the teleological argument) new life—one in the area of biology and the other in cosmology. The first line—discoveries made in cellular biology and genetics—has provided a breakthrough in our understanding of living cells, and arguments based on these discoveries have garnered the most attention. We are beginning to understand the digital information contained within the DNA molecule and the information processes operating within cells. Since the only known source of information is intelligence, then the best inference for information's existence within cells would be that it was put there by intelligent design. Also, researchers have begun to discern that many of the systems within creatures are irreducibly complex. That is, living things possess interworking components that require an amazing level of intricate organization. If any one portion of a certain component is lacking, then that component will not merely fail to work properly—it will not work at all. In addition to these two discoveries, it is also noted that Darwinism has failed entirely to provide any credible hypothesis for the commencement of life. It is one thing to argue that life evolves; it is another to explain how life came about in the first place. These three lines of evidence—information theory, irreducible complexity, and the initiation of life—form the basis for the current biological argument for intelligent design.

The second line of discoveries—recent findings in cosmology— have not received as much attention, but they may present an even more powerful case for intelligent design.[3] This is because these discoveries lend themselves more readily to precise mathematical formulation and verification than does much of the biological evidence. In addition, one finds broad agreement among physicists, astronomers, and cosmologists about these findings—regardless of their religious affiliation. The gist of these discoveries is that the universe has been formulated with a level of precision that is quite literally astronomical. For this reason, these findings are often called "the fine-tuning argument." The evidence overwhelmingly indicates that Someone has balanced the physical constants of this universe on a razor's edge and has orchestrated things in such a way that intelligent life—human life—could thrive on Earth. This essay intends to highlight the basic features of the fine-tuning argument—also known as the anthropic principle. Some features of this argument do not fit well with the typical young-earth creationist model, but the fine-tuning argument is so fruitful that it warrants further attention from all who take the biblical doctrine of creation seriously.[4]

The fine-tuning perspective is a far cry from what has been the standard understanding of the universe during much of the modern era. For at least a century and a half, the principle of mediocrity (otherwise known as the Copernican principle) has reigned as the prevailing zeitgeist within the academic and scientific community. The principle of mediocrity states that there is nothing special or privileged about our place in the universe. Our home, planet Earth, is a nondescript world that revolves around a typical star and is but one of billions and billions of similar planets. The Copernican principle holds that, rather than occupying the center of the universe, humans live on the third rock from the Sun. There is nothing special about humans or the home we inhabit. Before he died in 1996, well-known astronomer and atheist Carl Sagan wrote *The Pale Blue Dot* (1994). The title for the book came from a famous picture taken of Earth in 1990 by the Voyager 1 satellite. As Voyager 1 was leaving our solar system, NASA scientists had the satellite turn its camera back towards Earth. From a distance of nearly 4 billion miles, Earth appeared as a faint, bluish dot against a backdrop of darkness. However, because of the way sunlight struck the camera's lens, Earth also seemed to be bathed in a narrow band of light. To Sagan, the photo highlighted our misguided tendency to see ourselves as somehow important, when the reality is that we are cosmically insignificant. He expressed his conviction this way:

> Because of the reflection of Sunlight off the spacecraft, the Earth seems to be sitting in a beam of light, as if there were some special significance to this small world. But it is just an accident of geometry and optics. . . . Our posturings, our imagined self-importance, the delusion that we have some privileged position in the Universe, are challenged by this point of pale light. Our planet is a lonely speck in the great enveloping cosmic dark. In our obscurity, in all this vastness, there is no hint that help will come from elsewhere to save us from ourselves.[5]

For Sagan, Earth's loneliness was exceeded only by its insignificance.

In marked contrast to Sagan, many other scientists are coming to a very different conclusion. In the 1960s and '70s, some astronomers and physicists began to note that the cosmos seemed to exhibit an "anthropic principle"—that a number of independent physical constants were precisely calibrated to allow intelligent life to exist somewhere in the universe.[6] As Schnall put it, "It is not merely that the constants are right; it is that the constants are *just right*."[7] Over the last quarter century, a plethora of books have come out highlighting this phenomenon. The first work to significantly bring the observations about fine-tuning into the broader popular market was John Barrow and Frank Tipler's *The Anthropic Cosmological Principle* (1986). Other books have followed: Hugh Ross, *The Creator and the Cosmos* (1993); Peter Ward and Donald Brownlee, *Rare Earth* (2000); Guillermo Gonzalez and Jay Richards, *The Privileged Planet* (2004); Paul Davies, *The Goldilocks Enigma* (2008); and Alister McGrath, *A Fine-Tuned Universe* (2009), just to name a few of the more accessible works.

Some who marvel at our "goldilocks Universe" have not or will not face the implications of such a world. Several will acknowledge that the most reasonable conclusion is to infer design, but because of a prior commitment to philosophical naturalism, they will not take the next logical step. However, there are some scientists and scholars, as we will see, who credit nature's fine-tuning for convincing them of the viability of theism.

ID advocates often discern two levels of fine-tuning: local and universal. As noted earlier, examples of local evidences of design are such things as the complexity of living cells or the information contained within cells. But fine-tuning proponents generally point to local evidences of a cosmological sort, namely, the remarkable characteristics of Earth and its place in our solar system. Gonzalez and Richards's book, *The Privileged Planet*, is a good example of an argument based on localized fine-tuning. At the universal level, ID proponents point to the precise calibration of the fundamental constants of nature necessary for life to exist anywhere in the cosmos. Ross listed no less than 25 such constants as he made the case for universal fine-tuning.[8] Local and universal approaches show that ID proponents can make arguments from both the trees and the forest. I look first at a few of the local arguments and then examine some of the universal ones.

Evidences of Local Fine-Tuning

In their book *Rare Earth*, geologist Peter Ward and astronomer Donald Brownlee have bad news for *Star Trek* fans. Even though Ward and Brownlee are Darwinian evolutionists, they are convinced that it is highly likely that Earth is the only place in the galaxy, and perhaps even the universe, where intelligent life resides.[9] They suspect that single-cell organisms are probably rather common throughout the cosmos. But they conclude that the necessary prerequisites for complex life—and specifically intelligent life—are so extraordinary that not only is the earth exceptional, it is reasonable to conclude that our home is one of a kind.[10] Astronomer Guillermo Gonzalez and philosopher Jay Richards come to a similar conclusion in their work *The Privileged Planet*, although they write from an overtly theistic perspective.[11] They contend that our world is special, not only because it is uniquely habitable, but also because it is exceptionally situated for the scientific enterprise. Both sets of authors present impressive cumulative cases that Earth is an extraordinary example of localized fine-tuning. From their extensive compilations of evidence, I have highlighted just a few notable examples.

First, the location of Earth's orbit in the solar system turns out to be just right. Given the sun's size and energy output, there is only a relatively narrow band in which Earth could orbit the sun and still be habitable for life. The distance from the Earth to the sun turns out to be optimal. Initial studies indicated that if our planet were just 1 percent closer to the sun, the additional heat would cause the oceans to evaporate. However, if the Earth's orbit were just 5 percent farther away from the sun, all the world's oceans would be frozen solid. As Hugh Ross put it, Earth's biosphere is "poised between a runaway freeze-up and a runaway evaporation."[12] In addition, the average temperature had to be such that water would be retained while other greenhouse molecules such as methane and ammonia would largely dissipate. Though recent studies show that the parameters may be broader than originally believed, the range of the habitable zone still is "quite narrow."[13]

Second, our planet exhibits characteristics that uniquely suit it for life. For example, Earth is the only planet in the solar system found to have plate tectonics.[14] Plate tectonics cause earthquakes, but they also play a surprisingly important role in sustaining life. As it turns out, plate tectonics play a key role in such things as maintaining stable global temperatures and a stable ocean environment. Another example of Earth's unique status is its lunar partner. Our moon is remarkably large for a planet the size of Earth. It is one-fourth the size of its host planet. All the other planets of our solar system have moons that are much smaller in relation to their respective sizes. Along with factors such as plate tectonics, the moon's influence on the Earth's attitude and rotation acts to stabilize the Earth's temperature. Our moon maintains the Earth's tilt of 23 degrees. Without the presence of the moon, the Earth's rotation would be wobbly. These examples are just a few of what could be cited, but it is not hard to get the idea.

Hugh Ross listed 33 parameters that must be met in order for a planet to support life. He calculated that the probability of all 33 parameters occurring in one planet is one in 10^{42}. However, astronomers estimate that the maximum possible number of planets is 10^{22}. Ross concludes that the odds of a planet such as Earth existing by chance are "much less than one in a quintillion."[15] Our terrestrial ball really is a special place.

Third, our sun itself is just right for habitable life on Earth. One would get the impression from many astronomy textbooks that the sun is a rather ordinary and undistinguished star. Ward and Brownlee pointed out that actually our sun is not typical at all. Rather, 95 percent of all stars are smaller than the sun. In fact, the majority of stars are M-class luminaries that are only 10 percent the size of the sun.[16]

If the sun were smaller than it is presently, then its habitable zone would also be much smaller, which would require the Earth to orbit closer than it does now. However, the closer orbit would mean that the sun's gravity would have a much greater effect on the Earth's rotation on its axis. In short, rather than rotating every 24 hours, our planet's rotation would slow to the point it would turn only once per year. Then Earth's rotary motion would resemble that of Mercury (the closet planet to the sun) which rotates only one and a half times per revolution around the sun. Think of the similar effect Earth's gravity has on the moon. The moon rotates only once per orbit around the Earth (i.e., once per month), and so we see only one side of the moon (the other side faces the Earth only during the dark phase of the lunar cycle). So the end result of the Earth orbiting closer to the sun would be that the same side of the planet would face the brunt of solar heat for extended periods of time. That side would be hundreds of degrees hot while the dark side would be hundreds of degrees below zero (which are the conditions on Mercury). Life on Earth would not be able to exist.[17]

However, if the sun were much larger than it is, that too would prove catastrophic for life. A larger sun would put out much higher levels of ultraviolet light—too much ultraviolet light, in fact, for life to survive.[18] Life on Earth is sustained by a "goldilocks star" (i.e., neither too hot nor too cold—"just right").

The sun provides the Earth with more unique properties than just its size. Most stars in the Milky Way (two-thirds, in fact) are binary stars or are grouped in clusters of three or more stars. Any planet that belongs to binary stars has an orbit too erratic to provide the stable and temperate environment necessary to sustain life, and the energy that planet receives would vary too much. The solitary status of our sun is an essential quality for life.[19]

Fourth, our neighboring planets are just right. As it turns out, Earth benefits greatly from having large sibling planets such as Jupiter and Saturn patrolling the outer regions of the solar system. And both planets are needed. Saturn and Jupiter are the right size and distance to keep each other in a stable orbit. If either planet were substantially different, Jupiter would sling Saturn out of the solar system and Jupiter would go into an elliptical orbit, which could eventually cause it to crash into us.[20] As it is, Jupiter acts as a cosmic vacuum sweeper for Earth. If Jupiter did not exist, Earth would be struck by space debris at a rate 10,000 times greater than it is. As it is, "extinction-causing projectiles" strike our planet at the rate of once every 100 million years. Without Jupiter the rate would be once every 10,000 years, which would not give life enough time to recover.[21]

Fifth, our location in the Milky Way is just right. Our galaxy, the Milky Way, is 85,000 light years across. We are located about 25,000 lights years from the center. This turns out to be ideal for life. Just as our solar system has a habitable zone, so does our galaxy.[22] On the one hand, if we were closer to the center of the Milky Way, then we would be irradiated by cosmic rays and the particles emanating from exploding supernovas. On the other hand, if we were farther from the center, then there would be no heavy elements available. The outer bands are made up almost entirely of hydrogen and helium. The heavier, essential building blocks of life—oxygen, nitrogen, carbon, iron, and so on—are absent. Earth is located in the optimal region of the Milky Way: far enough from the center to escape most of the radiation yet near enough for all the major elements to be available.

There are basically three types of galaxies in the universe: spiral, elliptical, and irregular.[23] The Milky Way is a large, spiral galaxy that has major spiral arms composed of stars and dust. We are located in a relatively open part of the Milky Way (our nearest star is four light-years away), between two spiral arms. Most stars are in globular clusters—tens of thousands of stars grouped within a small region—and these clusters are generally contained within the spiral arms of the Milky Way. Whatever planets might be located in these clusters are constantly bombarded with radiation and particles that would make life impossible.[24] Since our solar system resides in an open region between the spiral arms, Earth is spared this high-intensity barrage.

In addition, Gonzalez and Richards pointed out that if our planet were situated within one of the spiral arms, then our night sky would be dramatically different from what we see now.[25] The cosmic dust would obscure everything. Rather than a canopy of stars, every evening would be shrouded in a dull fog. We would have had no reason to investigate beyond our planet since nothing else would be visible. Gonzalez and Richards contended that, in such a dreary setting, the scientific revolution more than likely would never have gotten off the ground. Our actual location is felicitous for astronomical investigations. Situated in "our highly accommodating perch," we enjoy "the best seating in the galaxy" for viewing the starry sky.[26]

Evidences of Universal Fine-Tuning

Beyond the local characteristics of our planet and its surrounding environment, the universe as a whole displays a number of remarkable examples of fine-tuning. The cosmos contains a long list of universal initial conditions and constants, each independent from the others, each essential for life to occur, which together exhibit a level of calibration that is astounding. Our universe is poised on a razor's edge.

A dilemma faces any writer hoping to communicate the full scope of these evidences to a popular audience. The subject matter at hand is by definition rather esoteric. And, in the typical discussion on universal fine-tuning, proponents present a plethora of scientific facts in a barrage that seems intended to overwhelm the reader. And they often succeed. Barrow and Tipler devoted 450 pages of their book to example after example of fine-tuning taken from the fields of physics, astrophysics, biochemistry, quantum mechanics, and more.[27] Others, such as Hugh Ross, listed dozens of the "cosmic coincidences" in brief bullet points that cover only about 15 pages.[28] Either way, the presentations are both impressive and intimidating to those for whom science is not their home turf. I intend to offer a few of the more salient examples in everyday language so that (hopefully) the reader can get the gist of the universal fine-tuning argument.

For example, consider the constants of nature. There are four fundamental forces: the strong-nuclear force, the weak-nuclear force, the electromagnetic force, and gravity. It turns out that the relationships between them must be exactly what they are to an amazing level of precision. John Lennox explains that if the ratio of the nuclear strong force to the electromagnetic force were different by one part in 10^{16}, then the stars would not be able to form. This, of course, would mean there would be no sun. Also, if the ratio of the electromagnetic force to the gravitational force were different by one part in 10^{40}, then only very small or very large stars would be able to form. Again, this would mean a star like our sun could not exist.[29]

Stephen W. Hawking noted that, on the one hand, if the expansion of the universe had been less by one part in 10^{10}, standard Big-Bang models show that the universe would quickly have collapsed. On the other hand, if the expansion had been more by one part in 10^{10}, then the universe today would be essentially empty.[30]

Paul Davies and Hugh Ross gave a great deal of attention to the precise relationship between protons, electrons, and neutrons. These, of course, are the building blocks of molecules, and physicists have discovered that an amazing accuracy was required in the ratio of one to the other in order for stars and planets to exist. For example, if the number of electrons were slightly different from the number of protons, then the electromagnetic forces would have overpowered the gravitational forces to the point stars and planets would not be able to form. How slight of a difference are we talking about? In other words, what level of exactness was required? The answer is astounding. Davies and Ross report that it has been determined that the number of electrons must equal the number of protons to an accuracy of one part in 10^{37}.[31]

At this point it is helpful to consider how large a number 10^{37} really is. Simply put, 10^{37} is unimaginable. A number of this magnitude is beyond everyday human experience, so it risks losing any true significance to us. So Paul Davies came up with an illustration that helps to put things into a little better perspective. Imagine a marksman who is so skilled that he is able to shoot a coin with a pistol from a distance of 100 yards away. The odds of the typical person managing to pull off such a stunt are small, but there are sharpshooters who can make this type of shot with regularity. But what if the distance were not 100 yards, but rather the distance were across a major city—say Atlanta? Now the trajectory traveled is measured not in yards but miles. Supposing he had very special bullets that could travel such lengths, what would be the odds in this case? But before we calculate those odds, let's progressively move the target farther away. What if the distance was across the entire state of Georgia? Or what if the marksman in Georgia hit the coin even though it was located in California, across the entire United States? What are the chances? And what if that eagle-eyed person in Georgia hit the quarter even though the coin was perched on the moon? Then the odds would be truly astronomical. Or what if the coin was on Pluto? Or across the Milky Way? Or on the other side of the universe? Now we are talking about odds so absurdly high that we dismiss them as impossible. But as Davies explained, that is the odds of 1 in 10^{37}.[32] Incredibly, the ratio of electrons to protons exhibits a level of calibration, that, if random, would be as if a person using a pistol managed to shoot a coin located at the opposite side of the known universe.

Ross gave another illustration designed to show just how amazing the odds of 1 in 10^{37} really are. Imagine the United States covered in dimes. And this pile of dimes is so high it reaches to the moon. Now imagine 1 billion piles of the same size and magnitude. Suppose, out of that immense number of mounds of coins, a single dime is painted red. Now envision the challenge, while blindfolded, of having to pick out that red coin from all those coins and having only one chance to get it right. That is the odds of 1 in 10^{37}.[33] Sir Fred Hoyle, who coined the phrase "Big Bang," admitted that discoveries of such astronomical precision shook his atheism "to the core." He observed that the universe appeared as if a "super intellect has monkeyed with physics, as well as chemistry and biology."[34] Indeed.

Yet the cosmos exhibits a level of precision that makes the previous examples pale into insignificance. Stephen Hawking discovered that the rate of the expansion of the universe cannot be different from what it is by one part in 10^{55}. If it were any faster, there would be no stars, galaxies, or planets. If the rate were any slower, the universe would be simply a giant black hole.[35] Roger Penrose, who was Hawking's collaborator in his initial work on black holes, demonstrated that the entropy of the universe exhibits a precision of one part in $10^{(10)^{123}}$. Keep in mind the number $10^{(10)^{123}}$ far exceeds the number of atoms in the universe. Penrose stated, "I cannot even recall seeing anything else in physics whose accuracy is known to approach, even remotely, a figure like one part in $10^{(10)^{123}}$."[36]

The above instances are just a sampling from the long list of examples that could be provided. After surveying the evidence of the universe's precise calibration, Davies concluded, "It seems as though someone has fine-tuned nature's numbers to make the Universe. . . . The impression of design is overwhelming."[37] Arno Penzias, winner of the Nobel Prize in physics, concurred: "Astronomy leads us to a unique event, a universe which was created out of nothing, one with the very delicate balance needed to provide exactly the right conditions required to permit life, and one which has an underlying (one might say 'supernatural') plan."[38] Either we "hit the cosmic jackpot" (Davies' phrase), or we are the recipients of extraordinary providential care. At the end their discussion covering much of the same evidences just given, Ward and Brownlee quoted a Clint Eastwood line from the movie *Dirty Harry*: "Do you feel lucky? Well do ya?"[39] Well, actually, no. I feel blessed.

Objections to the Fine-Tuning Argument

Objections to the fine-tuning argument can be grouped into two categories: (1) arguments that the discovery of fine-tuning is attributable to "the observation selection effect"; and (2) arguments that appeal to the anthropic principle itself (and for that reason are often called "the anthropic principle objection").[40] The first objection is fairly easy to answer, and as for the second objection, more than one Christian philosopher has expressed his surprise that the argument gets much traction.[41]

The "observation selection effect" objection claims that the fine-tuning argument is based on the tendency to notice remarkable coincidences while ignoring other mundane yet pertinent data. Opponents claim that advocates of the fine-tuning argument are like the fisherman who, after fishing in a lake using a net with 10-inch holes, concludes that the lake contains no fish smaller than 10 inches.[42] In other words, the "observation selection effect" contends that the theist sees evidence of fine-tuning because his biases have colored his perspective.

In response, it must be admitted that the tendency to see evidence through jaundiced eyes is always a very real possibility. However, that does not appear to be what is happening in this case. The first discoverers of the universe's fine-tuned characteristics were not looking for any such evidence. Many, in fact, were initially skeptical of their own findings. Only after example after example of the fine-tuned constants accumulated independently did scientists call attention to the phenomena.

Richard Swinburne answered the "fishing net analogy" with the "firing squad analogy"—an illustration repeated by William Lane Craig.[43] Imagine standing before a firing squad of 100 marksmen. They fire simultaneously on command, but you find that you are still standing. How did this happen? Though it is possible that all 100 trained sharpshooters unintentionally missed, it is highly improbable. Ockham's razor (the principle that states, all things being equal, the simplest solution should be preferred) points to a more likely explanation: someone orchestrated a fake execution. The "observation selection effect" objection argues that we are amazed about something that may be merely fortuitous, but the objection seems to suffer a similar slashing by Ockham's blade. Craig likened the objection's reasoning to be similar to that of a silk merchant whose thumb just happened to have covered the moth hole of the cloth he just sold you. "My thumb had to be somewhere," he explained, and each place on the garment was equally improbable.[44] The "observation selection effect" objection does not apply to the fine-tuning argument.

The second argument, the "anthropic principle objection," is more subtle and is even more unconvincing. It states that, given the fact we exist, we should not be surprised that the conditions necessary for our existence also exist. In other words, proponents of the argument are pointing out that our existence logically entails that the conditions for our existence also must exist. We are here, so the constants necessary for our existence must also be here. In his presentation of the "anthropic principle objection," Sober concluded that, since we exist, "the constants must be right, regardless of whether the Universe was produced by intelligent design or by chance."[45] The conditions for our existence are logically required by the fact we are here. Therefore, he concluded that the initial fine-tuned conditions were logically necessary.

In response, it must be pointed out that the "anthropic principle objection" confuses logical necessity with causality. Yes, the fact that we are here necessitates that the conditions for our existence also exist. But it does not follow that those conditions were necessary. For example, if a car accident occurs, then obviously the conditions for the accident to happen also existed. But those conditions did not necessarily exist. The problem with Sober's presentation of the anthropic objection is that he has the arrow of causality pointing the wrong way. Schnall gave an example that illustrates how easy it is to confuse causal relations.[46] Imagine determining the height of a flagpole by measuring the length of its shadow. By measuring the shadow and noting the angle of the sun at the time, calculating the flagpole's height is a simple process. Once the shadow's length and the sun's angle are ascertained, then the flagpole's height can be determined. However, logical necessity does not show causality. The shadow's length does not determine the flagpole's height. It is the other way around. Rather, the flagpole causes the shadow to be the length that it is. And so it is with the initial conditions of the universe. Our existence logically necessitates that the constants are what they are, but our existence does not cause them to exist. Schnall made an additional significant point in his response to Sober. The fact that we exist entails that the conditions necessary for our existence also exist, but it does not entail that those conditions are fine-tuned.[47] If a turtle is atop a fence post, then we can assume that someone put him there. And if the universe is poised on a razor's edge, then we can believe it is because Someone willed it so.

Conclusion

In 2004 the news that Anthony Flew had converted from atheism to theism hit the philosophical world like a thunderclap. In an interview with Gary Habermas, Flew gave intelligent design and fine-tuning arguments as the reasons why he had changed his mind. "I think that the most impressive arguments for

God's existence are those that are supported by recent scientific discoveries. . . . I think the argument for intelligent design is enormously stronger than it was when I first met it."[48] Perhaps the persuasiveness of ID arguments such as the case for fine-tuning is the reason certain atheists have reacted in such a shrill manner.

Flew published his book *There Is a God: How the World's Most Notorious Atheist Changed His Mind* in 2007, and in it he devoted a chapter to the fine-tuning of the universe. I close with an illustration given by Flew in that chapter:

> Imagine entering a hotel room on your next vacation. The CD player on the bedside table is softly playing a track from your favorite recording. The framed print over the bed is identical to the image that hangs over the fireplace at home. The room is scented with your favorite fragrance. You shake your head in amazement and drop your bags on the floor.
>
> You're suddenly very alert. You step over to the mini-bar, open the door, and stare in wonder at the contents. Your favorite beverages. Your favorite cookies and candy. Even the brand of bottled water you prefer.
>
> You turn from the minibar, then, and gaze around the room. You notice the book on the desk: it's the latest volume by your favorite author. You glance into the bathroom, where personal care and grooming products are lined up on the counter, each one as if it was chosen specifically for you. You switch on the television; it is tuned to your favorite channel.
>
> Chances are, with each new discovery about your hospitable new environment, you would be less inclined to think it was all a mere coincidence, right? You might wonder how the hotel managers acquired such detailed information about you. You might marvel at their meticulous preparation. You might even double-check what all this is going to cost you. But you would certainly be inclined to believe that someone knew you were coming.[49]

After contemplating our marvelous situation, Antony Flew realized that Someone had prepared the universe for us as an elaborate and lavish accommodation. Flew decided he no longer had enough faith to be an atheist. I agree with him. The best explanation from inference is intelligent design.

Notes

1. The paper can be found in A. Flew and A. MacIntyre, *New Essays in Philosophical Theology* (New York: Macmillan, 1964). Flew based his parable on an illustration given by J. Wisdom, "Gods," in *Philosophy and Psychoanalysis* (Berkeley: University of California, 1969).

2. Ibid., 97.

3. I. M. Schnall, "Anthropic Observation Selection Effects and the Design Argument," *Faith and Philosophy* 26 (October 2009), 4:361–62.

4. A number of evangelical writers have attempted to reconcile the fine-tuning argument with the Genesis account of creation by arguing that a faithful interpretation of Genesis 1 does not require holding to a young earth. Here are some of the more recent books arguing for an old earth: J. Sailhamer, *Genesis Unbound: A Provocative New Look at the Creation Account* (Portland: Multnomah, 1996); H. Ross, *A Matter of Days: Resolving a Creation Controversy* (Colorado Springs: NavPress, 2004); D. Snoke, *A Biblical Case for an Old Earth* (Grand Rapids: Baker, 2006); C. J. Collins, *Genesis 1–4: A Linguistic, Literary, and Theological Commentary* (Phillipsburg: P&R, 2006); J. H. Walton, *The Lost World of Genesis One: Ancient Cosmology and the Origins Debate* (Downers Grove: IVP, 2009); and W. A. Dembski, *The End of Christianity: Finding a Good God in an Evil World* (Nashville: B&H Academic, 2009). A quick survey of these works reveals that there is no consensus yet among those who hold to some version of ancient Earth creationism.

5. C. Sagan, *Pale Blue Dot: A Vision of the Human Future in Space* (New York: Random House, 1994), 8–9. My attention was drawn to this quote by Dembski, *The End of Christianity*, 41.

6. See N. A. Manson, "Introduction," in *God and Design: The Teleological Argument and Modern Science*, ed. N. A. Manson (New York: Routledge, 2003), 4. Manson called the phenomena "anthropic coincidences."

7. Schnall, "Anthropic Observation Selection Effects and the Design Argument," 369.

8. H. Ross, *The Creator and the Cosmos: How the Greatest Scientific Discoveries of the Century Reveal God* (Colorado Springs: NavPress, 1993), 111–14.

9. P. D. Ward and D. Brownlee, *Rare Earth: Why Complex Life Is So Uncommon in the Universe* (New York: Copernicus Books, 2000), xvii.

10. "In this book we will argue that not only intelligent life, but even the simplest of animal life, is exceedingly rare in our galaxy and in the Universe" (ibid., xviii). According to Ward and Brownlee, the Rare Earth Hypothesis postulates "the paradox that life may be nearly everywhere but complex life almost nowhere" (xxv).

11. G. Gonzalez and J. W. Richards, *The Privileged Planet: How Our Place in the Cosmos Is Designed for Discovery* (Washington, DC: Regnery, 2004). "Simply stated, the conditions allowing for intelligent life on Earth also make our planet strangely well suited for viewing and analyzing the universe" (x).

12. Ross, *The Creator and the Cosmos*, 127.

13. Ward and Brownlee, *Rare Earth*, 18.

14. Ibid., 220.

15. Ross, *The Creator and the Cosmos*, 134.

16. Ward and Brownlee, *Rare Earth*, 23. "It is often said that the sun is a typical star, but this is entirely untrue."

17. Ibid., 23–24.

18. Ibid., 22.

19. Ibid., 25.

20. Ibid., 21–22.

21. Ibid., 238–39.

22. Ibid., 27.

23. Gonzalez and Richards, *Privileged Planet*, 144.

24. Ward and Brownlee, *Rare Earth*, 25–27.

25. Gonzalez and Richards, *Privileged Planet*, 146–51.

26. Ibid., 146. I thank John Burkett for his help with this paragraph.

27. J. D. Barrow and F. J. Tipler, *The Anthropic Cosmological Principle* (Oxford: University Press, 1986), 122–576.

28. H. Ross, *The Fingerprint of God* (Orange: Promise, 1991), 119–32.

29. J. C. Lennox, *God's Undertaker: Has Science Buried God?* (Oxford: Lion, 2007), 69.

30. Cited by A. E. McGrath, *A Fine-Tuned Universe: The Quest for God in Science and Theology* (Louisville: WJK, 2009), 85.

31. Ross, *The Creator and the Cosmos*, 109.

32. Cited by Lennox, *God's Undertaker*, 69.

33. Ross, *The Creator and the Cosmos*, 109.

34. Cited by Lennox, *God's Undertaker*, 69.

35. Ross, *The Creator and the Cosmos*, 110.

36. Cited by W. L. Craig, "Design and the Anthropic Fine-Tuning of the Universe," in Manson, *God and Design*, 157.

37. Cited by Lennox, *God's Undertaker*, 70.

38. Ibid., 57.

39. Ward and Brownlee, *Rare Earth*, 257.

40. Schnall, "Anthropic Observation Selection Effects and the Design Argument," 361–77.

41. Ibid. "I must admit that I still find the AP objection somewhat puzzling. I only hope that my analysis will prompt others to respond in a way that will allay the puzzlement" (362). W. L. Craig made a similar statement ("Design and the Anthropic Fine-Tuning of the Universe," 168–71).

42. The fish-net analogy comes from E. Sober, "The Design Argument," in Manson, *God and Design*, 43–44. Schnall's article drew my attention to Sober's chapter.

43. Craig, "Fine-Tuning of the Universe," 170.

44. Craig, "Design and the Anthropic Fine-Tuning of the Universe," 161.

45. Sober, "The Design Argument," 44–45.

46. Schnall, "Anthropic Observation Selection Effects and the Design Argument," 370–71.

47. Ibid., 369.

48. A. Flew and G. Habermas, "My Pilgrimage from Atheism to Theism: A Discussion between Anthony Flew and Gary Habermas," *Philosophia Christi* 6 (2004), 2:200. In the interview, Flew embraced a version of deism.

49. A. Flew, *There Is a God: How the World's Most Notorious Atheist Changed His Mind* (New York: HarperOne, 2007), 113–14.

Chapter 12

How Science Works and What It Means for Believers

Robert B. Stewart

The August 15, 2005, *Time* magazine cover proclaimed "Evolution Wars: The push to teach 'Intelligent Design' raises the question: Does God have a place in science class?" To many this captures the essence of the conversation concerning science and faith today—science and religion are at war. This idea is absurd. It makes as much sense to say that science and religion are at war as it does to say that mathematics and English are at war or that history and philosophy are quarrelling. There is no doubt, however, that some scientists see religion as the enemy of good science, while some religious persons see science, or at least Darwinian evolution, as an enemy of faith. So some scientists and some religious leaders are fighting with one another. But that is an entirely different issue.

Most of the contemporary debate revolves around biological evolution, that is, the neo-Darwinian synthesis. In other words, much of the debate focuses on only one biological theory. Nobody, so far as I know, has ever objected to belief in the HIV virus or Einstein's theories for religious reasons. From the day Darwin's *Origin of Species* was published, evolution has been both heralded and opposed. Several noted atheists, such as Richard Dawkins and Daniel Dennett, hold that one cannot consistently follow Darwin on this issue and at the same time hold to the Christian faith in any meaningful sense. Other non-theists, like Michael Ruse, think otherwise.[1] And numerous Christian theologians embrace some form of theistic evolution while others oppose Darwin's theory with a passion. It is not even as simple as saying that Christians oppose Darwinism—or as many websites would say, that religion opposes science or vice versa.

So, how should a thoughtful Christian understand the relationship between science and Christianity? I cannot in this brief essay address this question in detail or comprehensively; nevertheless, I do speak to some issues related to the topic. In particular, I hope to help those concerned with understanding the implications of a Christian worldview bring these two important ways of interacting with reality into a harmonious relationship that does justice to both without distorting either. I also hope to help others begin to devise an effective strategy for living out one's faith in today's world in this regard.

There are multiple issues involved in coming to an understanding of the relationship between science and religion. First, there is no universally accepted definition of either term. Not all scientists agree on the nature of science. Not all religious persons agree on the nature of religion. And it is certainly true that there is no scientific consensus on the essence of religion, nor a religious consensus on the essence of science.

Not surprisingly, there are philosophical issues involved in coming to an understanding of either discipline. In fact, the fundamental issues in the debate are philosophical rather than scientific, hermeneutical rather than empirical. This is because there is a difference between science and *philosophy* of science. No scientist works without accepting certain axioms that are philosophical in nature. Similarly, no human can live without thinking scientifically, that is, without forming hypotheses about the nature of the material world and testing those hypotheses on the basis of repeated experience. Furthermore, we all benefit from the results of science on a regular basis. Science is truly one of God's good gifts to humanity.

Nobody understands perfectly how science works, but surprisingly enough, on a fairly regular basis I talk to people, including some working scientists, who do not recognize or understand the philosophical issues involved in the scientific method. This should not really surprise us. After all, we want scientists to *do* science, not to sit around reflecting on meta-scientific questions.

What do I mean by the term metascientific? Simply that there are two types of questions: first-order questions and second-order questions. The question "Does God exist?" is a first-order question. The question "What does it mean to ask if God exists?" is a second-order question. Science cannot answer second-order questions about science; that is the role of philosophy, and to that we now turn.

What does it mean to be scientific? Or to put it more simply, what does it mean to speak of science? To give a definitive answer to this question would require much more than can be done in one article. In this essay, when I speak of science I generally refer to the activity in which scientists working in the hard sciences (biology, chemistry, physics, geology, archaeology) engage, or at least to the goals they attempt to achieve. My use of the term is therefore more pragmatic and common sense in nature than it is theoretical. Most importantly, I am attempting to describe why and how they work as they do.

In part, when we say "science" we are talking about a way of investigating the physical world. Martinez Hewlett expressed this well when he said of science, "It's a very powerful way of examination, supported by a methodology that incorporates observation, hypothesis building, experimentation, and hypothesis revision. But this does not make it an *exclusive view* of the natural world. There is also the view of the artist, the writer, the philosopher, or the theologian to consider."[2] Unfortunately, many view science as the *definitive* way of seeing reality.[3] But science is not only a way of *viewing* the world. It is a system of *representing* what the world looks like.[4] Niels Bohr, a physicist whose work led to quantum theory, said, "It is wrong to think that the task of physics is to find out how nature *is*. Physics concerns only what we can *say* about nature."[5] What is true of physics is also true of other sciences. Science presents us with models of reality. By model I mean a way of conceptualizing and symbolizing the realities to which scientific statements refer. Hewlett provided some useful examples:

> The periodic table of Mendeleev models the relationship of all of the elements, including hydrogen, to all other elements. In this description, hydrogen occupies the upper left beginning position of the table, with the symbol and atomic properties described as ^1H. This table has explanatory value and its predictive value was so fruitful that all of the elements, as they were discovered, could fit into this same scheme. But, ^1H is not the gas; it is only a useful model.

> The nature of the atom itself was first described by Niels Bohr as a small planetary system. In this model, hydrogen is

drawn with a central spherical nucleus (the proton) around which orbits the small, spherical electron. This is a model with such important explanatory value that it still appears in elementary textbooks as a way to depict how two atoms join together to form a chemical bond. And yet, no physicist would think that this is what hydrogen actually looks like. To a physicist, hydrogen, or at least the ground state of the electron in the first orbit, would look like this:

$$\Psi_{1s} = p^{-0.5}\left[z/a_0\right]^{1.5}e^{-s}$$

Is this wave equation, then, the reality of the gas? No, but it is a very useful model, both explanatory and fruitful.[6]

Examples like this help us to understand that *science is inescapably a semiotic system*. A semiotic system is a system of *signs* that stand in the place of other realities. We use them all the time. Music, language, mathematics, and logic are just a few of the sign systems that we use. A sign—whether it be musical, linguistic, mathematical, or logical—stands in place of and represents something else. Some philosophers have argued that even thought itself cannot take place apart from some sort of sign system. Please note: the fact that something is represented via a sign system does not mean that what is represented is not real, or that what is represented does not or cannot exist apart from the sign system. The sign system allows us to talk about reality, but the sign system is not the basis of reality.

The effect of this realization is that science cannot be elevated to the level of the super-discipline or the highest way of knowing. There is no discipline that can rightfully claim this honor, not even philosophy—even though terminal degrees are "doctor of philosophy" degrees, and in many ways philosophy is presuppositional to the application of most, if not all, disciplines. Practice without theory is blind, but theory without practice is empty. Simply put, the quest for knowledge is ultimately an *interdisciplinary quest*. This is not to lessen the importance of science, but to emphasize the interrelated nature of all human knowledge. In other words, one cannot approach science (or any other discipline) with an Orwellian attitude that says, "All the disciplines in the academy are equal but science is more equal than others."

Many people labor under the false impression that since science always involves observation, particularly repeated observation, it is therefore purely an exercise in induction, that is, it is an exercise in repeated experience. The fact that science necessarily *involves* observation does not mean that science is *based on* observation. Simply put, science proceeds on the basis of inferences. These inferences are of different natures and involve different types of reasoning. The first inference is abductive or creative in nature; the second is deductive or logical in nature; the third is inductive or observational in nature.

(1) At the ***abductive stage*** a scientist creates or tentatively adopts a hypothesis that, if true, *would explain* certain phenomena. For instance, he might infer that the behavior of materials would be explicable if they were made up of tiny particles that could react to other tiny particles of different materials, sometimes combining, sometimes behaving in other ways.

(2) The ***deductive stage*** involves using logic to infer *testable consequences* of the hypothesis being true. On the basis of these consequences, predictions can be made.

(3) The final stage, the ***inductive stage***, involves the testing—through experimentation—of the predictions inferred at the deductive stage. In this way a hypothesis is *verified* or *falsified*.[7]

The idea of falsification is one of the most important of all concepts in the philosophy of science. Karl Popper held that *the proper mark of a scientific theory is falsifiability*. If a theory cannot be falsified, it is, according to Popper, a *pseudo-scientific* theory or a myth. He even insisted that science does not proceed by *proving* theories but by *falsifying* them.[8] Philosophers of science are quick to point out that Popper was using falsification to distinguish between science and nonscience, not between true and false theories. One has to wonder, though, whether earlier scientific advances, which did not couch their research in Popper's terms, were for that reason *pseudo-scientific*. I suspect that Popper would say that the fact that they *did not* state their position in his terms does not mean that they *could not have*, and thus many landmark moments in the history of science were indeed scientific. Yet one has to ask, "Can Popper's theory of what distinguishes science from pseudo-science be falsified?" I do not see how. But if we accept his premise, and his theory cannot be falsified, then are we not faced with a situation where *pseudo-science* is dictating the terms upon which *science* is to be conducted? Nevertheless, Popper's emphasis upon falsification has strong intuitional support. It seems clear that at the very least a falsifiable hypothesis is preferable to one that is not.

We must realize then that science is always theory-laden: no theory of science, no science. The theory-laden nature of science means that science is always driven by *paradigms*. A scientific paradigm is a set of axioms, that is, accepted theoretical assumptions that together form an overarching background for understanding reality. The history of science has been one of progress, but not a slow and steady progress from one individual idea to another, but of relatively small advances from within a dominant paradigm interspersed with periodic leaps forward as one paradigm is replaced by another. The most important names associated with these advances are familiar to most educated people: Copernicus, Kepler, Galileo, Newton, Darwin, Einstein, to name but a few. To these other important second-tier names could be added that scientists and historians would immediately recognize. The important thing to understand is that *science cannot take place apart from a paradigm*. One simply cannot work from nowhere, accepting nothing. There must be some first principles that together form a structure upon which the scientist can investigate and build—and within which he operates. When a paradigm changes we have a scientific revolution on our hands.[9]

How do scientific revolutions take place? Why do paradigms change? Simply put, scientific paradigms collapse when a crisis in knowledge takes place. How does such a crisis come about? A paradigm crisis never takes place on the basis of one experiment but as the cumulative effect of a growing awareness that the operating paradigm is insufficient to handle problematic data that is becoming more widely evident, the implications of which challenge the paradigm in an unacceptable way.

Is this all that is required? No. One does not and should not do away with a paradigm that has allowed progress to take place without sufficient reason to do so. Paradigms are judged according to their *explanatory power*, that is, by their fruitfulness, their coherence, their simplicity, their ability to produce testable predictions, and so on. So long as the paradigm functions well enough, experiments that seem to contradict the paradigm are considered anomalies for which there is no present explanation but for which there may be at a later time. In fact, these anomalies have often stimulated the most important science—sometimes leading to a revision or refinement of the operating paradigm, at other times leading to its collapse and replacement. But even a great amount of problematic data cannot produce a paradigm shift on its own. Only when a new paradigm is put forward to take the place of the old will such a revolution take place. And revolutions—whether they be political or scientific in nature—are always accompanied by revolts *and* establishment attempts to put them down. Sometimes attempts at revolution fail for good reasons. Not every proposed paradigm can deal with the data as well as the incumbent. The one thing that a scientific paradigm cannot survive, however, is the advent of a new paradigm that has more explanatory power, one that makes predictions that can be falsified but are not, and one that is simpler than the incumbent. The bases upon which scientific paradigms are judged are thus quite *pragmatic* and even a bit *subjective* in nature.[10] But this is as it should be; after all we *do* want *to use* our scientific beliefs.

One cannot overestimate the importance—at least in today's world—of peer review. Simply put, peer review is a requirement for scientific validation in today's scientific community. For the most part, peer review is a post-WWII process—Newton, Darwin, and Einstein did not have to survive the fires of peer review. Furthermore, peer review does not and cannot *produce* anything scientific; *scientists* produce science. Peer review never kept an honest and gifted scientist from doing ground-breaking research. But peer review can often hinder the publication of contrary views. Human nature being what it is, we should expect this. Accordingly, peer review functions more like a gatekeeper than a trailblazer in that it tends to filter new ideas rather than inspiring them. None of this matters even a little bit. Peer review is the way the game is played today. No scientific theory or operating paradigm that does not have the seal of peer review is even going to qualify for serious consideration in the contemporary scientific community.

I hope this brief summary of how science is actually conducted today helps one to understand why scientists often appear baffled by statements from nonscientists. Given that Darwinian evolution is the elephant in the room when science and religion are discussed, I examine the interaction when an often-heard retort occurs: "Darwinism is *only a theory*." True enough, as far as the statement goes. But what sort of theory is it? Is it a theory that is testable, fruitful, from which we can make predictions, and that has explanatory power? Or is it simply something Charles Darwin thought up after being too long away from home on a sea voyage? The answer to this question is that by the standards laid out above, Darwinian evolution has been a hugely successful theory of biological development. I am not arguing for Darwinism. I am trying to state clearly how the scientific enterprise is conducted today. Non-Darwinists need to understand that *Darwinism is **the** operating paradigm in the biological sciences today*—and it will remain so until it is replaced by a more pragmatically effective paradigm.

Fiery sermons can be preached, scores of books on creation science or intelligent design can be published, and an innumerably large number of websites decrying the inconsistency of a Darwinian worldview can be made available online, but until the proposal of a body of peer-reviewed scientists from which a more productive paradigm can be framed, Darwinism will continue to hold the scientific (and political/legal) high ground. This is neither an entirely good or bad thing. No doubt the broad acceptance of better science may at times be delayed as a result of peer review, but on the other hand peer review prevents the too-easy acceptance of bogus science. Security and quality control have their price, but all things considered they are worth the cost.

This does not mean that Darwinism, or the neo-Darwinian synthesis, will always hold this privileged position. In 1900 Newtonian physics was the most-successful, well-confirmed scientific paradigm ever developed. For over 200 years its laws had been unfailingly corroborated by literally *millions* of scientific tests. Based on its principles, civilization had seen the most impressive technological advances in human history. *Surely it could never be replaced.* But Albert Einstein did not believe that

Newton's laws were beyond critique, and instead he built on the work of Albert Michelson and Edward Morley and disproved some of them in his special theory of relativity.

How can we as Christians engage the sciences in a way that is culturally relevant without being theologically vacuous? The first step is to involve ourselves in scientific research. We need evangelical Christian scientists who can engage in meaningful research work. This requires a paradigm shift in how Christians as a group think about our place in society. As a group, Christians have made the mistake of abandoning for the most part the two most important shapers of our culture—science and entertainment.[11] Instead we have settled comfortably into our Christian ghettos and been content with Christian music, Christian movies, and a type of Christian popular science—all produced and distributed by Christian sources and outlets, and all summarily dismissed by the broader culture, thus becoming effectually irrelevant. We need a generation of Christians who will see the lab as every bit as much of a mission field as far-away continents and the scientific community as a largely unreached people group.[12]

What is required of these missionary-scientists? These believer-scientists must first commit themselves to being the best scholars and researchers possible because a first-rate outcome will never be the result of second-rate preparation and/or effort. They also must understand that they are going to be swimming upstream, but so be it. Paradigms crumble bit by bit, just as superstructures are built piece by piece. These believer-scientists will need to be patient and industrious, and to do solid work that is supported by scientific observation rather than theological belief. Those who are not called or equipped to be working scientists must pray for those who are.

There is, of course, a role for philosophers to play as well. As we have seen, science proceeds on the basis of philosophical beliefs as well as observation. Tough-minded philosophers are therefore required to hold scientists' feet to the fire at the presuppositional level. Many scientists have presuppositions about science that are not supported by good science or rational thought. A case in point is the somewhat prevalent belief that good science, or more particularly that Darwinian evolution, demands atheism. Darwinism proper does not address issues such as why there is something rather than nothing, or the age of the universe, or even the question of *abiogenesis*—how to get life from nonliving substances. Simply put, even if one should accept every tenet of Darwinian evolution *with relation to biology*, there is no scientific or logical reason to think that Darwinism *requires* atheism. As Hewlett noted, "There is no step in the scientific method where it says 'at this point, abandon belief in God.'"[13] To do so is simply to impose a nontheistic worldview over science.

Besides praying for scientists (and philosophers), what strategic moves do I recommend? First, I recommend that we not fight each other over issues that, while important, are not central to our main challenge. Our primary challenge is metaphysical naturalism. I see no good reason for Christians to battle over the age of the earth, or whether we should understand the days of Genesis 1 as consecutive 24-hour days, or whether Adam and Eve had navels. These are simply intramural debates. We have more important battles to fight. Our primary focus should be scientific or metaphysical naturalism, á la Dawkins, Dennett, and Harris, not specific issues of evolutionary theory. My experience tells me that even if we can do a credible job of challenging a single issue related to biological evolution, the naturalists will generally move on to another point and then the debate starts all over again. Instead, I suggest that we first take on naturalism. If naturalism is true, then Christianity is false. On the other hand, it does not follow that if Darwinism is false, then Christianity is true. But it does follow that if naturalism is false, then Christianity is possibly true—and is thus a worldview that must be seriously considered. We must use our time and energy wisely. A single well-placed rifle shot is often more effective than several generally directed shotgun blasts.

As a matter of fact, I can see how Darwinism and Christianity *might both be true*, so long as one does not buy into the atheistic shrink-wrap that evolutionary theory is so often wrapped in. In fact, there are many Christian scientists and theologians who accept the basics of Darwinian theory and believe the Bible. Francis Collins, the former director of the human genome project, and the late pope John Paul II are examples in our day; the evangelical Calvinist theologian B. B. Warfield is an example from around the turn of the century. I am not saying that simply adding the word "God" or "theistic" to a flawed scientific theory makes it a sound scientific theory. I am insisting that if Darwinism is not our primary challenge—and it is not, naturalism is—then surely theistic evolution is not our primary challenge and thus should not be our primary focus.

I am suggesting that we use *a fortiori* arguments at least some of the time. An *a fortiori* argument is an argument "from the stronger." For example, if I am too old to play in the Little League World Series, then *a fortiori* my father is also too old. The late Mortimer Adler gave us a useful example of how to argue *a fortiori* in his book *How to Think About God*.[14] In this book, he argued for the necessity of God as the first cause of *an eternal universe*. If God is necessary for an eternal universe to exist, then certainly He is necessary for a noneternal universe to exist. Why not then argue that if Christianity is not unreasonable, even if Darwin's theory of biological development is true, then it is certainly reasonable if Darwinism is false. This is no cop out; it is sound logic coupled with good rhetoric. I am simply suggesting that we be as wise as serpents and as gentle as doves.

There is one more issue to cover. Is methodological naturalism *always* the appropriate stance for a scientist to take? I suspect that the answer is yes—and no. What do I mean? I mean that we dare not forget that the scientific enterprise involves abduction, deduction, and induction. The deductive (logical) step and the inductive (observational) step must proceed in public, and thus one must not appeal to special or private knowledge such as divine revelation, even if one believes that such a claim is just that; appeal should be made to knowledge rather than mere belief. But the abductive (creative) step demands that we bring all our beliefs about reality to bear on the question, even those beliefs that are nonscientific—yes, even those that are religious in nature. It is never a good epistemic idea to attempt to answer a question with less truth rather than more. One is never wise to behave as though he were ignorant when in fact he believes himself to be knowledgeable. And though the Bible is not a science textbook, it is a book that purports to tell us numerous things about the material world and the nature of the God who created it. The Bible even indicates that there is a connection between God's nature and what can be observed in nature.[15] To ignore these truth claims is not wise. So, if Christianity is true, then at the abductive moment, the theistic scientist finds himself in a superior position to that of the nontheist, and the Christian in a superior position to that of the mere theist.

The Christian scientist thus need not and should not operate like a non-Christian, and particularly not like a naturalist. Contrary to Christian faith being an enemy of science, it is in fact an aid to scientific understanding. This is still our Father's world and all truth is His truth. Thus, believers should embrace science and seek to think God's thoughts after Him as they study His creation and thereby love Him with their minds as well as their hearts.

Notes

1. See M. Ruse, *Can a Darwinian Be a Christian? The Relationship Between Science and Religion* (Cambridge and New York: Cambridge University Press, 2001), especially 217–19; and id., *The Evolution-Creation Struggle* (Cambridge, MA: Harvard University Press, 2005), 190–213.

2. M. Hewlett, "The Evolution Wars: Who Is Fighting with Whom about What?" in *Intelligent Design: William A. Dembski and Michael Ruse in Dialogue*, ed. R. B. Stewart (Minneapolis: Fortress, 2007), 45.

3. The position that holds that science is the only source of true understanding of the physical world is often referred to as "scientism" or "scientific reductionism." A weaker form of scientism would admit that there are other ways to understand the physical world but still insist that science is the best way to do so.

4. Philosophers tend to distinguish between "realist" theories of science and "antirealist" theories of science. I am presenting a critical-realist position with reference to the nature of science. A critical realist affirms that there is actual truth to be known (thus realism), but he necessarily insists that one's conclusions be open to revision upon further hypothesis testing, which must take place (thus critical). Therefore, when evidence counter to an explanatory theory is produced, it cannot be ignored. At such time, one must determine whether a particular explanatory theory fails or if it merely needs to be adjusted at some point(s) and/or more finely tuned. Particularly related to the science and religion question is N. H. Gregersen and J. W. van Huyssteen, *Rethinking Theology and Science: Six Models for the Current Dialogue* (Grand Rapids: Eerdmans, 1998). For more on critical realism, see R. Bhaskar, *A Realist Theory of Science*, 2nd ed. (London: Verso, 1997); id., *Reclaiming Reality* (London: Verso, 1989); id., *Scientific Realism and Human Emancipation* (London: Verso, 1986); A. Collier, *Critical Realism: An Introduction to Roy Bhaskar's Thought* (London: Verso, 1994); P. Manicas, *A History and Philosophy of the Social Sciences* (Oxford: Blackwell, 1987). Cf. A. Collier, "Critical Realism," in *Routledge Encyclopedia of Philosophy*, vol. 2., ed. E. Craig (London: Routledge, 1998); C. F. Delaney, "Critical Realism," in *The Cambridge Dictionary of Philosophy*, ed. Robert Audi (Cambridge: University Press, 1995); id., "New Realism," in *The Cambridge Dictionary of Philosophy*. For a useful introductory discussion of critical realism especially related to history but also with some importance for science per se, see N. T. Wright, *The New Testament and the People of God*, vol. 1, *Christian Origins and the Question of God* (Minneapolis: Fortress, 1992), 32–37. For useful introductory discussions of scientific realism versus scientific antirealism, see J. P. Moreland and

W. L. Craig, *Philosophical Foundations for a Christian Worldview* (Downers Grove: InterVarsity, 2003), 307–45; and S. B. Cowan and J. S. Spiegel, *The Love of Wisdom: A Christian Introduction to Philosophy* (Nashville: B&H Academic, 2009), 101–41.

5. A. Petersen, "The Philosophy of Niels Bohr," in *Niels Bohr, A Centenary Volume*, ed. A. P. French and P. I. Kennedy (Cambridge, MA: Harvard University Press, 1985), 299.

6. Hewlett, "The Evolution Wars: Who Is Fighting with Whom about What?" 46.

7. C. S. Peirce famously presented this schema in "The Fixation of Belief," *Popular Science Monthly* 12 (November 1877): 1–15.

8. K. R. Popper, "Science: Conjectures and Refutations," in *Conjectures and Refutations: The Growth of Scientific Knowledge* (New York: Basic, 1962), 43–65, esp. 46–48.

9. The view that I am advocating is in part consistent with the one that T. S. Kuhn presented in his influential *The Structure of Scientific Revolutions*, 3rd ed. (Chicago and London: University of Chicago Press, 1996).

10. Kuhn insists that there is no commensurability between scientific paradigms, and that ultimately scientific paradigms are preferred for non-rational reasons. See T. S. Kuhn, "Objectivity, Value Judgment, and Theory Choice," in *The Essential Tension: Selected Studies in Scientific Tradition and Change* (Chicago: University of Chicago Press, 1977), 320–39. As a scientific realist (albeit a critical realist), I disagree with him concerning the incommensurability of scientific paradigms. Further, though I agree that assessing the strengths of a paradigm is a somewhat subjective process, I do not think that subjectivity is *necessarily* determinative as to which theories are to be preferred over others.

11. I mention entertainment because Hollywood is the Mecca for storytellers in today's world, and stories shape our worldviews. Science and entertainment together speak to the total person—the right-brain and the left-brain, so to speak, the analytical and the artistic.

12. The same goes, of course, for the film industry, but this is an essay on science, not entertainment, though both desperately need Christian involvement and ultimately they both need to be redeemed.

13. Hewlett, "The Evolution Wars: Who Is Fighting with Whom about What?" 51.

14. M. J. Adler, *How to Think About God: A Guide for the 20th-Century Pagan* (New York: MacMillan, 1980).

15. Ps 19:1; Rom 1:18–20.

Christianity and Culture

Chapter 13

Art: Classical and Popular

L. Russ Bush

U sed bookstores are marvelous locations to find treasures. After an afternoon movie, my wife and I walked over to Mr. Mike's Used Books to look around, and there in prefect unused condition was William D. Romanowski's *Pop Culture Wars: Religion and the Role of Entertainment in American Life* (Downers Grove: InterVarsity, 1996). I had been looking for this for years. Someone "relocated" their copy to the store seemingly without ever having opened it for any serious study. I hope that someone was not one of my students.

Then on the same shelf sat Jane Dillenberger's *Style and Content in Christian Art* (New York: Dillenberger, 1965; New York: Crossroad Publishing, 1986). It was also unopened, like new. This was another long-sought-after title that had been recommended to me in the late 1960s by John Newport, my professor of philosophy and culture at Southwestern Seminary in Fort Worth. Unbelievable finds priced at $3.99 each. Mr. Mike, you better watch out; I am on my way back. For less than my movie ticket, I found two significant works. It would be a little off target to write typical reviews of these out-of-print titles, but most of my readership are book hounds, and we all know about libraries. So a few comments might be in order.

Dillenberger claimed that she would revise a few sections if she were to do a third edition. Maybe so, but the content is already so rich and intellectually rewarding that I doubt we are missing much. There are 10 chapters that range from a very helpful introduction to how to look at great religious art with insight and comprehension. Chapter 3 finds the roots of Christian art (the only art style that really mattered) in the Byzantine period. There are 80 photographs of the works she discusses throughout the book. Her writing style is clear and helpful at every point.

Chapter 4 opened my mind's eye to the medieval period (Romanesque and Gothic). Chapters 5 and 6 move to Giotto, Fra Angelico, da Vinci, and Michelangelo (examples from the Renaissance in Italy). Jan Van Eyck, Grünewald, Dürer, and Buegel illustrate Northern European art, while Tintorette, El Greco (one of my favorite painters), and Bernini take us into the world of Baroque art. A full chapter (and deservedly so) focuses on Rembrandt, a true genius. Finally, Nolde, Rouault, Manessier's "Crown of Thorns," and Henri Matisse's *The Chapel of the Rosary at Venice* round out the volume.

A valuable feature that I had simply overlooked over the years (I am ashamed to say) is the "up-to-date" bibliography listings with annotations coming from 45 years ago. "Out of sight—out of mind" is a truism. But the author has left us with a historical resource unmatched for doctoral research projects in our day that seek theologically sensitive sources on Christian art (1500–2000).

No other religious tradition has so rich a cultural treasure trove as does Christianity. To be reintroduced or (I am afraid in most cases in America at least) to be introduced for the first time to Rouault or Rembrandt is an exciting experience for sensitive believers who know how to appreciate the power of fine art.

I admit, I was like a child intellectually when Newport began making his efforts with me. I still feel very much a novice. Four museums have impacted my cultural growth more than any others. The Louvre is one, of course, but my time there was very limited. I recently purchased a Teaching Company series on the Louvre, and Cindy and I have enjoyed it very much. We saw most of the items used in the video series. Second on my list would be New York's Metropolitan Museum of Art. Third, the truly marvelous collection at the Smithsonian's National Gallery. And finally, I so much love the Philadelphia Museum of Art. (I could go on to Chicago, Toronto, London, and Fort Worth's Kimball. There is a lot of great art out there.)

But here is the interesting thing. When I opened Romanowski's volume, it began in 1977 when the 72 front steps of the Philadelphia Museum began to be crowded with imitators of *Rocky*, a blockbuster movie starring Sylvester Stalone as a comeback boxer, a hero for the common man. The film made Stalone millions of dollars, so he commissioned an artist to produce a sculpture of "Rocky." He had it put at the top of the steps leading into the museum to celebrate the 1982 sequel. He intended then to donate it as a gift to the city. It would take several pages to describe the reactions of the people (generally positive) and the museum and city officials (generally negative). The classic culture war broke out. Keep it right there at the famous museum entrance! Move it to the city's sports arena! Send it back to Hollywood! Plus there were a few other locations suggested!

This conflict between popular culture and classical styles

is often a conflict between the ordinary folks and the educated elite. It is a conflict between those who focus their entertainment on sports, TV, movies, and popular music versus those who attend theatrical plays, opera, concerts, and similar events. This description is not really very good. It is a very prejudicial way of looking at cultural differences, so throw those characterizations away. There are always counter-examples. But clearly there is a difference somewhere between Romanowski's pop culture and Dillenberger's classical interests.

Perhaps a good way to think about this is to characterize pop culture as entertainment, something done or viewed for fun, something that is not taken too seriously. Movies come and go. The advent of the DVD has enabled some longevity, but not many pop culture items survive for long. Classical art, however, is hung on a wall in the groupings set by the museum staff of art critics and historians. Classical art is assumed to be an item of significant quality that will remain in the museum perhaps for hundreds of years. Nothing in pop culture is likely to remain after a few decades. The quality is simply not there. Pop culture is quickly dated.

Many of us love both classical art and popular art. Harry Potter is a legendary story in modern film and literature. But it is Rembrandt's depiction of himself raising Jesus on the cross that explains the numerous references to Christmas (and even one to Easter holidays) at Hogwarts in the Potter story about the Deathly Hallows. (Actually, of course, it is the New Testament, not Rembrandt, that influences the boarding school known as Hogwarts; British popular culture has Christian roots even in the school for witchcraft and wizardry.)

How can classical and popular culture co-exist? First, we have to open our minds a little bit. Why can't I like both the monster movies and *Driving Miss Daisy*? Why can't I like comedy and action stories?

Popular culture has always been a means of passing along cultural information that tends to unify ordinary folks. Vaudeville began in the gutter, but it was not long until it transformed itself into inoffensive family entertainment. This led to family-friendly TV sitcoms. The lack of bad language and other offensive behaviors in modern movies and TV remains due to the rating system, but the fact that we now have literally hundreds of cable channels and multiplex movie theaters virtually guarantees that we will have a choice for our entertainment preferences. I believe the sinfulness of man will always assure that we will have few clean and moral choices, but we will have some. Christians need to support that which is good, or at least that which is reasonable. We will never get a TV show or a movie that we could all support, but we must not move into and live in cultural isolation. Because of sin, there is an uncanny backdrop to almost everything. But I do not believe that Jesus never laughed or that He never enjoyed aspects of popular culture or that He could not appreciate tradition or classical human cultures. That is not central to the gospel, of course, so the New Testament says little about this aspect of Jesus' life, but I can easily imagine hearing the apostles laughing.

Worldliness and worldly amusements should be avoided. Elitist snobbery about art is of no value and may actually be sinful. Human beings are in God's image, and they can and do produce much beauty, but we also can turn our thoughts to ugliness.

The Bush Center for Faith and Culture hopes to promote the good, seeks to support understanding between conflicting cultural norms, and seeks to lead people to submit all things to the mind of Christ as we seek to share Christian culture and Christian truth with the world and with the diversity we find within the church.

Chapter 14

The Virtue of Friendliness

Mark Coppenger

Several years ago, as I was about to enter my local bank in Wilmette, Illinois, I saw an older woman coming out. I moved to the side, held open the door, and smiled, only to have her walk past without so much as a glance or a perfunctory thank you. I wanted to follow her and ask, "Did you mistake me for a menace? Have you just gotten word that a loved one was stricken with cancer? Are you a feminist who finds men's courtesies patronizing? Did your parents tell you never to speak to strangers?"

And then there are those young people in the neighboring Chicago suburb of Rogers Park who meet us walking three abreast, the ones who run my wife and me off the sidewalk even though we have shifted to single file. They see us, but they show no interest in accommodating us. What is this? I have begun to wonder whether the problem is my own cultural captivity—my nostalgia for a small-town 1950s childhood where neighbors were solicitous and strangers were greeted with at least an amiable hello.

Of course, compared to the virtues of courage, reverence, honesty, and loyalty, the practice of amiability seems lightweight, more a matter of style than morality. But I submit that friendliness, affability, and warmth are praiseworthy as well as pleasing, and that a prevailing aloofness and coldness is even reprehensible and alien to the regenerate soul. Friendliness is not just a Boy Scout ideal;[1] it is a Christian virtue. In considering friendliness, this brief essay is only a sketch. Still, I hope it will suggest and commend more work on this topic, one which is typically marginalized in the realm of Christian ethics and apologetics. I discuss what friendliness is and what it is not; where it is valued and where it is ignored or shunned; how it is abused and how it is splendidly applied; where it connects with Scripture and where it disconnects from the world.

A *Via Negativa* to Understanding True Friendliness

One classic way to get clearer on a concept is to say what it is not. Plato used it in the *Republic* when he considered and discarded the notion that "might makes right." The medieval philosopher Moses Maimonides used it to describe God as nonfinite, nonignorant, and so on. Analogously, the Renaissance sculptor Michelangelo spoke of a figure, such as David, encased in the stone; his task, then, was merely to chip away whatever was not David. So, in sorting out friendliness, let us begin with a negative path, noting the corresponding positives along the way.

Not the Same as Friendship

Friendliness can manifest itself in a moment—in a wave to the person who lets you merge into a single lane or in kind eye contact when two strangers pass. Friendship takes longer than this, and unlike friendliness, it has a critical element, for as Prov 27:6 teaches, "The wounds of a friend are trustworthy" (HCSB).

Not Mere Courtesy, Etiquette, or Politeness

Every society has its social code, its standards of courtesy. There is even an academic *Journal of Politeness Research*, a publication that studies protocols and sensitivities. For example, one article traces the gradations of verbal gentility from "Will you stand over there?" to "I wonder if you'd mind standing over there for a second?"[2] This sort of shading occurs in every language, and friendly people typically honor these nuances.

The same goes for rules of the road, including bicycle and pedestrian paths. For instance, if you are overtaking someone from behind, you need to announce your presence and intentions, as with "Onyerleft."[3] Of course, friendly people are sensitive to such protocols, but propriety does not guarantee warmth.

Not Tribal

When I asked a representative of the Muslim student group at Northwestern University whether Islam addressed the matter of friendliness, she pointed me to one of Mohammed's sayings: "To meet your brother with a smiling face . . . [is] *sadaqah* [voluntary charity]."[4] But the emphasis is familial and tribal: "One's children, family, and relatives have precedence over others." And continuing, "When one of you is poor, he starts with himself. If anything is left, he spends it on his dependents. If anything is (still left) then on his relatives, and then, if more is left, he spends it here and there."[5]

Of course, one can smile at strangers without expense, but this Islamic counsel lacks the generosity of spirit that friendliness embraces. Better to pick up on the insight of Presbyterian seminary president Donald McCullough. An avid sailor, he sometimes takes his students out on San Francisco Bay, only to see them violate an unwritten code of the water, namely, *never* wave at motor boaters. He and his fellow sailors reason, "If you want to go fast, get in a car; if you want to smell exhaust, stand behind a bus. But if you want to enjoy the beauty of God's creation . . ." But one day he caught himself in this partisan conceit, concluding that the world needs more "people who wave to everyone; they are prodigal in cordiality, spendthrifts of good will."[6]

Not Commercial

Southwest Airlines proudly proclaims, "Our employees are famous for their warm hearts and giving nature."[7] This so-called friendliness is good business, since surveys show that "bad manners or lousy attitudes" have led most Americans to take their business elsewhere, even when the prices were higher and access more inconvenient.[8] We gravitate toward companies like the bank that pledged, "[A]ll telephone calls will be answered within ten seconds" and "customers will be serviced within five minutes."[9]

This works at the personal level too. Those who have a high EQ (Emotional Quotient as distinct from IQ, Intelligence Quotient), the ones adept at cordiality, can expect higher annual salaries,[10] though, of course, native social savvy does not ensure true friendliness.

Not Just Native Sociability

From ancient times, scholars such as Aristotle have recognized that men are inclined to congregate, even more so "than bees or any other gregarious animals."[11] Xenophon pictured Socrates saying much the same thing: "[M]en need one another, feel pity, work together for their common good, and, conscious of the facts, are grateful to one another." And despite inevitable conflicts, "friendship slips, and unites the gentle natures."[12] Be that as it may, the social tendencies do not ensure amiability, for cooperation may well be perfunctory.

The Christian Angle

To call friendliness a Christian virtue is not to insist that it is a uniquely Christian virtue or even distinctively Judeo-Christian. Like temperance, fortitude, prudence, and justice, it is found in the thought and life of admirable people in every age and region. To say it is a Christian virtue is to disassociate it from anti-Christian "virtues" (such as Nietzsche's intimidating guile in *The Genealogy of Morals*), to insist that Christians should not consider it trivial or optional, and to point out the resources of text and Spirit that are available to believers for its practice.

A Spiritual Matter

In his book on civility, Stephen Carter said that true warmth is more than a social lubricant. It has a strong spiritual component. He told the story of his family's move into a "lily-white enclave" in Washington, DC, in 1966. Since they were black, the reception was chilly, but then, "all at once, a white woman arriving home from work at the house across the street from ours turned and smiled with obvious delight and waved and called out, 'Welcome!' in a booming, confident voice I would come to love." That same day, she brought them sandwiches and made them feel welcome.[13]

Reflecting on the woman's socially risky generosity, Carter observed that "nothing in contemporary secular conversation calls us to give up anything truly valuable for anybody else. . . . Only religion offers a sacred language of sacrifice—selflessness—awe that enables believers to treat their fellow citizens as . . . fellow passengers." He called this sort of "civility" a "moral duty,"[14] a conviction that resonates with the witness of Scripture.

The Fall

Painfully aware of the fall, a true Christian finds it difficult to be "high and mighty." He understands that only God is properly magisterial and that he, a sinful creature, is not. So, in realistic humility, he meets others on another footing and with a different demeanor. Certainly, there are occasions for human reserve and even coldness, whether in solemn ceremony, the theater of diplomacy, or the discipline of child-rearing. But the person who styles himself imperial slips easily into the imperious, which ill suits the Christian walk. Better to lead with a friendliness that announces, "I'm not so special."

The Golden Rule

The Bible resonates with this assessment, for it teaches friendliness in a variety of ways. Certainly, the Golden Rule prescribes a measure of friendliness: "Just as you want others to do for you, do the same for them" (Luke 6:31 HCSB). In this connection, I think of a chilling experience my wife and I had in Coventry, England, back in the mid-1970s. After visiting the cathedral and checking in to our hotel, we walked next door to a little restaurant. We found ourselves among middle-aged and elderly Brits who scowled when we entered and looked askance at us repeatedly. We were not at all sure what bothered them about our touristy intrusion, but we resolved never to make others feel as we did at that moment.

On the other hand, I remember the account of my roommate at Fort Benning, an officer who had served on a missile site in New Zealand. One day, he left his overseas post on foot for a two-week vacation. Though he started out with only $35 in his pocket, he returned with a new suit and money to spare without working a single day. The New Zealanders were incredibly kind and welcoming. As they spied him walking down the road, they offered him a ride, invited him to dinner, searched out things they might give him, and sent him on his way with cash. Surely a Christian would prefer to emulate this sort of Golden Rule treatment.

Risk Taking

Then there is the matter of fear. It is one of the great causes of social coldness. Of course, we are reluctant to make ourselves vulnerable, but Scripture does not indulge cowardice. Rather, it teaches that "the one who fears is not made perfect in love" (1 John 4:18 NIV). Still, there are some very scary people out there, particularly in the "urban jungle."

Chicago's Joseph Epstein has captured the problem beautifully—and horrifyingly—in a short story about a Jewish stockbroker named Siegel who befriended a "homeless" man selling papers on a Loop sidewalk. In charity, Siegel progressed from buying a paper, to helping gather copies blown away in the wind, to sharing his own reading material, to taking the indigent to lunch, to giving him a cash gift at New Year's, to paying for emergency dental work. But things went badly as this man, a Canadian Muslim, sank into menacing delusion. Eventually, he found Siegel's house and tried to break in at 2:00 in the morning. As the police hauled him away, he screamed obscenities toward "cops" and Jews.[15]

It is a perfectly recognizable city story. I think of my own experience as a "stalkee," after experiencing an unfortunate encounter with a stranger on the L platform. I am not a woman, for whom fear of urban danger is even more understandable. And I live in a relatively tame neighborhood, unlike the gang-ridden districts where students learn tough survival techniques: "Avoid direct eye contact. Walk fast, but not too fast; you don't want anyone to think you are scared. Keep one hand free, so you can swing back if someone hits you. Above all keep your mean mug on."[16] Friendliness, then, can be courageous. Yes, there is room for prudence, but when fear trumps your amiability, you have gone sub-Christian.

Fruit of the Spirit

Furthermore, "the fruit of the Spirit" (Gal 5:22–23) legislates against churlishness, indifference, and peevishness. Rather, we are to manifest love, joy, peace, and so on; all of those suggest a certain readiness to meet the other person in an unmistakably upbeat, conciliatory, helpful, and positive frame of mind.

In Gal 5:22 the Greek word for "kindness" (*chrestotes*) could be used in the secular Greek of the day to mean "friendliness."[17] Of course, the other fruit also promote warmth toward others: In *love*, we try to lift downcast spirits. Our *joy* makes us smile. *Peace* erases a frown. In *patience*, we persist in cheerful encouragement. In *goodness*, we speak beneficently. In *faith*, we take risks for the sake of our neighbor's morale. In *self-control*, we "police" our faces, ensuring that our expressions are edifying, not depressing. (Of course, there are a time and place for solemnity or grief in one's visage, but the one who typically subjects the world to the facial reflection of his boredom or gloom is acting irresponsibly.) And, as Phil 4:5 teaches us, our disarming "graciousness" should "be known to everyone" (HCSB).

In contrast, the "works of the flesh" (Gal 5:19–21) generate coldness and even menace. No one wants to abide with those given to hatreds, jealousy, selfish ambitions, drunkenness, and the like.

Beyond this, there are many passages where biblical characters model and anointed spokesmen teach cheerfulness, hospitality, and mercy. For instance, the gentle speech taught in Prov 15:1 and the holy kiss prescribed in Rom 16:16 reflect this spirit. Indeed, Paul's many greetings and commendations in Romans 16 are redolent with the infectious delight and encouragement of friendliness.

Contrasting Spiritual Deadness

This Christian manner stands in stark contrast to the insolence, haughtiness, and coldness so common in the world. At one extreme is the strikingly unregenerate Goth look, with its blank stares and scowls and its roster of bands with names like Perfidious Words, Mothburner, and Die My Darling.[18] But you need not seek out eccentrics to find a culture of unfriendliness. Pouting and brooding fashion models in upscale magazines will do quite nicely. For instance, in a recent issue of *Gentleman's Quarterly*, we find that Channing Tatum is the "next big thing." Whether appearing shirtless in his Dior Homme jeans, or sporting his Burberry Prorsum trench coat, Versace jacket, or Dolce & Gabbana suit, he radiates indifference and even animosity.[19] One can hardly imagine his being saved, that this man is a Christian unless, perhaps, he is mulling over theological slippage in the mainline churches or the decline of respect for the Nicene Creed. (Despite appearances, perhaps he is a Spirit-filled Christian forced to look this way to collect a paycheck from the ad agency; if so, he ought to look for other work.)

Then there is surliness in the corporate world. In his book on power, long-time Simon and Schuster editor Michael Korda detailed, and essentially recommended, a variety of techniques for getting ahead or staying secure through intimidation. He noted with admiration the manager who called a meeting in his office, while making sure there were not enough chairs. This obliges "people either to go and carry their own down the hall or to sit on the floor [and] establishes one's power by making people uncomfortable."[20]

In short, believers who consider the offerings of the Goth culture, survey the cold faces common to fashion spreads, and trace Michael Korda's Machiavellian counsel may well recall the Eph 2:1 expression, "dead in your trespasses and sins" (HCSB).

Caveats

Those convinced that friendliness is a Christian norm must still hear words of counsel, for this virtue can be misapplied in practice.

Too Much or Too Soon

In fleeing the cold, we need to be careful not to overdo warmth. When we exercise the fruit of the Spirit, we need to have a sense of balance. Thus, the Bible cautions, "If one blesses his neighbor with a loud voice early in the morning, it will be counted as a curse to him" (Prov 27:14 HCSB). Too much vocal cheerfulness at that hour can be irritating.

Of course, there can be excess at any hour. The satirical newspaper, *The Onion*, picked up on this in a mock news story on Despondex, "the first FDA approved depressant for those who are insufferably cheery." Symptoms include "talking to people in line at the grocery store" and "organizing neighborhood potlucks." The story features the case of a woman who, before treatment, "was always smiling."[21] Yes, this is snide, but there is something there.

Privacy Concerns

Stephen Carter counseled, "We owe to every stranger the chance to remain a stranger, whether the stranger is a seatmate on an airplane who is more interested in that book in her lap than in conversation, or a coworker who has no desire to share with us the slightest details of his love life. So civility requires respect for the privacy of others."[22]

Judith Martin (aka "Miss Manners") made a similar point when she cited instances of "inappropriate friendliness," such as when a teller or checkout clerk holds up a line of customers with irrelevant chatter or when a room service waiter peppers the single woman guest with compliments and personal inquiries.[23] The former case is thoughtless and irritating, the latter unseemly.

A Threat to the Prophetic Task

A reputation for amiability can be seductive. While it is gratifying, and even evangelistically helpful, to be liked by the lost, we need to be cautious lest we abandon the confrontational and even censorious tradition of Elijah, Amos, and John the Baptist—cautious also that we do not despise those who maintain that tradition.

Of course, a loss of prophetic edge is understandable, for there is tremendous pressure from the world to mitigate one's righteous judgment. Consider, for instance, a scene in Bill Maher's contemptible movie *Religulous*, the segment in which he challenges the faith of the congregants in a truck stop chapel. One trucker soon has his fill and storms out. The others do their best to respond to Maher's questions and then freely admit they lack some of the answers. Finally, they pray for their guest, who has patronized them by saying he is fortunate his life has been so comfortable that, unlike them, he has had no need for a religious crutch. As they conclude, Maher praises them for being "Christlike" as well as "Christian."[24]

This is pleasant enough, but the church must not let enemies of the gospel like Maher define "Christlike" in strictly gentle terms. Indeed, allowed to take control of the dictionary, they would hasten, for starters, to label Romans 1 "homophobic" and Ephesians 5 "chauvinistic."

A Cover for Evil

A 1956 booklet sought indulgence for apartheid by praising the natural amiability of South Africans.[25] The writer tried to play on his readers' regard for friendliness, and their conviction that they exemplified it, to disarm their concerns over the impact of apartheid. But the apostle Paul warns of such seductive flattery. Though the Greek word *chrestotes* shows up as a fruit of the Spirit in Gal 5:22, a cognate term (*chrestologia*) appears in less favorable light in Rom 16:18. It literally means "kind speech," but in Rom 16:18 it is used to warn against "*smooth talk* and flattering words" that "deceive the hearts of the unsuspecting."[26]

Even the cruelest people can use graciousness to accomplish their ends. Corrie Ten Boom told of a Nazi camp interrogator named Lieutenant Rahms who offered her a chair, filled the pot-bellied stove with coal, and spoke with her about Dutch flowers. But then she realized, "All the friendliness, the kindly concern that I had half-believed in—all a device to elicit information."[27]

Regional Considerations

Populations are fluid and diverse, but generalities persist and are perennial subjects of conversation among tourists, comedians, journalists, and missiologists. The topic of friendliness surfaces frequently in these discussions.

The Southeastern United States

If true friendliness is a Christian hallmark, it should be the case that where Christians are concentrated, friendliness abounds. And this could bring honor to the faith. Ben Stein's columns in *American Spectator* point in this direction, for as he spoke at Christian colleges throughout the South, he praised their cordiality to the heavens. After visiting Liberty University in Lynchburg, Virginia, he observed, "For reasons I do not know, the Southeastern USA has the most polite and friendly people on this planet."[28] Then, of the University of the Cumberlands in Williamsburg, Kentucky, he wrote, "These people are the salt of the earth."[29] And when an official at Harding College in Searcy, Arkansas, wished Stein a safe trip home, he responded, "I am home."[30]

Other regions do not fare so well. Stein spoke of a "mean Brooklyn-Tehran fearfulness,"[31] and he noted that in Beverly Hills "no one even says 'hello' when you walk past."[32] Where he did find "super friendly" people in his Malibu circles, he figured they were "mostly Midwestern folks."[33] Still, for Stein, the South wins, for they are "amazingly polite people, the exact opposite of what you see in some other regions"; one should "Look Away, Look Away, Dixie Land."[34] As for the Midwesterners, native Minnesotan Garrison Keillor described them as "insular, industrious, abstemious, introspective people skittish about body contact."[35]

At this point, it is fair to mention three maps. The first reflects the Southern Baptist Convention's 2000 Evangelism Index, which shows that the greatest estimated concentration of lost people in the US is in the northeast and west.[36] The second comes from the Rand Corporation and shows America's highest percentage of evangelicals to be in the Southeast.[37] The third is published by the Roman Catholic Glenmary Home Missioners, which reveals that Southern Baptists are the leading group in this region.[38] This cannot be an accident. Given that "conversion" is a hallmark of evangelicalism,[39] it would be surprising to find a prevailing culture of peevishness and aloofness where the born-again people are concentrated.

A Friendly Confederacy?

One might object that the southeast United States honored for its evangelical friendliness was the home of the Confederacy during the Civil War. How could slaveholders be the models of friendliness?

For one thing, the center of mass for evangelicalism was farther to the north in the nineteenth century. The major theaters of the Second Great Awakening were New England (with Dwight, Beecher, Taylor, and Nettleton), New York (with Finney), and Kentucky (with Cane Ridge).[40] None of these states was in the Confederacy. As for cities, the prayer revival of 1857–58 in New York and the work of Dwight Moody in Chicago were singular, and, again, in the north.[41]

Still, the Lord had worked mightily in the south, such as through the revival-oriented Sandy Creek Baptists, who organized in North Carolina in the eighteenth century.[42] Many slaveholders claimed to be Christian. What shall we say about them? Then (as now) there were certainly many false professors. But among those who did own slaves, some were relatively amiable and thoughtful, and even saved. After all, the apostle Paul called the slave owner Philemon a "dear friend and co-worker," even while urging him to alter his relationship with his slave Onesimus.

James Petigru Boyce, the first president of The Southern Baptist Theological Seminary, provided an interesting example.

He owned a female maid, which had been a gift of his grandfather through his mother. When this "handsome mulatto about twenty years of age" fell in love with another slave, a skilled artisan owned by another man, Boyce paid a high price to acquire him so that the two could be together. At war's end, Boyce gave him an expensive box of tools, and their parting was amiable. When Boyce had occasion later to visit Memphis where the couple and their children lived, they invited him to dinner, and some years later she attended his funeral.[43]

Of course, Boyce's kindness did not excuse his slaveholding. Friendliness is not everything. But it is far from nothing. And to the extent he manifested charitable warmth, he showed forth the spirit that should mark every Christian and that does indeed emerge where believers gather.

Berlin and Hungary

In decidedly nonevangelical Germany, the city of Berlin is having image problems. In the spring of 2009 the city launched a friendliness campaign to help keep tourists coming her way during a time of economic downturn. Rene Gorka, who headed a group promoting the city, said, "Berlin has a reputation in Germany of being a rude city, but we're a rude city with a heart. . . . With the upcoming anniversary of the fall of the Wall and the World Championships in athletics, Berliners should be as friendly as they were in 2006 and not give any credence to our rude image."[44]

Hungarians also have a way to go. As one guidebook puts it, their formality "can be interpreted as aloofness, a desire to keep 'outsiders' (foreigners and other Hungarians) at a distance." We are assured, "This is not really the case; Hungarians simply need a while to make up their minds about people."[45] Unfortunately, few tourists are able to stay for the "while" that the Hungarians need to make up their minds.

Given Berlin's rudeness and Hungary's aloofness, it would be surprising to find these nations teeming with evangelicals, for they brighten things. In contrast, countries perfectly satisfied with a "national church membership" or wary of conversion are susceptible to coldness.

Density Instead of Regional Culture?

We should note, in passing, another explanation for "Southern hospitality," one suggested by *The American Spectator*'s Philip Klein. He believed that such friendliness is based on population density rather than religious orientation. When the cashier at a White Castle restaurant in Nashville cheerfully corrected a mistaken overcharge, even after Klein and his friend had driven away and returned to report the problem, he compared their behavior to that of New York, where "you're conditioned to expect that any consumer dispute will be a major hassle or a potential altercation." The result: "We were a pair of stunned Yankees." After some reflection, he concluded that "it was a matter of numbers. That is, the more people there are in a given area, the more likely it is that the people will come into conflict, and the less likely that they will treat each other with basic decency." This was his explanation both for the relative friendliness of Omaha and the selfish behavior of line-breakers in "some of China's congested cities."[46]

But how does this account for the difference between Danes and Swedes? Though the population density of Denmark is six times that of Sweden, the Swedes are reputed to be more "austere, formal, and affectively restrained."[47] And, as for Klein's examples, it is fair to ask whether the lostness of New York and Beijing compared to the stronger Christian presence in Nashville and Omaha might have something to do with the differences.

An Aristotelian Framework

I venture to propose that *wherever evangelical Christianity abounds, friendliness abounds*, but I need to be careful what I make of this. Using categories of Aristotelian logic, I briefly rehearse the implications of this claim. Very simply, the converse and inverse will not follow logically; the contrapositive will.

The Converse ("Friendly Peoples Are Evangelical") and the Inverse ("Nonevangelical Peoples Are Not Friendly")

There are simply too many apparent counter-examples for these two propositions to be sustained. For instance, on a list of do's and don'ts for visitors to predominantly Muslim Jakarta, we read, "Indonesians smile a lot. Smile back!"[48] So there are a lot of nonevangelicals who come off as friendly in Indonesia—and also, it appears, in Denmark: "[A]mong the Scandinavians, the Swedes see the Danes as smiling too much."[49] But how do we account for these perky Danes? Though they have a Lutheran state church, it appears quite dead; yet they remain relatively amiable. Perhaps this is simply a manifestation of a "cut flower civilization," wherein a culture retains some of the bloom from its Christian past. But whatever the reason, today they are both friendly and nonevangelical.

Then there are the Muslim Jordanians, who commonly greet strangers with *"Ahlan wa sahlan!"* meaning, "Be as one of the family and at your ease." The guidebook continues, "Arab traditions of hospitality and kindness are deeply ingrained in the psyches of most Jordanians, especially the Bedouin. Rooted in the harsh realities of life in the desert, these traditions have been virtually codified into all social behavior." Thus, one tourist reported, "After making it clear to a porter at the airport that we didn't want help, we were surprised when he shook our hands, told us his name, said, 'Welcome' and walked away!"[50]

The Contrapositive: "Nonfriendly Peoples Are Non-Christian" (India and Israel)

What then of the contrapositive? Well, the case of India serves it admirably. The nation is decidedly short of born-again believers (less than 2 percent), a situation reflected on a familiar color-coded map showing evangelical concentrations around the world.[51] Not only is it a non-Christian nation, but it is also a maddening and dangerous place to drive. Here, "an estimated 100,000 people die every year—one out of every ten road deaths in the world." In Delhi alone, "there are nearly 110 million traffic violations *per day*." The situation has been described as "anarchy on the roads,"[52] and the taxi driver's motto is "Good brakes, good horn, good luck."[53]

Then there is the study showing that American school children are more likely to return the smile of a stranger than are their counterparts in Israel. "American mothers smiled more than Israeli mothers, were more patient, were more expressive, and had a more positive ambience with their children than Israeli mothers."[54] Furthermore, research indicated that "in the United States smiling is normative and lack of compliance with the norm has social consequences," and that "in Israel teachers showed a slight tendency to identify nonsmilers as more socially competent than smilers."[55] It seems that Israelis think "they are authentic and genuine people who smile only when they really like the person and that Americans, with their empty smiles, are less genuine."[56]

As admirable as the Israelis may be on many counts, theirs is not a Christian nation, not even relatively so, as in the case of America. If it were, then one might well be surprised at the people's reluctance to return smiles.

But are we being fair to the Indians and the Israelis in suggesting that, were they Christians, they would be friendlier?

After all, Delhi's drivers have to cope with extremely crowded conditions, grinding poverty, and "forty-eight modes of transport, each struggling to occupy the same space on the carriageway"—from "green-and-yellow auto-rickshaws" to "slow-moving oxen-drawn carts" to "heaving buses,"[57] not to mention the cows resting comfortably in the middle of the street. And, as for the unsmiling Israelis, one might well note that "the small country of Israel is surrounded by less than friendly border countries which represent a constant threat, and these ever present strangers are not of the type to inspire or provoke smiling."[58]

Still, one cannot help but think that evangelicals forced into these situations would perform better. If Liberty, Cumberlands, and Harding students had endured a holocaust and were surrounded by hostiles, or if they were on the dangerous roads of India, it is reasonable to suppose that one still would see a better showing in terms of amiability and thoughtfulness. Being born again does that for people.

Conspicuous Christian Friendliness

Circumstances can weigh heavily on a citizen of this fallen world, and these burdens tend to discourage friendliness. But the vital Christian does not remain *under* the circumstances.

Christian Resiliency and Generosity

There are countless examples in the twentieth century alone: Corrie Ten Boom and her sister Betsie in the Nazi prison camps of Scheveningen, Vught, and Ravensbruck with their loving prayers for the man who betrayed them;[59] Eric Liddell in the Shantung Compound with his "spring of step" and "overflowing with good humor and love of life";[60] Gerardo, the "Brother of Faith," in Castro's hellish Isle of Pines prison, where he preached daily from a pulpit of salt-codfish boxes a message of love for their captors;[61]

and Rwandan pastor Yona Kanamuzeyi who prayed—just before being shot for helping Tutsi refugees—"help these soldiers who do not know what they are doing."[62]

True Christians are not just survivors. They are cheerful survivors—and even cheerful martyrs. For as James suggested in the opening words of his epistle (1:2–3), the redeemed are able to "consider it a great joy . . . whenever [they] experience various trials, knowing that the testing of [their] faith produces endurance"(HCSB). On the other hand, where a people are chronically insular or glum, it is hard to argue that they are genuinely saved.

The Counsel of Perfection

Jesus concluded the Sermon on the Mount with the command to be perfect, which includes the love of one's enemies. Love of friends is easy—even the tax collectors manage that—so the real perfection lies in returning love to the hateful (Matt 5:43–48).

By extension, we understand it is easy to be friendly to the friendly. But the serious Christian is one who answers churlishness, insolence, and callous indifference with astonishing friendliness. This more-than-reciprocal friendliness marks the path of sanctification.

Some men pride themselves on "not suffering fools gladly," and certainly there is a place for a no-nonsense approach in certain situations. But when one is overtaken by a spirit of brusque and sweeping contempt for those who "waste their time," "show little promise," or "don't have clue," then one misses the deeper wisdom of grace which manifests itself in durable friendliness. Indeed, there would be no church at all had God not suffered lost fools, showing them (us) the highest kindness at Calvary.

Notes

1. The Boy Scout Law requires that its members be "trustworthy, loyal, helpful, *friendly*, courteous, kind, obedient, cheerful, thrifty, brave, clean, and reverent." "Boy Scout Law," http://www.usscouts.org/ADVANCE/BOYSCOUT/BSLAW.ASP (accessed Oct. 19, 2009).

2. G. Leech, "Politeness: Is There an East-West Divide?" *Journal of Politeness Research* 3 (2007): 179.

3. M. Brown, "Word to Wise on Bike Trails: Onyerleft!" *Chicago Sun-Times*, July 28, 2009; http://www.highbeam.com/doc/1N1-129BC79BE91F86E0.html?key=01-421604517E1916606179 0516741B0E7E0A05737A77342050314949230A42333D5F71 18731A7B1D6B741700646D157926 (accessed Aug. 29, 2010).

4. S. Sabiq, "Types of Saddaq," *Fiq-us-Sunnah*, vol. 3, 99; http://www.jamaat.net/ebooks/Fus/fus3_48.html (accessed Oct. 12, 2009).

5. Ibid., 3:100.

6. D. McCullough, *Say Please, Say Thank You: The Respect We Owe One Another* (New York: Perigree, 1998), 261, 263.

7. "Doing the Right Thing: Southwest Lives by the Golden Rule," *Spirit* (July 2009): 136.

8. J. T. Ziegenfuss Jr., *Customer Friendly: The Organizational Architecture of Service* (New York: University Press of America, 2007), 119.

9. Ibid., 169.

10. T. Bradberry and J. Greaves, *Emotional Intelligence 2.0* (San Diego: TalentSmart, 2009), 21–22, 139, 193–94.

11. Aristotle, *Politics*, trans. B. Jowett, in *Great Books of the Western World* (Chicago: Encyclopaedia Britannica, 1952), 9:446.

12. Xenophon, "Memorabilia," *Memorabilia and Oeconomicus*, in *Xenophon in Seven Volumes*, vol. 4 (Cambridge: Harvard, 1923), 137. In other editions, see II.VI.21.

13. S. L. Carter, *Civility: Manners, Morals and the Etiquette of Democracy* (New York: Harper, 1998), 62.

14. Ibid., 74–75.

15. J. Epstein, "No Good Deed," *Commentary* (June 2006): 38–43.

16. K. Mack, "Violence Is Nothing a Teenager Should Ever Get Used To," *Chicago Tribune*, October 16, 2009; http://articles.chicagotribune.com/2009-10-16/news/0910151237_1_chicago-public-schools-students-gangs (accessed Aug. 29, 2010).

17. K. Weiss, "*chrestotes*," *Theological Dictionary of the New Testament: Abridged in One Volume*, ed. G. Kittel and G. Friedrich, trans. and ed. G. W. Bromiley (Grand Rapids: Eerdmans, 1985), 1321.

18. M. Mercer, *21st Century Goth* (London: Reynolds & Hearn, 2002).

19. L. DePaulo, "Channing Tatum Won the Lottery," photographs by Mario Testino, GQ (August 2009): 68–75.

20. M. Korda, *Power! How to Get It, How to Use It* (New York: Random House, 1975), 140.

21. B. Batista, "FDA Approves Depressant Drug for the Annoyingly Cheerful," Onion News Network, Feb. 11, 2009; http://www.theonion.com/content/video/fda_approves_depressant_drug_for (accessed July 6, 2009).

22. Carter, *Civility*, 72–73.

23. J. Martin, *Miss Manners' Guide for the Turn-of-the-Millennium* (New York: Pharos, 1989), 332, 384.

24. *Religulous*, DVD, directed by L. Charles (Thousand Words, 2008).

25. T. J. Haarhoff, *Why Not Be Friends? Natural Apartheid and Natural Friendliness in South Africa* (Parow, Cape Town: Cape Times, 1956), 2.

26. Weiss, *"chrestotes,"* 1322.

27. C. Ten Boom, *The Hiding Place* (New York: Bantam, 1974), 159.

28. B. J. Stein, "Liberty Weekend," *The American Spectator* (July-August 2009): 72.

29. B. J. Stein, "Not Cambridge," *The American Spectator* (June 2009): 64.

30. B. J. Stein, "From Coolidge to Harding," *The American Spectator* (April 2009): 64.

31. B. J. Stein, "Plugging Away," *The American Spectator* (September 2009): 65.

32. Ibid., 64.

33. Ibid., 65.

34. Stein, "Liberty Weekend," 72.

35. G. Keillor, "Take in the State Fair with Garrison Keillor," *National Geographic* (July 2009): 72.

36. *Evangelism Index 2000* (North American Mission Board, SBC).

37. C. Grammich, *Many Faiths of Many Regions*, Rand Corporation (December 2004): 7; http://www.rand.org/pubs/working_papers/2005/RAND_WR211.pdf (accessed Sept. 26, 2009).

38. "Largest Participating Religious Groups," Glenmary Research Center (2000); http://www.glenmary.org/grc/RCMS_2000/maps/Largest_Group.jpg (accessed Sept. 26, 2009).

39. D. A. Sweeney, *The American Evangelical Story: A History of the Movement* (Grand Rapids: Baker, 2005), 17–18.

40. Ibid., 66–73.

41. J. A. Carpenter, *Revive Us Again: The Reawakening of American Fundamentalism* (New York: Oxford University Press, 1997), 115.

42. B. J. Leonard, *Baptists in America* (New York: Columbia University Press, 2005), 17–18.

43. T. J. Nettles, *Stray Recollections, Short Articles and Public Orations of James P. Boyce* (Cape Coral, FL: Founders Press, 2009), 9.

44. F. Scheven, "Ich Bin ein Friendly Guy . . .," Reuters, March 10, 2009; http://www.reuters.com/article/oddlyEnoughNews/idUST RE5295RE20090310 (accessed June 11, 2009).

45. C. Turp, *Hungary* (London: Dorling Kindersley, 2007), 17.

46. P. Klein, "Density Is Destiny," *The American Spectator* (June 2009): 82.

47. T. Shapiro, "The Social Smile: Pride and Prejudice," in Y. E. Babad, I. E. Alexander, and E. Y. Babad, *Returning the Smile of the Stranger: Developmental Patters and Socialization Factors*, Monographs for the Society for Research in Child Development 48, no. 5 (Chicago: Chicago University Press, 1983), 72.

48. C. Draine and B. Hall, *Culture Shock, Indonesia: A Guide to Customs and Etiquette* (Portland: Graphics Arts, 1986), 268.

49. Shapiro, "The Social Smile: Pride and Prejudice," 72.

50. J. Walker and M. D. Firestone, *Jordan*, 7th ed. (Footscray, Victoria, Australia: Lonely Planet, 2009), 53.

51. "Evangelical Christianity," Missions Atlas Project, www .WorldMap.org (accessed Oct. 20, 2009).

52. T. Vanderbilt, *Traffic: Why We Drive the Way We Do (and What It Says About Us)* (New York: Knopf, 2008), 214.

53. Ibid., 213.

54. Babad et al., *Returning the Smile of the Stranger*, 54.

55. Ibid., 3.

56. Ibid., 6.

57. Vanderbilt, *Traffic*, 212.

58. S. Harter, "To Smile or Not to Smile: Issues in the Examination of Cross-Cultural Differences and Similarities," in *Returning the Smile of the Stranger*, 82–83.

59. C. Ten Boom, *The Hiding Place* (Grand Rapids: Baker, 1971 & 1984), 180.

60. L. Gilkey, *Shantung Compound: The Story of Men and Women Under Pressure* (New York: Harper & Row, 1966), 192.

61. A. Valladares, *Against All Hope: The Prison Memoirs of Armando Valladares*, trans. by A. Hurley (New York: Alfred A. Knopf, 1987), 201.

62. J. and M. Hefley, *By Their Blood: Christian Martyrs from the Twentieth Century and Beyond* (Grand Rapids: Baker, 2004), 280.

Chapter 15

Would the Elimination of Nuclear Weapons Make the World More Peaceful and Safe?

Richard Land

Ever since the first use of nuclear weapons in 1945 there have been those who, having witnessed the armament's previously unimaginable destructive power, have dreamed that someday mankind would find a way to eradicate such weaponry from the globe. Even committed Cold War warriors like former President Ronald Reagan and former Secretary of State George Shultz have expressed a desire for a nuclear-free world. In 2009 President Barack Obama committed his administration to putting the United States and the world on a "trajectory" toward "a world without nuclear weapons."[1]

One can immediately identify with the almost utopian ideal of such a vision. This is perhaps especially true for those like myself who are at the front end of the Baby Boomer generation (born 1946–64). Many of us experienced the so-called "duck and tuck" drills and wore metal, government-issued ID tags so authorities could identify our incinerated bodies after a nuclear conflagration. The desire to undo the nuclear magic, to put the destructive genie back in the bottle, to rewind the nuclear clock to a time when humanity did not possess the power to blow itself back into the Stone Age in a matter of hours is almost hypnotic in its appeal.

The recent upsurge in interest in eliminating nuclear weapons has been driven by the asymmetrical threat posed by radical Islamic jihadists for whom the threat of nuclear retaliation is not a sufficient deterrent to their use of nuclear bombs as terrorist weapons. However, the larger appeal of an envisioned world free of nuclear weapons is the assumption that such a world would be far more peaceful, with far less bloodshed and suffering. Would that indeed be the outcome?

Questions of Prudentiality

In any ethical debate, Christian or otherwise, at some point one must ask questions of prudentiality. Is this course of action prudent? Is it wise?

In this particular case, it is my purpose to take issue with those who would argue that the elimination of nuclear weapons would in actuality lead to a safer world. While there are many elements that can be used to determine what is prudent and biblically sound wisdom, given that the argument for nuclear disarmament is based largely on the projected consequence of a safer world, I must challenge the prudence of such an argument through an analysis on pragmatic and consequential grounds.

This is not to say that other elements necessary to demonstrate biblical prudence are unimportant or could not be applied to this issue. Rather, my goal is to show the lack of foresight, the inadequate representation of facts related to a policy of non-proliferation, and the overly optimistic view of human nature that too often underlie the arguments of those calling for a safer world through nuclear disarmament. In other words, my discussion pursues whether this course of action would in reality lead to the desired goal of a safer world.

Such questions involve far more than merely questions of practicality or pragmatism. Questions of prudentiality are not a retreat into utilitarianism. In utilitarianism, what works for the greatest good and for the greatest number is the ultimate arbiter of action. Questions of prudentiality operate in ethical systems that have other ultimate values than mere pragmatism. In such systems they serve as a check against utopianism, the polar opposite of utilitarianism, in which the questions of reality are never allowed to intrude on the vision of what ought to be or the way one wishes things to be.

Questions of prudentiality are necessitated in Christian ethical debate by recognition of certain painful realities in the present fallen world, such as the sinfulness of man and his world. Holy Scripture teaches us about the human condition: "The heart is deceitful above all things, and desperately wicked: who can know it?" (Jer 17:9 NKJV). Given the fallenness of man's nature and his consequent ability to deceive himself, we must always and forever raise questions of prudentiality.

Therefore, we are compelled to ask, would the elimination of nuclear weapons be possible in the world in which we actually live, as opposed to the world as we wish it were? If so, would such elimination lead to a more peaceful, safe world?

Perhaps the best place to begin is to ask, what did the world look like before the introduction of nuclear weapons in 1945? Before the advent of nuclear weapons, was warfare more or less common? Did human beings make war on each other only at intermittent and more civilized levels?

In fact, the first 45 years of the twentieth century produced unparalleled bloodshed among human beings in what are known to history as World War I (1914–18) and World War II (1939–45).[2] Nuclear weapons were used for the first time in human history by the United States when two were dropped on the Empire of Japan in August 1945. The use of these weapons brought the massive, unprecedented slaughter of World War II to an abrupt and accelerated end.

In reality, the illusory, dream-like vision of a return to a world free of nuclear weapons is a mirage, a myth, a chimera. *Webster's* defines a "mirage" as "something that falsely appears to be real" and a "chimera" as "an impossible or idle fancy."[3] A "myth" is defined as "a fiction or half truth, especially one that forms part of an ideology."[4] All these words aptly describe the dangerous delusion that a return to a pre-nuclear weapon world is feasible and would lead to a safer and more peaceful world.

The goal of returning to a world free of nuclear weapons is a well-intentioned notion, but one that is misguided. If such an illusory goal were ever even temporarily met, it would lead in a fairly short order to a world wracked by conventional armed conflicts with ever more lethal and sophisticated non-nuclear weaponry. This in turn would lead to the reintroduction of nuclear weapons into a dangerously unstable environment of armed conflict among belligerent nations, which would be far more likely to use those nuclear weapons against their enemies, especially if they were losing the conventional war. Thus, the actual *use* of *reintroduced* nuclear weapons would be *far more likely* than in the present status quo or in the foreseeable future.

False Presumption

The mirage advocating the abolition of nuclear weapons is based primarily on the false presumption that the ability to build nuclear weapons can be permanently unlearned.[5] Even if, after Herculean efforts among the world's nations, one could come up with a regime that could ensure the elimination of all existing nuclear arsenals, with the agreed upon diminution of national sovereignty that would be necessitated to ensure proper verification of such elimination, what then?

Could any treaty, agreement, or other mechanism erase from humanity's collective memory the knowledge and technology necessary to produce nuclear weapons? One cannot "un-invent" something. You cannot put toothpaste back into the tube once it has been squeezed out. In the Internet Age it is impossible to keep such knowledge from proliferating virally throughout the world.

Surely it must be acknowledged that the possibility that the world would ever actually achieve a system whereby nuclear arms would be *completely eliminated* is, at best, remote. In discussing this issue with a nuclear ban proponent, one hopeful individual said to me, "Well, we have eliminated slavery; we can eliminate this!" "Unfortunately," I replied, "according to the United Nations there are more people actually living in slavery in the world today than the number enslaved in the nineteenth century before the American Civil War emancipated the three million slaves in America."

Declaring something illegal and attempting to have the governments of the world enforce a ban on that activity does not mean that it ceases to exist in the dark corners of human society. Such is the fallen, sinful nature of man in a fallen, sinful world (see Rom 3:23; 8:22–23).

False Assumption

The mirage of the elimination of nuclear weapons is a seductive attraction based on the false assumption that a denuclearized world would be a less warlike and more peaceful world. It is reported that Mark Twain once presciently observed that while history does not always repeat itself, it often rhymes.[6] Based on the history of the first half of the twentieth century, one would have to conclude that a world without nuclear weapons would be a world in which nations would be far more likely to go to war with each other in ever more technically lethal, non-nuclear ways.

The Twentieth Century's Two Halves

Between 1900 and 1945, the nations of the world engaged in two catastrophic world wars. World War I was a terrible bloodletting, primarily, though not completely, confined to the nations of Europe, their colonies and dominions, and the United States. It is estimated that approximately 16.5 million human beings lost their lives in World War I (9.7 million military deaths; 6.8 million civilian deaths).[7] World War II was even more barbaric in the savagery of the conflict and the tremendous advances in the technology of the weaponry in the one-generation hiatus between the two wars. It is estimated that at least 50 million people lost their lives in the Second World War, with 27 million to 30 million of the deaths being designated as civilians.[8]

World War II ended with the Japanese surrender to the Allied Forces on August 14, 1945. Previously, the United States dropped an atomic bomb on Hiroshima, Japan, on August 6, 1945, followed by a second atomic bomb being dropped on Nagasaki, Japan, on August 9, 1945. The death toll from these two nuclear attacks was horrendous. At Hiroshima, it is estimated that between

70,000 and 100,000 people were killed by the initial blast and the five-year death total, including those from radiation-related illnesses, rose to between 130,000 and 200,000.[9] At Nagasaki, it is estimated that approximately 40,000 were killed by the initial blast and the five-year death toll rose to 140,000.[10]

It should be remembered, however, that the American Air Force had already killed far more Japanese civilians in conventional aerial bombardment of Japanese cities with concentrated incendiary bombing raids. It should also be remembered that the American military's estimates of causalities to invade and defeat Japan were approximately 500,000 American casualties and as many as 4 million Japanese dead. Given the fanatical defense mounted by the Japanese at Saipan, Iwo Jima, and Okinawa, such estimates are hard to challenge. Furthermore, the war would have been prolonged until approximately November 1946; this would have meant 15 additional months of intense warfare in which the home islands of Japan would have been ravaged as savagely as Germany had been in 1944–45.[11] Thus, nuclear weapons likely saved about 4.5 million Japanese and American lives in their first and only use in human history.[12]

When one examines the atomic or nuclear half of the twentieth century from 1945–2000, one finds a very different history of armed conflict when compared with the one that predominated from 1900–45. While there were bloody conflicts, Korea (1950–53) and Vietnam (1945–54 against France and then 1962–75 against America) being the bloodiest, they were essentially limited flash points in the global American policy of containing the expansion of Soviet and Chinese communism in what was known as the Cold War.

The key phrase is "cold" war, as opposed to "hot." Most realistic and informed observers of the twentieth century's last six decades would agree that absent the fact that both the United

States and the former Soviet Union possessed sufficient nuclear weapons to destroy each other from the early 1950s onward, America and its allies would have become engaged at some point in a Third World War with the Soviet Union, China, and their allies. While certainly the presence of two huge nuclear arsenals was not the only contributing factor, there is no question that the threat of mutual annihilation greatly diminished the temptation to engage in another world war.

The potential flash points for such a war to start were many, including, in no particular order, Berlin, Korea, Taiwan (Quemoy and Matsu), Vietnam, Western Europe, and the Middle East. Derek Leebaert, in his riveting history of the Cold War, described in compelling fashion the moments when the world came perilously close to World War III, despite the threat of nuclear annihilation.[13] Even without nuclear weapons, this conventional Third World War would have been far more lethal in its death toll than World War I and World War II combined.

Consequently, it could be argued convincingly (but certainly not proven) that up until this moment in world history, nuclear weapons, for all their destructive power, have in all likelihood saved far more lives than they have cost. Granted, that calculation could change at any moment if a new situation erupted in the Middle East or between the Indians and the Pakistanis on the Indian subcontinent. But up until this moment, it is my belief that the existence of nuclear weapons has, in all probability, saved the lives of tens of millions of human beings around the globe and prevented a grotesquely destructive Third World War from igniting. Such a global war would undoubtedly have made the twentieth century's second half far bloodier than even its first half. The existence of nuclear weapons created what proved to be a very stable balance of power, which made the twentieth century's second half far less bloody in terms of warfare than its non-nuclear first half.

Non-Nuclear Fantasy

The most dangerous aspect of the non-nuclear fantasy is the belief that it would lead to a less warlike and dangerous world. Given the twentieth century's example, a world without nuclear weapons would rather rapidly become far more likely to see wars beginning in flash points such as the Middle East or Asia. These wars could quickly escalate into a war, say, between the United States, Japan, and South Korea on one side and China and her allies on the other. In such a war, fought over control of the Korean Peninsula, Taiwan, or disputed regions of Indochina or the Indian subcontinent, the war and the world would remain nuclear weapon-free *only* until one side began to lose the conventional war. At that point, the losing side would initiate a crash program to produce nuclear weapons to defend themselves against impending defeat. It is not unimaginable that the "other side," anticipating this, would initiate a crash nuclear rearmament program as well. Soon, both sides would have enough nuclear weapons to devastate the other, and already being at war, they would be much more likely to initiate a first-use doctrine for their weapons.[14] Once nations are at war, cooler heads are far less likely to prevail in counseling against such use than they would have been before hostilities had actually commenced. Ironically, the elimination of nuclear weapons would, sooner rather than later, lead to a greater likelihood of nuclear war than the present situation in which the world finds itself.

The Terrorist Dilemma

The terrorist threat of asymmetrical warfare in which terrorists manage to acquire nuclear weapons through barter, cash, theft, or state sponsorship—and seek to blackmail America in particular or Western nations in general—has energized the recent increase in attempts to mobilize for a world free of the scourge of nuclear weapons. The theory and reasoning are that the threat of nuclear retaliation or annihilation is not an effective or reliable deterrence against radical Islamic jihadists who believe that the instigation of a catastrophic nuclear exchange would trigger the purported return of the Twelfth Imam and the consequent triumphant Islamic consummation of world history. Therefore, unlike Soviet and Chinese communist leaders, radical jihadist leaders would not be deterred by the threat of nuclear retaliation in response to a nuclear attack.

As former Secretary of State George Shultz asked me during a discussion of this issue, "Richard, how would you feel if jihadist terrorists announced that they had placed atomic bombs in the four largest American cities (New York, Los Angeles, Chicago, and Houston), plus Washington, DC, and threatened to detonate those bombs unless America complied with their blackmail demands?" "Mr. Secretary," I replied, "I would feel terrible! However, I would feel even more terrible if the jihadists had the only five nuclear weapons in existence and the civilized world had none."

Why? First, if the civilized family of nations disarmed itself, it would embolden the jihadists to try such nuclear blackmail. Remember, you cannot "un-invent" the technology and knowledge of how to build such weapons.

Second, while there are certainly jihadist terrorists whose belief system makes them capable of, or perhaps even predisposes them to, making such a blackmail threat, the people who most often finance them and manipulate them are susceptible to the threat of a credible nuclear deterrence. Why? Call me cynical or a skeptic if you will, but I suspect that those mullahs who are in sympathy with jihadist terrorists quite enjoy the perks of power their position offers and are therefore far less willing to put their faith beliefs to the immediate test of thermonuclear annihilation.

The current spate of interest in eliminating nuclear weapons is based on the best of intentions. However, the road to perdition is too often paved with good intentions. After all, when a patient is in pain he does not want a doctor with good intentions, but an excellent diagnostician with a superb record of successfully treating patients.

As mentioned earlier, at some point one has to ask questions of prudentiality. In other words, is the position being advocated likely to achieve its desired and stated goals, or is it more likely to have negative results? The answer in this case is that the attempt to eliminate nuclear weapons completely from the globe is extremely unlikely to produce the intended result of a more peaceful and safe world. Instead, it will be far more likely to produce, in a rather short period of time, a far greater likelihood not only of a significant increase of warfare among nations, but also the very nuclear warfare it seeks to prevent.

Alternative Courses of Action

Spending time and energy on the mirage of eliminating nuclear weapons detracts from the opportunity to engage in more productive processes that will help to reduce the possibility of nuclear weapons actually being used against human beings anywhere in the world. If the goal of eliminating nuclear weapons from the planet is a dangerous mirage and a practical impossibility, then where should peace-loving people of goodwill direct their attention and energies?

Based on the evidence of the last half century, a more prudential position would be to support a vigorous international effort to stop further proliferation of nuclear weapons and to work for the further significant reduction of existing nuclear arsenals. Both these efforts have produced significant results in the recent past, and both hold the promise of making meaningful progress in the near future.

International efforts to stop proliferation of nuclear weapons to countries beyond the circle of those nations who entered the nuclear club early on (the United States, the United Kingdom, the Soviet Union, France, and China) have been largely successful. In the last half century the only acknowledged or suspected additional nations thought to have acquired nuclear weapons are India, Pakistan, and possibly North Korea and Israel.[15]

Clearly, the world community of nations is currently at a critical crossroads. If the Islamic Republic of Iran manages to obtain nuclear weapons, then the world will become a significantly more dangerous place. Iran, the world's chief sponsor of terrorism, would be truly frightening as a nuclear power. A nuclear Iran would almost certainly lead in short order to a nuclear-armed Saudi Arabia, Egypt, and Syria, and to the subsequent destabilization of the region and the world (given the global significance of the oil that passes through the Persian Gulf). Prudence would recommend focusing the world's major efforts on stopping this scenario from playing out by agreeing to put truly meaningful sanctions in place to force Iran to abandon its dangerous and destabilizing course. Furthermore, the world's current nuclear powers should continue their negotiations to reduce further their stockpiles of weapons and nuclear warheads. It should encourage all people of peace and goodwill that the world is, in fact, in far less danger of nuclear war than it has been in the fairly recent past.

Historians tell us that the two most dangerous moments in the nuclear age to date were the Cuban Missile Crisis in 1962 and the Yom Kippur War in the Middle East in 1973. In both instances, the United States and the former Soviet Union came very close to miscalculating their way to a full-on exchange of nuclear weapons.[16] Since the fall of the former Soviet Union, Russia and the United States have continued the nuclear arms reduction process. This action was started during the latter years of the Soviet Union and has produced truly significant reductions in nuclear arsenals and such things as the de-targeting of both countries' cities and military installations by the other. I have actually talked with a former member of the Russian missile forces whose assignment was to blow up my hometown—Houston, Texas. He certainly gave evidence of detailed familiarity with the topography of the Greater Houston area.

A great majority of the people who lived through the Cold War (1946–91) would vigorously agree that the world is far less likely today to experience a civilization-destroying nuclear war than during most, if not all, of the years of the Cold War period. The bottom line: nonproliferation works when it is vigorously pursued by the major international actors, and nuclear arms reduction is capable of producing remarkably positive results.

On many ethical issues one should avoid making the perfect the enemy of the good. This is one of those issues. In a fallen and sinful world, we are not going to beat all of our nuclear missiles into plowshares until the Lord Jesus returns (Isa 2:4). In the meantime we must dedicate ourselves to being "salt" and "light" (Matt 5:13), and we must always ask the prudent questions about any proposed ethical goals. A goal without a plan is just a dream. Prudent questions make any proposed goal or plan better.

Notes

1. Speech given in Prague, Czech Republic, April 5, 2009; http://www.whitehouse.gov/the_press_office/Remarks-By-President-Barack-Obama-In-Prague-As-Delivered (accessed Sept. 2, 2010).

2. N. Ferguson, "The Next War of the World," *Foreign Affairs* 85, no. 5 (Sept–Oct 2006): 61. Fergusson commented, "The twentieth century was the bloodiest era in history. World War I killed between 9 million and 10 million people, more if the influenza pandemic of 1918–19 is seen as a consequence of the war. Another 59 million died in World War II. And those conflicts were only two of the more deadly ones in the last hundred years. By one estimate, there were 16 conflicts throughout the last century that cost more than a million lives, a further six that claimed between 250,000 and 500,000. In all, between 167 million and 188 million people died because of organized violence in the twentieth century—as many as one in every 22 deaths in that period."

3. *Webster's Universal Unabridged Dictionary*, 2nd ed. (New York: Simon and Schuster, 1983), s.v. "Mirage," def. 3, and "Chimera," def. 1b.

4. *The American Heritage College Dictionary*, 3rd ed. (Boston: Houghton-Mifflin, 1993), s.v. "Myth."

5. United Nations Secretary General B. Ki-moon called nuclear disarmament "the only sane path to a safer world," while speaking at the Summit on Nuclear Non-Proliferation and Nuclear Disarmament at the United Nations headquarters in New York, Sept. 24, 2009; http://www.un.org/News/Press/docs/2009/sgsm12485.doc.htm (accessed Sept. 2, 2010). The Two Futures Project, a coalition of Christians from diverse denominations and directed by Tyler Wigg-Stevenson, states as its mission "the abolition of all nuclear weapons." It "support[s] the multilateral, global, irreversible, and verifiable elimination of nuclear weapons, as a biblically-grounded mandate and as a contemporary security imperative"; http://twofuturesproject.org/about. For further study and commentary on this idea see G. P. Shultz et al., "Toward a Nuclear-Free World," *Wall Street Journal* (Jan. 15, 2008); http://www.nti.org/c_press/TOWARD_A_NUCLEAR_FREE_WORLD_OPED_011508.pdf (accessed Sept. 2, 2010); G. P. Shultz et al., "A World Free of Nuclear Weapons," *Wall Street Journal* (Jan. 4, 2007_; http://www.fcnl.org/issues/item.php?item_id=2252&issue_id=54 (accessed Sept. 2, 2010); "Anti-nuke set courts religious leaders; Sam Nunn group, which advocates disarmament, makes diplomatic effort," *Atlanta Journal-Constitution* (May 11, 2009); "Evangelicals: Nuclear weapons are 'direct affront' to God," *USA Today* (April 30, 2009); http://www.usatoday

.com/news/religion/2009-04-30-evangelical-nuclear_N.htm (accessed Sept. 2, 2010).

6. See http://en.wikiquote.org/wiki/Mark_Twain (accessed Sept. 2, 2010).

7. Verifiable figures giving hard and supported estimates are difficult to attain; however, the following sources are helpful accounts of this claim: PBS' Great War Series states that 8,528,831 military personnel were killed (from both sides) in WWI. This does not appear to factor in civilian deaths; http://www.pbs.org/greatwar/resources/casdeath_pop.html (accessed Sept. 2, 2010); White's Twentieth Century Atlas, "World War I casualties," compiles data from a variety of sources. He puts the total deaths at approximately 15,000,000. Total military deaths range from 8,364,712 to 12,599,000. Total civilian estimates range from 9,000,000 to 13,000,000. See http://users.erols.com/mwhite28/warstat1.htm (accessed Sept. 2, 2010); FirstWorldWar.com's casualty list seems close to the 8 million+ military deaths. The site notes: "[T]hese statistics reflect military casualties only; no reliable figures are available for civilian casualties throughout the world"; http://www.firstworldwar.com/features/casualties.htm (accessed Sept. 2, 2010). See also http://en.wikipedia.org/wiki/World_War_I_casualties.

8. http://warchronicle.com/numbers/WWII/deaths.htm (accessed Sept. 2, 2010).

9. http://www.cfo.doe.gov/me70/manhattan/hiroshima.htm (accessed Sept. 2, 2010).

10. http://www.cfo.doe.gov/me70/manhattan/nagasaki.htm (accessed Sept. 2, 2010).

11. L. Morton, "The Decision to Use the Atomic Bomb," in *Command Decisions*, ed. K. R. Greenfield (Washington, DC: Center for Military History, Department of the Army, 1959), 493–518; http://www.history.army.mil/books/70-7_23.htm (accessed Sept. 2, 2010). For more information supporting this idea, consider the following. Henry L. Stimson, Wartime Secretary of War, argued that dropping the bomb would save American lives and reduce the need for protracted ground warfare (507–8). After the Potsdam Conference, the military made future projections. "November 15, 1946 was accepted as the planning date for the end of the war against Japan" (512). This comes from the Combined Chiefs of Staff Report to the President and Prime Minister, 24 July 1945, quoted in Cline, *Washington Command Post*, 346, and reproduced in *The Entry of the Soviet Union into the War Against Japan: Military Plans, 1941–1945* (Washington, DC: Department of Defense Press Release, 1955), 89–91.

General MacArthur argued that the pre-bomb strategy would probably have taken well into 1946 to ensure the surrender of Japan (501–2).

12. The 4 million estimate is reached by taking the 4.5 million lives estimated to have been killed in invading and subduing Japan and then subtracting the approximately 200,000 and 140,000 five-year death totals at Hiroshima and Nagasaki respectively.

13. D. Leebaert, *The Fifty-Year Wound: How America's Cold War Victory Has Shaped Our World* (New York: Back Bay Books, 2003), 275–82.

14. For an interesting argument closely related and indirectly in support of this idea, see M. Walzer's *Just and Unjust Wars: A Moral Argument with Historical Illustration*, 4th ed. (New York: Basic Books, 2006). Walzer makes the case that under "supreme emergency" conditions the use of nuclear weapons may be justifiable.

15. K. Sutcliffe, "The Growing Nuclear Club," Council on Foreign Relations, Nov. 17, 2006; http://www.cfr.org/publication/12050/ (accessed Sept. 2, 2010).

16. Leebaert, *The Fifty-Year Wound*, 506–12.

Chapter 16

Nature Is Given, People Create Culture

Udo W. Middelmann

B y the time we intentionally consider the world around us, we are already imbedded in a real world. Nature guards us in a cradle of things and neighbors in our time-space experience. Culture, in a basic meaning, is a description of what we do with these elements, which are boundaries and challenges to each person. Culture reveals the distinctions we make between stuff and persons, whether we submit to or harness and overcome limitations of place, time, and knowledge. Some cultures encourage conformity in rituals and rites with an emphasis on repetition. Others promote individuality and unique efforts. Some cultures accept the normality of what is, and others struggle to grasp what ought to be from an awareness of an unsatisfactory present.

Where nature is considered the root of all things, societies will venerate it as mother and model, perhaps vicious, but always victorious in controlling its victims. Life in such cultural contexts follows the circular patterns of seasons, life cycles from birth to death, the ups and downs of the ocean's tides, and the eat and get eaten of the food chain.

In a more distinct definition, culture requires an effort over nature, a deliberation and distinction between what is and what ought to be, revealing a tension between the physical factors of the real world (the "givens") and the mental, spiritual, and intellectual longing for control. Culture in this sense involves judgment and praise, critique and rewards.

Such judgment is made possible, without its being a childish discontent, from the biblical perspective. The present situation for all of us is flawed, imperfect, and not as originally intended. While the longing for more, better, and fulfilling situations is common to everyone, only the biblical description of the real world gives an explanation and mandate to create: to impose culture on nature, both the impersonal stuff around us and our own human nature.

Without that biblical perspective nature is the final horizon and stage on which life unrolls. Religions embrace that natural scenery, while Christianity found a different text. It answers basic questions coherently and enables us to promote a life reflecting the image of God.

For example, Plato looked at the night sky and Aristotle delighted in the regular motion from potentiality to actuality of all things in nature. They thought they had found in these regular patterns the essential character of the universe. That regularity in the firmament above and in nature around them gave them the model of what society should adopt for it to be orderly, and for the individual to know his place in the larger scheme of things. So it is not surprising when both derived models to emulate from the example of eternal passages of heavenly bodies and steady motion of natural processes.

The effect would be, according to Plato,[1] a harmonious program of a state, and for Aristotle,[2] a society modeled on nature. For the sake of an ideal order, Plato "disallowed" artists and poets with their troubling lines, provocative ideas, and unpredictable and disturbing influence over the citizens' minds. For a similar ideal order, Aristotle demanded of people a conformity to virtues modeled on patterns observed in nature. He subsumed people's moral concerns to political ideals. From an urgency to fit in, people were expected to give up and to avoid such "extremes" as moral judgments.

The pursuit of either ideal of conformity came with a price—in dependent thought, creativity, and personal responsibility. They were buried in concerns (maybe "interests") of the *polis* as a whole. Greek tragedy and a generally fatalistic outlook in Greek culture made it easy for many later idealistic totalitarian cultures to refer back to Greece as their model.

Only in the small Jewish cultural context on the eastern shore of the Mediterranean do we find an alternative to such a system orientation. The God of the Bible describes a very different relationship between individuals, and between them and God. The contrast could not be more powerful. This model shaped a culture of responsibility, personal conscience, innovation, and repentance, of which we are heirs with our present worldview. It did not arise spontaneously, nor does it continue with a life of its own. It requires from us constant effort and affirmation. Without it we likewise would slide into patterns of life that are more marked by resignation than by purposeful exhibitions of moral courage. We shall observe in what follows the "difference of YHWH and the difference he makes."[3]

Athens had undergone violent civil war, chaotic popular democracy, and rivalries among oligarchs and rulers. The search for a harmonious interplay between man and nature, the state and the soul of man, and layers of society had become a major concern for Greek thinkers and poets. Gradually they began to replace an often immoral pantheon of contradictory divinities in Homer's writings with a system of justice, logical consistency, and social harmony. At first such order was sought in impersonal elements, or what are described, in the words of some modern philosophers, "ground of being." They suggested water,[4] air,[5] fire,[6] and a boundless everything.[7] Plato sought the stability in eternal forms (Greek idea), models or permanent ideals, which he believed to exist outside our circle of transient existence and could be understood by the mind.

Applying these forms to reality would make the shadows they cast from the particular shapes and events on Earth somewhat more real, and thereby bind society and virtue to absolutes beyond the ups and downs of current troubles. An appeal to eternal and perfect forms, to ideals, gets rid of opposition, discussion, and cultural vitality. When the ideal is *assumed* and the perfect is already known, nothing is out of place or inferior. The result is habits of repetition rather than innovation. When it is believed that we already live in the best of all possible worlds, challenges no longer exist. There are no invitations to create variety. The unfinished, untidy reality of the human and natural context is denied. Culture is reduced to what people already do, not what should be done to address the boredom of repetitions.

This appealing source of order in ideas of eternal perfect forms was often assumed by Alexandrian Christians like Origen and Clement to be an indication of how close the pagan Plato was to a Christian understanding of God. In that they failed to make the weighty distinction between a permanent ideal of "love" and "justice" and the consistently loving and just God of the Bible. Plato's forms are permanent and static, while God is continuously dynamic. God is not justice, but always in every situation just.

We should remember that the embrace of such ideals, such visions of perfection, has become, according to Karl Popper, the justification of multiple totalitarian political and religious systems. Visions of a pure race, of an egalitarian new humanity, of an exclusive religion, variations of nationalisms, or a pre-industrial "nativist" world have been pursued up to our own days at the cost of enormous bloodshed.[8] The image, the imagination of perfection, is so appealing that the messiness of an untidy real and present world should be suppressed until all signs of individuality, thought, or discussion are annihilated. Stalin, Hitler, Mohammed, Pol Pot, at times the Popes in Rome, and more recently a multitude of Protestant quasi-popes want their people to fall in line. They find a controlled, repetitive, and aligned public an ideal, finished, perfect, impersonal culture under a "great leader," whether Father Stalin, Hitler ("who had such a warm way with children"), or Mr. Kim.

What Plato described in *Timaeus*, a dialogue with his account of the origin of the visible world, gives a vision of permanence. Plato's mind and his recent experiences in Athens craved an order, a logical and practical way to resolve uncertainties of events and conduct. Yet he and others were not lonely philosophers with odd ideas. In fact, every person in his time and place would attempt to find something reliable to attach to in the world he first encountered. Until we do, we are alone, insecure and unable to relate to the various events and impressions we face. Conformity to something or someone in the immediate world outside (ourselves) brings confirmation, comfort, and eventually community. Hence the importance of culture in its definition as what is already and habitually done by a group of people.

Rest in such habits, rites, and formulas is offered for each individual in the fundamental nature of all transcendent and immanent *religions*, whether they are secular and naturalistic or spiritual and revealed religions: each person seeks to *relate* to something bigger than himself, something bigger, of longer duration, and greater weight than himself. We all seek to fit in, to go with the approved and traditional, in order to avoid alienation and isolation. Our personal world is too small, our experience too limited, our need for care and protection, for explanations and repetitions too urgent when we start to become aware of ourselves in early childhood. Our minds expect answers soon after we have instinctively expected food for our bodies; warmth, protection, and eventually conversation make us experience belonging, a sense of home in the human race.

We relate with obvious benefit when we learn the vocabulary of our family, the meaning and innuendoes of words, the figures of speech and the metaphors of the people around us. Only through adjustment to their social patterns and behavior do we understand and communicate adequately to find the way for life to go ahead.

In bigger questions we also attach ourselves to whatever is assumed to direct the world. In Islam one accepts the orders and the perfect will of Allah. In African tribal religions, as John Mbiti pointed out so well,[9] the authority of the ancestors and the power of the spirits determine life and behavior in colorful variations. In Marxism and dialectic materialism, history is the energy behind the inevitable progress through struggle that determines one's place and obligations at every turn of life. The material conditions of a person determine his behavior. The material weight of the stars determined his personality, including the outcome of one's marriage. Buddhism calls for increasing disciplines of denial in order to lose oneself in the undifferentiated ONE of Being.

Man enters the waters and causes no ripple on undifferentiated Oneness. Hinduism suggests a fundamental justice in the way the die is cast for the Karma of a person's position and life. In Greek thought Fate directed what people would experience.

There was nothing that Electra could have done to escape the impending judgment.[10] All things are controlled, determined, and inevitable. Antigone had to die for reasons of state, for reasons of the gods, and of "necessity."[11] In some expressions of Protestant religion, a similar acceptance of all events and disturbances is justified from a peculiar understanding of divine sovereignty. The only difference from Greek or Islamic determinism is that a benevolent purpose is thought to exist even in the most hideous tragedies and injustice. These views produce cultures of the "again and again," symbolized by the wheels of fate and the dictates of gods that rule without awakening a conscience—life is seen to be controlled by necessities.

The price for belonging or relating to such a bigger "whatever" is not just the abolition of personal uniqueness, creativity, and enterprise. It also demands the denial of moral discernment, though not of judgmental pronouncements. Characteristic of every one of these attachments is an assumption that the reality is already final, that everything is in order. The use of power for adjudication, the appeal to necessity, the praise of collective thinking, and practice are virtues that assume, if not require, one's moral abdication through conformity—the abandonment of a person's distinctive and critical evaluation.

Problems arise only from the presence of a mind that stands outside the collective, the fates, the necessity, and looks at problems with a moral, critical, and discerning perspective. In other words, this is a mind that has not concluded that whatever exists is all there ever could or should be. Such a mind comes alive from the obvious contrast between birth and death, between distinct individual personalities, and between the multiple contradictions encountered in a life, from a deceptive or illogical use of language to promises not kept, to death as a violation of everything one previously struggled for in life.

The mind of this person thinks, evaluates, discerns, and complains. It understands that a remedy or improvement of a painful situation can only come through repentance, imagination, and enterprise. In turn, this person steps out of the circle of "that's just life" in order to bend life into a different shape. Plato's firmament is impersonal, cold, and distant; Aristotle's nature is amoral and silent. Looking around us at the stars above or the flowers in the field below can serve as a reference only at the expense of our becoming less than human ourselves. Only an infinite person with an accessible and defined character can serve as a standard and confirmation that being a human being is not a cosmic mistake.

It comes as no great surprise when cultures with a closed sky above them or nature's morbid model around them will be blind to human needs such as intellectual insight, moral orientation, and personal motivation. The result is often material and cultural poverty from intellectual and religious darkness, where the human being is seen to serve as an accidental phenomenon in an impersonal and therefore uncaring nature, time, and death.

In a fascinating lecture, Professor Thomas A. Long of Emory University examined Greek and other fatalistic views of life and proposed the biblical view.[12] Although Plato in *Timaeus* looked to the closed heavens as an anchor for his thoughts and as a model for human order and virtue, the Jew and the Christian look to the God of heaven who is the infinite-personal God of the Bible. The biblical idea is not to lie low, to deny true humanity, and to silently and without moral motions accept what comes along from the past. He is not squeezed to serve the needs of an ideal state, an image of harmony or peace. No ideal assigns him a role as philosopher-king, soldier, or peasant in the service of an idea.

Instead, Jews and Christians find a text from God, who made the firmament below Him, and opened it and addresses us with words "through it" (Matt 23:17; Mark 1:9–11; Luke 3:21; John 1:31ff). He came for lunch to talk with Abraham (Gen 18:1), took a body from Mary (Luke 1:30ff) in which He revealed the character, being, and interest of God in real history. The Word is singled out as "the exact representation of His [God's] nature" (Heb 1:3 NASB) at Jesus' baptism; we are told this with audible language, following rules of grammar and syntax. God in the flesh (Jesus) argued with the blind acceptance of the human condition by the Pharisees. He revolted against the tragic world of sin and its manifestation in sickness, evil spirits, death, and despair. He refused dinner with Herod and fed the 5,000 on the hillside, first a decent lunch and then with words that tell us how we can be fed in body, soul, and mind to receive comfort, confidence, and hope in dark times (John 6).

In perhaps the most startling text, Bar-Timaeus, who was physically, philosophically, and culturally blind and knew it, pleaded with Christ for his eyes to be opened as Christ, the "son of David" in distinction from the blind "son of Timaeus," has opened heaven (Mark 10:46–52). Where Christ came from and where He now sits (and at dramatic moments even stands [Acts 7:56]!) at the right hand of the Father are no ideal and static forms of Plato, but the personal-infinite God. At each moment in time God loves, agonizes, intervenes, and pleads with us to believe Him instead of all the temptations to see the earthly horizon among the stars, nature in motion, and social habits and beliefs of a people group and culture as the final measure of things.

The Word from a personal-infinite God explains both the order of the universe and the chaotic moral confusion of the present human experience. That Word, in and with Christ, invites man to understand that the tie-in—our first and most basic, original, and satisfying relationship—is with God, not creation. We relate to God through language, which brings understanding of purpose. We receive answers, not a reprimand or even an obstruction to our questions. We receive mandates to create, so that no day is a repetition of the previous one—no age merely traditional.[13] We are invited to talk with God and now, in a more problematic situation after the fall, even to argue with God. Moses, Job, Jeremiah, and Jesus are not reproached for wondering out loud how to proceed, when a fallen reality creates a conflict between what is seen and what is known. We know God's goodness and see a messy history in the real world.

Yet precisely because of that tension between Word and imperfect reality, we understand something of the content of our calling: that nature is to be transformed through culture. Creative discernment rather than repetitive obedience should characterize the person made in the image of God the Creator. We are addressed as people not to seek fusion, but a conscious particularity; not to find a place in the impersonal order or motion of the world, but to develop the capacity to be oneself; not to accept what happens in the impersonal universe or from perverted human power, as if all were decided ahead of time, from incestuous love to inevitable death, in contrast to, among others, Euripides.

We are not the leaf on the river of time, carried by the water in a disinterested displacement, but rather a stick stuck into the river to cause ripples all the way to the shore. We have a heavenly Father; an indifferent nature is not our mother.

There is no corresponding word in Plato or Demosthenes for "guilt," "obligation," or "responsibility," notions which weave a personal, subjective bond between a moral agent and an act attributed to him. For Plato and many Greek philosophers, justice and virtue are not imperative but related to an eternal order of the cosmos—the mute, servile, and almost mechanical contemplation that suffices to regulate a life with as much precision and rigor as the revolution of a star. Horizontality is maintained, but nothing more. The very bedrock of Greek civilization and all totalitarian religions is an ontological flattening out within the horizon of a general cosmology.[14] As revelation of omnipresent powerful forces and fate, they lack the word that addresses an individual consciousness. They fail to startle people to action with intellectual freedom for moral and creative engagement.

Contrast this to the biblical teaching in the Old and New Testaments. The view presented there is uniquely different. It breaks the bond of ontological slavery and establishes continuity between God and man. The Bible is based on debate and not on a programmed drama; on transcendent words of justice and encouragement, creating an encounter between the personal Creator and the person made in His image: "He created them male and female" (Gen 1:27 HCSB). It sets the person in an impersonal nature, but it affirms that there is something of Man in man, the opposite of an object or a category *of* Being. It is rather a point of view *on* Being for one who is essentially an image bearer of the Creator. This gives birth to a perspective on the world from a critical distance, a position of *response-ability* to God and man, as well as resistance after the fall against evil and death and any tempting merger with impersonal matter, history, or fate.

The Jew and the Christian stand in dependency on God. We do not crawl with humility across the earth. The Bible addresses us on the level of our minds and informs us how to employ our lives. Our calling is to be human beings.

God Himself had prepared meticulously the garden of Eden where He placed our first parents. He acted very deliberately, making increasingly distinct shapes of things and forms of life over much time. The Bible describes the care, intentions, thoughtfulness, and artistic pleasure in variety as much as the power of the Creator. It was not just done "in one fell swoop," but thought through, deliberated in the give-and-take between the members of the Godhead over however much time, to conclude with the wonderful, peaceful, and harmonious "Let Us make" (Gen 1:26 HCSB). A day of rest followed, not from fatigue, but for enjoyment.

When God made man, male and female, He gave them the mandate to create for themselves. He made them creatures with the finite attributes of the Creator. He gave them the dignity of a cause. God's world was not a finished product, calling only for admiration and maintenance. There is no picture of a status quo, of completeness without possible addition, variation, and innovation. Perfection is not an ideal, but a moral and aesthetic judgment that expands to include what Adam and Eve were to discover. Who they were and what they wanted to become in their relationship, with their abilities and in the training of their priorities, is all part of a perfect world: to have dominion over creation, over their choices, over themselves, so that every day their world was to be the result of God's original creation and their unique contribution to it. They were to have children, which God would not create. They were to name the animals, which names God would then also call them (Gen 2:19)! No "admiration collective" here, no fear of change, no hurt feelings on the part of God that His creature, man, would choose to continue creativity. God saw it as a continuing expression of the God in whose image man was made in the first place. They were to draw sustenance for the power of their will from God's encouragement, to express their derived sovereignty in enterprise, aesthetic sensitivity, and moral discernment.

Work through the agency of the freely creative creature is not a consequence of the fall. It was and is an expression of our creativity, of human significance, of the power of ideas over material circumstances and as a stamp of our existence on the real world. Additional burdens arose from the fall, such as frustration, difficult decisions with limited resources, and temptations to blame others for our hardships. These are consequences of what went wrong at the fall. Extra effort is now demanded in a painfully flawed world. It was an effort on the part of God, as He went back to work to redeem man from guilt and His creation from a state of sin. That work is partially accomplished, like the firstfruit of a harvest, when Christ rose on the eighth day—that is, the first day of the new week.

Adam and Eve had to believe God for hope in a future Savior (Gen 3:15), for working the fields in spite of nature's encroachments (Gen 3:18), for having babies as an effort (Gen 3:20). It was even a form of resistance to their own bodies now inevitably to return to dust (Gen 3:19). Isaac had to dig a well for water to provide for his sheep (Gen 21:25–30; 26:12 ff). Elijah had to confront the king over his unacceptable wickedness (1 Kgs 17:1). Prophets were sent to trouble those who thought they could get away with terrible views on truth, law, and the mistreatment of the poor (e.g., Amos). They had read into God's patience a sign of His indifference or even absence (Mal 2:17; Rom 2:1–6).

This understanding, with a focus on enterprise against abandonment, of work against waiting, of force against fatalism, is central to the cultural mandates inherited from the biblical perspective. It frees us from merging with a gender, class, or national consciousness, from any "amor fati"[15] inherent in any submission to the "order of things" or the inevitable flow of history, "the scientific dialectic," or, as Cicero suggested, "to live according to the science of what happens," or to live in conformity to nature (Zeno). Marx said that history is "a second nature," "the natural science of humanity." Well, that was Marx, and we saw not only what it led to, but also how his totalitarian ideals were imposed to break the human spirit in order to accomplish those ideals.

Christianity and biblical Judaism understand the human being as dependent on God's Word, the Scriptures, from which all history, all nature, all personal and social situations are to be evaluated, judged, and formed. It is a position in which *what is* is neither simply to be maintained in an attitude of "again and again" (as if nature were a museum and society an academic exercise or a culture mired in its traditions), nor is it always already *what ought to be* (as if everything were good enough or as if the will of God had been worked out).[16]

The result is a practice of innovation, invention, and development in opposition to the maintenance of a status quo, in other words, transforming culture. Continuing God's sequential creation in seven Genesis days with increasing distinctions leads to an understanding of a welcome and, after the fall of man, a continuing dynamic of review and change. The Bible speaks of a linear history, planned, executed, and teleological. We wait for more, including the accomplishments of better governments, technologies, compositions in music and paintings, novels, automobiles, marriages; and we also wait for the return of Christ whom God raised from the dead (1 Thess 1:10).

A Christian culture is marked by a concentration on the human being, the crown of creation. Men and women are our central focus in obedience to what God has said about being bearers of His image. We share our amazement that God would be mindful of us in multiple ways (Ps 8:4), and we are therefore mindful of both our tremendous greatness and our real brokenness. We seek a rule of justice under law, not the constraints and herding of people under power. We encourage the dignity of skillful work on any level as a means to express how much we are in the Creator's image. We leave our name everywhere, with delight in all the different possible services to others and ourselves; and at times with arrogance as followers of "Zorro." We take from God the authority to amputate limbs, vaccinate an organism to precede a hostile incursion from unfriendly bacteria, and poison malign cancer cells as an expression that biology, nature, and circumstances are not our lord and will have their claim of mastery opposed. We recognize that human beings can cause enormous problems, but that also without their discerning effort there would be neither judgment nor improvement, no discovery of fault, no remedy or repair. Only human beings trained by Scripture directly or by way of a sensitized inheritance of biblical ideas would notice the possible extinction of endangered species, the pollution of the environment, the unfairness of natural blight and catastrophes. They then attempt to do something about it.

What one believes about life in the real world will create a culture, a sum total of attitudes and practices that a group of people embrace and pass on to the next generation. That belief is a choice, born out of the alternatives of vision, ideas, and experiences. A choice always contains an element of separation. A good life is not self-evident. We have a feel for it, but it is a puzzle, filled with tragedy and contradictions. But in the end the Scriptures and Christianity alone enable us to separate from the stars and stones:[17] we are alive. We are not like wilting flowers, which are composted; human beings compose, love, and invent. We are at home intellectually and intelligently only in the world that has an open heaven, where the God of the Bible is our point of reference to give shape, purpose, hope, and redemption.

From that source we seek to fulfill the point of it all against all adversity. To God we can complain in search of solutions, which He explains and delivers, so that we are able to be human beings who express their examined faith about reality in deliberate actions for their satisfaction and glory to God.

It is worth the effort—the discipline and persistence—involved for the experience and exhibition of true humanity. Such effort alone makes us unlike the stones below or the stars above. Our calling is to be persons, who choose to bring order to what is merely natural. Culture to our benefit does not come about naturally. It wants[18] to be chosen wisely, nursed and tended, or it will kill the soul of man, waste his mind and starve his body. By this a culture is formed that exhibits true humanity or humanness.

Notes

1. Plato's *The Republic* was written for that purpose.

2. See Aristotle's *Nicomachean Ethics*.

3. I lean here on the title from M. A. Adler, *The Difference of Man and the Difference It Makes* (New York: Fordham University Press, 1993).

4. Thales suggested water.

5. Anaximenes thought it was air.

6. So thought Heraclitus.

7. Anaximander of Miletus.

8. R. Issac and E. Isaac, *The Coercive Utopians* (Chicago: Regnery Gateway, 1983).

9. J. S. Mbiti, *African Religions and Philosophy* (New York: Praeger, 1969).

10. Sophocles' *Electra*, child of the murdered Agamemnon.

11. Sophocles' *Antigone*, where the curse of Oedipus haunts a younger generation: "For once a family is cursed by God, disasters come like earthquake tremors, worse with each succeeding generation."

12. T. A. Long, "Tearing the Heavens Apart: The Big Ideas in Mark's Gospel," Calvin Seminary; http://www.calvin.edu/worship/events/past/2008/preaching_mark.php (accessed Oct. 9, 2008).

13. See the progression from Genesis 1 (take dominion of self and creation) to Genesis 2 (name the animals and discover Eve's distinct full humanity) to Genesis 3 (put your hands to the plow and work).

14. B. Levy, *The Testament of God* (New York: Harper & Row, 1980), 68–73.

15. Latin: "Love of fate"

16. I borrow the term "again and again" from Daniel Boorstin's repeated use of it. See D. Boorstin, *The Discoverers: A History of Man's Search to Know His World and Himself* (New York: Random House, 1983), 16, 122, 566.

17. Genesis 1 makes such a point of the fact that the sun and moon were created late. The first light of day, separate from the night, was from God, not from a creation that Plato observed in the firmament.

18. I say "wants" not due to an assumed personality of nature, but because failure will create a lack, a want!

Scripture Index

Afterword

As one of the editors of this volume dedicated to honor L. Russ Bush, I am privileged to write a few lines regarding his ongoing legacy. Over two years ago, the leadership of the L. Russ Bush Center for Faith and Culture first discussed the desire to honor the legacy of this exceptional servant of God. Now three years after Dr. Bush's death what began as a good idea has developed into a collection of exceptional essays in his honor. The list of contributors to this volume reveals the breadth of his interests and the scope of his influence reaching beyond the Southern Baptist Convention. Everything about this volume, its content and presentation, reveals that those contributing to this project succeeded in crafting a lasting tribute to Dr. Bush's legacy.

Beyond this volume, surely his legacy will continue through many of us who knew and were taught by him. The Center for Faith and Culture, however, is specifically dedicated to continuing the work and spirit of Dr. Bush. The Center exists today as part of Southeastern Baptist Theological Seminary because of the vision Dr. Bush had for a center that would responsibly defend the Faith and engage the culture. It must be noted that while his vision gave birth to the Center, it was his life that gave definition to that vision. It is precisely this vision for which the Center exists as an exemplar of the spirit and passion of Dr. Bush as revealed in his classroom lectures, publications, and tireless efforts within the community of Faith both at home and abroad. I believe the work of the Center, if true to its commitments, will assure his enduring legacy for years to come.

Dr. Bush was known for teaching that cultural artifacts should matter to Christians, especially film. In this way, his thinking was shaped by the late Francis A. Schaeffer. In his philosophy class he made regular use of the Schaeffer film series "How Should We Then Live?" and taught students how to think about culture Christianly. One saw in his life (whether it came from Schaeffer or his own study I do not know) the idea that people matter because they are made in the image of God. I think this explains the gracious spirit he exhibited especially in controversy. Consequently, the Center, from its inception, has sought to engage culture in a way that respects humanity while speaking theologically to all areas of the human experience and to do so with a winsome tone. This is what we learned from Dr. Bush.

Furthermore, Dr. Bush had an inexhaustible passion for the work of Christian apologetics. Understandably, the first two conferences organized by the Center highlighted two great apologists: C. S. Lewis and Francis A. Schaeffer (and that, incidentally, was the first ever conference on Schaeffer). Although taking place after Dr. Bush's death, the work of the Center proved instrumental in SEBTS' receiving custodianship of the vast collection of the papers and tapes of Francis Schaeffer. This marvelous and important gift from the Francis A. Schaeffer Foundation stands as a wonderful testimony to the ongoing legacy of Dr. Bush.

The Center, as inspired and modeled by Dr. Bush, seeks to bring the Christian faith to bear upon all areas of culture through helping others to think and to act Christianly in both private and public discourse. The prayer is that the legacy of Dr. Bush will not fade from either the evangelical memory or experience.

Bruce A. Little, director of the L. Russ Bush Center
for Faith and Culture